BURLINGTON COUNTY NEW JERSEY

DEED ABSTRACTS

Books A, B and C

Richard S. Hutchinson

HERITAGE BOOKS
2006

HERITAGE BOOKS
AN IMPRINT OF HERITAGE BOOKS, INC.

Books, CDs, and more—Worldwide

For our listing of thousands of titles see our website
at
www.HeritageBooks.com

Published 2006 by
HERITAGE BOOKS, INC.
Publishing Division
65 East Main Street
Westminster, Maryland 21157-5026

Copyright © 2000 Richard S. Hutchinson

Other books by the author:
Abstracts of the Council of Safety Minutes, State of New Jersey, 1777-1778
Middlesex County, New Jersey Deed Abstracts: Book 1
Monmouth County, New Jersey Deeds - Books A, B, C and D
Abstracts of the Deaths and Marriages in the Hightstown Gazette, *18 April 1861-28 December 1871*
Abstracts of the Deaths and Marriages in the Hightstown Gazette, *4 January 1872-27 December 1877*
Abstracts of the Deaths and Marriages in the Hightstown Gazette, *3 January 1878-29 December 1881*
Abstracts of the Deaths and Marriages in the Hightstown Gazette, *5 January 1882-31 December 1885*
Abstracts of the Deaths and Marriages in the Hightstown Gazette, *7 January 1886-26 December 1889*
The Mercer County Genealogical Quarterly, Volumes 1-6
CD: Mercer County Genealogical Quarterly [New Jersey], Volumes 1-6

All rights reserved. No part of this book may be reproduced or transmitted in any form or by any means, electronic or mechanical, including photocopying, recording or by any information storage and retrieval system without written permission from the author, except for the inclusion of brief quotations in a review.

International Standard Book Number: 0-7884-1452-6

Table of Contents

Introduction v

Book "A" 1

Book "B" 37

Book "C" 69

Index 119

BURLINGTON COUNTY DEED ABSTRACTS
BOOKS "A", "B", "C"

Burlington County, New Jersey, one of the state's early counties, was formed in 1694 from what was then known as West New Jersey, with its northern boundary extending to the top of the state. Today, the county is located in the south-central part of the state, with its present boundaries abutting the counties of Atlantic, Camden, Mercer, Monmouth and Ocean, while its western boundary is the Delaware River. The county also reaches the Atlantic Ocean where its southeastern boundary meets the boundary lines of Atlantic and Ocean counties.

The abstracted information has been gleaned from the county clerk's copies of the recorded deeds maintained at the Burlington County Court House, in Mount Holly, New Jersey. These early deed books contain the county clerk's handwritten recordings of the deeds as they were presented to him for recording. Other documents were also recorded in these books; such as Release of Dower, Creditor's Agreements, Division of Property amongst heirs, etc. With this county also having a large Quaker influence, these early deed books also contain numerous records of slave manumissions which name both the slave and the owner.

The majority of the documents recorded in these books pertain to deeds from the 1750s through the 1790s, but contain a rich source of genealogical information from the early 1700s. These documents are listed in the order in which they were recorded, and contain (as available) pertinent dates, the names of wives, children, siblings, parents, previous property owners, the adjoining property owners, and the witnesses.

Many names recorded within these documents differ in spelling from the signatures. The abstracts of this book record all of the above information including how the person signed the document or whether they simply 'made their mark'. Every readable name in the recorded document is included in the Index."

BURLINGTON COUNTY DEEDS - BOOK "A"

BURLINGTON COUNTY, NEW JERSEY
DEED ABSTRACTS
BOOKS "A", "B", "C"

DEED BOOK "A"

[p 1] **DANIEL ELLIS to JOHN POPE**

9 March 1774 - Between Daniel Ellis Esquire High Sheriff ... county of Burlington ... and John Pope of Mansfield ... County aforesaid, Merchant ... Whereas Daniel Cooper in the Inferior Court of Common Please ... [November 1773 Term] ... by the Judgement of the Said Court recovered against Peter Marr, James Brixton and Hannah his wife late Hannah Tallman (which Peter and Hannah were Administrators of Goods ... which were of Thomas Tallman deceased) ... And Whereas Samuel Burroughs in the Supreme Court ... by Judgement ... recovered against the aforesaid Peter and Hannah Talman Administrators ... And Whereas Benjamin Pine in the Supreme Court ... by the Judgement ... recovered against the aforesaid Peter and Hannah Talman Administrators ... And Whereas a certain Writ ... called Fieri Facias ... Which the Said Sheriff was commanded that ... the Goods ... which were of the said Thomas Talman at the Time of the Death in the hands of the said Peter Tallman James Brixton and Hannah his Wife ... he should cause to made the Debt and Damages aforesaid ... And Whereas in the lifetime of the said Thomas Tallman, Peter Talman and Margaret his Wife by Indenture ... [13 January 1768] ... did grant ... unto the said Thomas Talman ... and two Lots of Land ... in Mansfield ... [Adjacent land owners or names - Corner of Burlington and Mansfield Roads; Mansfield Meeting House; Land formerly Lyndon Browns now ... Peter Tallman; Joseph Gibbs Land] ... [.5 acre and 12 perches] ... The other Lot ... [.25 acre] ... which Lots the said Peter Talman purchased of John Hutchins ... and the said John Pope ... by bidding [343 pounds] ...; [Witnessed by - John Heulings, Thomas Rodman one of the Judges of the Superior Court of Common Pleas; Recorded- 16 March 1785.]

[p 4] **JOHN BUFFIN, SEN to JOSEPH GIBBS**

28 November 1766 - Between John Buffen Senr of the Township of Mansfield ... county of Burlington ... Yeoman ... sold to Joseph Gibbs of the same Place Yeoman ... Lands ... being in the Township of Mansfield ... [Adjacent land owners or names - Black House tavern ... near a Black Walnut Tree which is in the Middle of the Road that leads from the said Black House Tavern to the Meeting House of the People called Quaker in Mansfield; Pope's Corner] ... [Deed was created to correct the boundaries between the two parties]; [Witnessed by - Thomas Richards, Arthur Edwards, Michael Buffin; Recorded - 16 March 1785.]

BURLINGTON COUNTY DEEDS - BOOK "A"

[p 6] HENRY DELATUSH to NATHANIEL POPE

4 July 1776 - Between Henry Delatush...Township of Mansfield ... and Nathaniel Pope ... of the same Place ... Whereas Isaac Gibbs the elder late of Mansfield aforesaid deceased ... was in his lifetime seized ... of ... Certain lands situate in Mansfield aforesaid ... and by his last Will ... bequeath unto his Grandson Joseph Gibbs ... as by that said Will ... [18 January 1742/3 ... recorded in Book U-6, folio 318] ... And the said Joseph Gibbs ... [31 July 1769] ... did convey a Part of said recited Lands unto Henry Delatush the present Grantor. NOW this Indenture ... the said Henry Delatush for ... [300 pounds did sell] ... Land or piece of Meadow Ground and Upland being a Part of the said Isaac Gibbs Land ... [Adjacent land owners or names - George Folwell; Nathaniel Pope formerly William Nutts; Thomas Curtes's Line; (formerly Philip Nutts)] ... [23.5 acres and 27 perches]; [Witnessed by - John Pope, David Robeson; Recorded - 1 February 1885.]

[p 8] JOHN POPE to MARMADUKE CURTES

Between John Pope Executor to the Estate of William Delworth late of Mansfield deceased ... Merchant ... and Marmaduke Curtes of Chesterfield ... [sold for 106 pounds] ... land situate in Mansfield aforesaid near the black House ... [Adjacent land owners or names - Edward Thomas; Joseph Gibbs; the Black House] ... [.25 acre] ... Which said ... [.25 acre] ... of Land is part of a larger tract bequeathed by Isaac Gibbs the eldest to his Grandson Joseph Gibbs ... and the said Joseph Gibbs and Wife conveyed unto William Delworth ... 5 January 1782 ... and by the said William Delworth was Ordered to be disposed of by his Executor John Pope ...; [Witnessed by - Jacob Vansciver, John Imlay; Recorded - 19 July 1783.]

[p 10] JOSEPH GIBBS to JOHN POPE

3 February 1784 - Between Joseph Gibbs of the Township of Mansfield ... Yeoman and Elizabeth his Wife ... and ... John Pope of the same Place Merchant ... Whereas Joseph Potts and Mary his wife ... did convey unto Joshua Gibbs and Lyndon Brown ... Lots of Land ... being at a Place ... by the name of the Black House in Mansfield ... [Adjacent land owners or names - Mansfield Meeting House; Lyndon Brown; Joseph Gibbs now Thomas Kerlins land] ... [.5 acres and 12 perches and .25 acre] ... conveyed by Joshua Gibbs and Hannah his wife and Lyndon Brown unto John Hutchins; and by John Hutchins and Sarah his Wife Conveyed unto Peter Tallman and by Peter Tallman and Margaret his Wife Conveyed unto Thomas Tallman and their deed dated ... [13 January 1768] ... and the said Thomas Tallman dying intestate and not leaving sufficient personal estate to discharge his just Debts ... Now the said Joseph Gibbs and Elizabeth his Wife ... [for 5 shillings] ... sold to John Pope ...; [Witnessed by - Isaac Gibbs, Jacob Vansciver, J. Imlay; Recorded - 5 February 1784.]

BURLINGTON COUNTY DEEDS - BOOK "A"

****

[p 12] **NATHANIEL POPE to JOHN POPE**

1 February 1785 - Between Nathaniel Pope of the Township of Mansfield ... and Sarah his Wife ... and John Pope of the same Place Merchant ... [sold for 148 pounds] ... land ... being Part of the Real Estate of Isaac Gibbs ... bequeathed unto his Grandson Joseph Gibbs ... [and Gibbs to Henry Delatush 1769 and 1776 to Nathaniel Pope] ... [Adjacent land owners or names - William Wright (formerly George Folwells); Nathaniel Pope] ... [10 acres, 3 rods, and 35 perches]; [Witnessed by - William P [?], Senr; Peter Tallman; Recorded - 14 February 1785.]

[p 14] **JAMES FENIMORE to JOHN POPE**

7 April 1784 - Between James Fenimore ... Mansfield Township ... Carpenter and Elizabeth his wife and John Pope of the same Place Merch't ... [sold for 20 pounds] ... Piece of Ground (being Part of a larger Lot purchased by the said James Fenimore of Mathais Kerlin & wife ... [23 July 1781] ... and which ... said ... Kerlin purchased of his Grandfather John Buffin ... [13 June 1772]) ... being in the Township of Mansfield ... [Adjacent land owners or names - John Imlay Junr; Mount Pleasant Road; James Fenimore; Thomas Kerlin] ... [3,276 square feet of land] ...; [Witnessed by - William Black, Jacob Vansciver, Thomas Kerlin; Recorded - 7 April 1784.]

[p 16] **JOSEPH & ELIZABETH GIBBS to MARMADUKE WATSON CURTIS**

3 September 1783 - Between Joseph Gibbs and Elizabeth ... his wife of the Township of Mansfield ... and Marmaduke Watson Curtis of the same place Hatter ... [sold for 13 pounds and 10 shillings] ... Lot of Land ... in ... Mansfield Township near the black House ... [Adjacent land owners or names - the Black House; Edward Thomas; Corner of the Widow Delatush] ... [land of 48 rods] ...; [Witnessed by - Edward Thomas, J. Imlay; Recorded - 3 September 1783.]

[p 18] **JOSEPH GIBBS to JOHN POPE**

16 November 1782 - Between Joseph Gibbs of Mansfield Yeoman and Elizabeth his wife ... and John Pope of the same Place Merchant ... Whereas Isaac Gibbs the Elder of Mansfield aforesaid deceased ... and by his last Will ... bequeath unto his Grandson Joseph Gibbs ... the son of his Son Richard Gibbs all the Eastern Part of Said ... Land ... [dated 18 January 1742] ... NOW this Indenture ... Joseph Gibbs and Elizabeth his Wife ... [sold for 22 pounds and 10 shillings] ... [Adjacent land owners or names - Nathaniel Pope, Joseph Gibbs, George Folwell] ... [2 acres of land] ...; [Witnessed by - Jacob Walcott, George Saville; Recorded - 18 November 1782.]

[p 20] **JOSEPH IMLAY to JOHN POPE**

16 November 1782 - Between Joseph Imlay of Mansfield ... Quit Claims unto John Pope of the Place

BURLINGTON COUNTY DEEDS - BOOK "A"

aforesaid ... the Within mentioned Lot of Land as the same is Conveyed by Joseph Gibbs and Elizabeth his Wife ... [for 5 shillings] ...; [Witnessed by - Jacob Wolcott, Peter Tallman; Recorded - 18 November 1782.]

[p 21] JOHN BLACK to JOHN POPE

13 April 1784 - Between John Black late of the Township of Mansfield ... Burlington ... New Jersey but at present of the City of Philadelphia Board & Merchant and Mary his Wife ... And John Pope [of the same place] ... Merchant Witnesseth that the said John Black and Mary his Wife ... [sold for 88 pounds] ... the following described Lot and Piece of Woodland being Part of a larger Tract of Land devised unto the said John Black by the last Will ... of his Father William Black ... situate ... in the Township of Mansfield ... [Adjacent land owners or names - Line of John Black's other land, to Land of John Atkinson, Line of Aaron Robins, to Nathan Folwells Land] ... [land consisted of 7 acres, 3 rods and 35 perches] ...; [Witnessed by - Jacob Walcott, William Black; Recorded - 13 April 1784.]

[p 23] TRIPARTETE DEED

This Indenture Tripartete made ... [18 July 1782] ... Between Joseph Ellison ... County of Burlington ... New Jersey Yeoman and Hannah his Wife One of the Daughters of Robert Hartshorne of the said County of Burlington, Attorney at Law deceased of the first part, Richard Wells of the City of Philadelphia ... Pennsylvania Merchant, which said Richard Wells and the said Hannah Hartshorne are Trustees named in an Indenture here after mentioned of the second Part And Benjamin Chew of the said City of Philadelphia Esquire of the third part. Whereas by Indenture ... [22 January 1752] ... made between Joseph Allinson of the City and County of Burlington Yeoman and Elizabeth his Wife of the one Part and the said Robert Hartshorne of the other Part ... for the Consideration therein mentioned, they the said Joseph Allinson and Elizabeth his Wife ... [sold unto] ... Robert Hartshorne ... A certain Lot of Land called a Water Lot in the said City of Burlington ... [Adjacent land owners or names - Matthew Allen, near Henry Berchanes] ...And Whereas by Indenture ... [9 January 1731] ... made between Simon Nightingale of the Town and County of Burlington and Sarah his Wife of the One Part and Peter Baynton of the said City of Philadelphia Merchant of the other Part ... they the said Simon Nightingale and Sarah his Wife ... [sold to] ... Peter Baynton ... dwelling House and Lot of Land situate in the Town of Burlington fronting the River Delaware ... [Adjacent land owners or names - Peter Bard, Esq, to Pearl Street] ... [Recorded in Liber E, folio 210] ... And Whereas the said Peter Baynton by his last Will ... [made 11 December 1742] ... did give and bequeath all the residue ... of his Estate ... to his oldest Son John Baynton ... [Will recorded Liber 5, fol 15 Perogative Court] ... And Whereas by virtue of a Certain Agreement in Writing ... between the above named Robert Hartshorne ... and the said John Baynton ... [1752] ... the said John Baynton ... [sold] ... to the said Robert Hartshorne ... And Whereas the said Robert Hartshorne ... having paid to the said John Baynton ... afterwards departed this Life Intestate leaving a Widow Named Hannah and their Infant Daughters Namely Catharine Margaret and Hannah before any Deed or Conveyance was

BURLINGTON COUNTY DEEDS - BOOK "A"

executed by the said John Baynton to the said Robert Hartshorne ... according to the true Intent and Meaning of the said recited agreement to Which said Catharine Margaret and Hannah Daughters of the said Robert Hartshorne deceased, descended the said Hannah the Widow being entitled to the Right of Dower therein And Whereas by Indenture tripartete ... [1753] ... between the said John Baynton and Elizabeth his Wife ... of the first part And Samuel Smith of the said County of Burlington Esquire and Hugh Hartshorne of the same County Yeoman ... of the second part And the said Hannah Hartshorne Widow and Relict of the said Robert Hartshorne deceased And Catharine Hartshorne, Margaret Hartshorne and Hannah Hartshorne Daughters of the said Robert Hartshorne deceased of the third part ... the said John Baynton ... [sold] ... unto the said Samuel Smith and Hugh Hartshorne ... All that ... last above described Lot of Land ... To hold to them ... in trust as to One third Part thereof to the use ... of the said Hannah Hartshorne the Widow ... and after her decease to the use of the said three Daughters Catharine Margaret and Hannah ... And as to the other two third Parts whereof to the Use ... of the said Catharine Margaret and Hannah ... as Tenants in Common ... And Whereas Hannah Hartshorne the Widow of the said Robert Hartshorne deceased is since deceased. And Whereas Margaret Hartshorne One of the Daughters of the said Robert Hartshorne deceased is also dead Intestate unmarried and Without Issue Whereby all her ... Share ... in the Estate ... descended unto and vested in her two Sisters the said Catharine and Hannah. And Whereas the said Catharine afterwards intermarried with a certain Benjamin Fordham and the said Benjamin Fordham and Catharine his Wife by Indenture bearing ... [date 10 August 1771 sold] ... All the Right and Interest of her the said Catharine in the Estate Real and Personal of the said Robert Hartshorne deceased unto the said Richard Wells and Hannah Hartshorne (the Daughter) ... In Trust to sell and dispose of the same to any Person ... by the last recited Indenture ... [Book A-E, Fol 381] ... And Whereas the said Hannah Hartshorne (the Daughter) afterwards intermarried With the said Joseph Ellison. Now this Indenture Witnesseth that for and in consideration of ... unto the said Joseph Ellison and Hannah his Wife and Richard Wells in hand ... paid by the said Benjamin Chew ... [sold to said Benjamin Chew] ... All that the said Lot of Land (called a Water Lot) situate in Burlington aforesaid ...; [Witnessed by - Isabella Kearney, Richard Smith; Recorded - 18 July 1702 (sic)].

[p 29]   **BENJAMIN CHEW to FREDERICK KESSELMAN**

8 October 1784 - Between Benjamin Chew of Burlington ... County of Burlington ... New Jersey Esquire and Elizabeth his Wife of the One Part And Frederick Kesselman of the City of Philadelphia ... Pennsylvania Merchant ... Witnesseth that the said Benjamin Chew and Elizabeth his Wife ... [sold for 1,400 pounds] ... A certain Lot of Land Called a Water Lot in the said City of Burlington ... [Adjacent land owners or names - the Lot Late of Matthew Allen, Henry Birchams, fronting the River Delaware, Land late in possession of Peter Bard Esq, Pearl Street] ... and two described Lots of Land Joseph Ellison of the said County of Burlington Yeoman and Hannah his Wife, and Richard Wells of the said City of Philadelphia Merchant by Indenture tripartite ... [dated 18 July 1782] ...; [Witnessed by - John Abm. Debrmandie, Rd. Shettell [?] Jones; Recorded - 8 October 1784.]

BURLINGTON COUNTY DEEDS - BOOK "A"

****

[p 32] MATTHIAS KERLIN to JOHN POPE

4 August 1783 - Between Matthias Kerlin of the Town of Mansfield ... county of Burlington ... New Jersey Cordwainer of the One Part. And John Pope of the same place Merchant of the other part ... [sold for 22 pounds and 10 shillings] ... the following described piece of ground being part of ... [1300 acres] ... located by Percival Forole [?] late of the City of Burlington ... in several Tracts all lying in the Town of Mansfield ... and the sd Percival Toule [?] being so seized did by his last Will ... [dated 26th day of the 8th Month 1691 Recorded in Register's Office] ... give and devise ... unto Frances Davenport George Hutchinson & John Woolston the aforementioned tract ... in Trust for the uses expressed in Sd Will recourse being thereunto had well appear: And the Saide Frances Davenport George Hutchinson & John Woolston being so thereof Seized did by their Deed ... [dated 20 May 1696 - Public Records at Burlington - Book 13, Page 665] ... Convey the same to Richard Gibbs then of Long Island in the State of New York Hatter And the Said Richard Gibbs being so whereof Seized & dying intestate his Son Isaac Gibbs the elder Became invested with the aforesaid tract of land as his only Son & Heir at Law: & the said Isaac Gibbs the Elder being so whereof seized did convey the Eastermost part of the aforesaid Tract unto his Son Richard Gibbs by Deed ... And Richard Gibbs being so whereof Seized did By his Deed ... [dated 1 April 1735] ... convey the same to his Brother John Gibbs & Sd John Gibbs being so whereof seized did by his Deed bearing date ... [3 March 1738/9] ... convey two Acres part of the aforesaid tract (and ... the premises ...) unto Jacob Hugg of Mansfield & the Sd Jacob Hugg ... [sold on 1 September 1739 by deed the above 2 acres] ... to Isaac Gibbs the Younger & the Sd Isaac Gibbs the Younger ... [sold to] ... John Buffin: And the Sd John Buffin ... did by his Last Will ... [dated 20 April 1771] ... bequeathed the aforesd two Acres of Land unto his Grandson Matthias Kerlin grantor to these presents ... [Adjacent land owners or names - Road Leading from Mount Pleasant by the Black House, by the Land of Matthias Kerlin, Road leading from the Black House to Martin Gibbs] ... [consisting of 7 rods of land or 1400 & 40 square feet] ...; [Witnessed by - Jacob Wolcott; Recorded - 26 August 1783.]

[p 35] PHILLIP NUTT to NATHANIEL POPE

26 March 1771 - Between Phillip Nutt of Chesterfield ... county of Burlington ... New Jersey Yeoman of the One Part And Nathaniel Pope of Mansfield ... [of the same place - sold for 160 pounds] ... A certain piece ... of Meadow Ground Situate ... in Mansfield aforesaid ... [Adjacent land owners or names - Corner of Henry Delatush which was late Joseph Gibb's corner, Joseph Tallman's Corner, George Folwell] ... [consisting of 9 acres, 1 rod and 7 perches] ... Land The Said Phillip Nutt purchased from John Harvey & Ann his Wife ... [dated 1 August 1758] ...; [Witnessed by - Joseph Pancoast Junr, Thomas Richards, Jos Imlay; Recorded 1 Feb 1785.]

[p 38] PHILLIP NUTT to NATHANIEL POPE

26 March 1781 - Between Phillip Nutt of the Township of Chester ... county of Burlington ... New

BURLINGTON COUNTY DEEDS - BOOK "A"

****

Jersey (Yeoman) ... And Nathaniel Pope of Mansfield (Joyner) ... Whereas Isaac Gibbs ... [sold on 20 January 1720] ... unto his Son Richard Gibbs a Certain Quantity of Land in the Township of Mansfield Aforesaid And the said Richard Gibbs ... [sold on 1 April 1745] ... to his Brother John Gibbs ... And whereas the Said John Gibbs ... [sold on 21 April 1744 [?] did] ... Convey the same ... unto Michael Buffin ... & the said Michael Buffin & John Gibbs being so thereof Seized ... [sold on 19 January 1744 [?]] ... fifty acres of the above Recited Land unto Thomas Nutt And whereas Thomas Nutt ... [sold on 26 June 1747] ... the same unto the Sd Phillip Nutt the present Grantor. Now this Indenture the Sd Phillip Nutt ... [sold for 171 pounds, 5 shillings] ... to Nathaniel Pope ... the above Recited fifty Acres ... Situated ... [Adjacent land owners or names - Blacks Land, Isaac Gibbs land, in the line of Thomas Curtis, Mount Pleasant Road, to John Buffins Corner] ... [amounting to 50 acres] ...; [Witnessed by - Joseph Pancoast Junr, Thomas Richards, Joseph Imlay; Recorded - 1 Feb 1785.]

[p 42]   **JOSEPH GIBBS** to **HENRY DELATUSH**

6 January 1776 - Between Joseph Gibbs Yeoman ... and Henry Delatush Cooper ... both of the Township of Mansfield ... county of Burlington ... New Jersey Whereas Isaac Gibbs the Elder late of Mansfield afd. Dec'd ... Seized ... in Certain Lands Situate in the Township of Mansfield ... And ... did ... by his last Will ... bequeath unto his Grandson Joseph Gibbs (party to these presents) the son of his son Richard Gibbs all the Eastern part of Said Tract of Land & Plantation to ... the said Joseph Gibbs ... & by the Sd Will before given the Western part of the Said Plantation the Said Joseph Gibbs ... Expressed as by the Will ... [dated 18 January 1742/3 - Book 6, folio 31] ...Witnesseth that the Said Joseph Gibbs ... [sold for 11 pounds, 5 shillings] ... [Adjacent land owners or names - George Folwell, Henry Delatush, Nathaniel Pope's Land] ... [amounting to 2 acres] ...; [Witnessed by - Job Emans, Jno Black, Recorded - 2 Feb 1785.]

[p 45]   **JOSEPH GIBBS** to **JACOB VANSCIVER**

10 May 1784 - Between Joseph Gibbs and Elizabeth his Wife of the Township of Mansfield ... county of Burlington ... New Jersey Yeoman ... [sold to] ... Jacob Vansciver of the same place Innkeeper ... [for 165 pounds [?]] ... Land ... in the Township of Mansfield ... [Adjacent land owners or names - Road ... from the Black House to the City of Burlington, Corner to Edwd Thomas Tanyard Lot, Joseph Gibbs] ... Land ... Whereas Isaac Gibbs Grandfather to the afd. Joseph Gibbs ... [was seized] ... in ... a Certain Plantation ... in the Township of Mansfd .. and by his last Will ... bequeath unto his Grandson Joseph Gibbs party to these Presents the Son of his Son Rich'd Gibbs all the Eastern Part of the said Tract ... And by Virtue of the Bequeath from his Grandfather Isaac Gibbs ... to him the said Joseph Gibbs doth sell ... the above described One Acre and 38 perches of Land ...; [Witnessed by - Jacob Wolcott, Peter Tallman, Joseph Imlay; Recorded - 26 May 1784.]

BURLINGTON COUNTY DEEDS - BOOK "A"

****

[p 47]   **JOSEPH IMLAY** to **JACOB VANSCIVER**

26 March 1785 - Joseph Imlay of the Township of Mansfield ... county of Burlington ... New Jersey hathe granted ... quit Claimed unto Jacob Vansciver ... [for 5 shillings] ...; [Witnessed by - John Phillips, John Imlay; Recorded - 5 April 1785.]

[p 48]   **JOHN CAMPBELL** to **EPHRAIM CLARK**

13 Dec 1784 - Between John Campbell of Timber Creek ... county of Burlington ... New Jersey Storekeeper & Elizabeth his Wife ... [sold to] ... Ephraim Clark of the City of Philadelphia ... Pennsylvania Watchmaker ... [for 100 pounds] ... Land ... on the Northside of Mill Street in Mount Holly ... county of Burlington New Jersey ... [Adjacent land owners or names - Josiah Whites house now or late in the Tenure of Peter Chiras [?], Micajah Walls Land] ... Which ... Lot Jaber Woolston of Mount Holly ... Taylor & Esther his Wife by Indenture ... [dated 25 January 1776 sold to] ... Alexander Wills with Ann his Wife ... [on 7 January 1779] ... Granted ... the same (Interlia) unto the said John Campbell ...; [Witnessed by - Rich'd Thomas, Solomon McNair, Elizabeth Campbell, Wm Harrison, Jsh Hugg; Recorded - 31 December 1784.]

[p 52]   **MARMADUKE WATSON CURTIS** to **JOHN POPE**

13 September 1784 - Between Marmaduke Watson Curtis ... Township of Mansfield ... county of Burlington ... New Jersey Hatter and Mary his Wife ... [sold to] ... John Pope of the same Place Merchant ... [for 142 pounds, 10 shillings] ... A Certain House and two Lotts of land adjoining each other situate in Mansfield ... [Adjacent land owners or names - the black House, Edward Thomas, Joseph Gibbs, Road that leads from the Black Horse to Burlington] ... [consisting of .25 acres] ... The other Lot ... [Names of adjacent land owners - Marmaduke W.Curtis's, from Black Horse, to Edward Thomas, Corner of the Widw Delatush] ... [consisting of 68 rods] ... said two Lots of Land is part of a larger Tract bequeathed by Isaac Gibbs the elder to his Grand son Joseph ... [dated 18 January 1742/3] ... One Whereof Conveyed unto William Dilworth ... [on 5 January 1782] ... and by the said William Dilworth was Ordered by his last Will ... to be disposed of by his Executor John Pope ... The other Lot was Conveyed by Joseph Gibbs and Wife unto Marmaduke Watson Curtes ... [on 13 September 1783] ... the front Lot being also conveyed unto ... Curtis by John Pope ... [on 19 July 1783] ...; [Witnessed by - John Nutt, John Black Jun'r; Recorded - 14 September 1784.]

[p 55]   **JOHN FORMAN** to **EXECUTORS OF JOHN RIDGWAY**

2 February 1778 - Between John Forman of the Township of Little Egg Harbor ... county of Burlington ... New Jersey & Phoebe Ridgway Executrix & John Ridgway Executor to John Ridgway Deceased ... [of the same place for 322 pounds] ... All them several Tracts of Land & Cedar Swamps lying in the Township & County Aforesaid the Tract that the said Forman now doth live on ...

BURLINGTON COUNTY DEEDS - BOOK "A"

[Adjacent land owners or names - Ridgeway Creek, Mill Creek, Line Creek, North side of the Meeting House Road, Corner of James Freelands land, Bridge Creek, Daniel Shourds line] ... [consisting of 250 acres] ... Bounded Southerly by ... [Adjacent land owners or names - Ridgeway Creek, Calsep Carr, James Freeland, Daniel Shourds, Mill Creek] ... And Also a tract of Cedar swamp Lying on the southeasterly Branch of Bass River that part of said swamp that Mordicai Andrews did give to his son Isaac Andrews by Will ... the said Phoebe Ridgeway & John Ridgeway Executrix & Executor ... To Grant which the sd John Forman has ... by a Deed of sale from Isaac Andrews ... [on 23 September 1777] ... we the sd John Forman & Elinor Forman Wife of the sd John Forman hath hereunto set their hands ...; [Witnessed by - John Gaunt, Daniel Shourds; Recorded - 23 June 1785.]

[p 59]   **PETER TALLMAN** to **THOMAS TALLMAN**

13 January 1768 - Peter Tallman ... Township of Mansfield ... Burlington ... New Jersey ... Yeoman & Margaret his wife ... [sold to] ... Thomas Tallman ... Township of Evesham ... Yeoman ... [for 500 pounds] ... Lotts of Land situate in Mansfield ... [Adjacent land owners or names-Burlington & Mansfield Roads, Road to Mansfield Meeting House, Lott of Land formerly Lyndon Browns now of Said Peter Tallman, Joseph Gibbs, Burlington Road] ... [.5 acres and 12 sq perches] ... Also other Lott ... [Adjacent land owners or names - Mansfield Road] ... [.25 acres] ... both ... Lotts ... Peter Tallman Purchased of John Hutchins & Sarah his Wife by Deed ... [dated 15 Sept 1764] ... The first mentioned Lott was by sd John Hutchins purchased of Joseph Gibbs & Mary his Wife by deed ... [dated 15 June 1763] ... & the other Lott ... purchased of Linden Brown by Deed ... [dated 16 Feb 1764] ...; [Witnessed by - John Cox, Willm Cox, Junr, Eliz^h Imlay, Benj^a Talman.]

[12 December 1774 - Peter & Margaret Tallman appeared before Robert Field, Judge of Inferior Court, Burlington.]

[p 64]   **DANIEL ELLIS** to **JOHN POPE**

7 May 1779 - Daniel Ellis ... City of Burlington ... Burlington ... New Jersey Esqr ... [sold to] ... John Pope of Mansfield ... [for 3 pounds] ... [20 acres] ... of Inappropriated Land to be taken up & Surveyed to him the sd. John Pope ... [which land] ... is part of a Warrant granted ... unto the sd Daniel Ellis for ... [208 and 1/3 acres] ... anywhere in the ... [Western Division] ... below the fall of Delaware as by sd. Warrant ... [dated 4 November 1778] ...; [Witnesses - Robert Burchan, Henry Ridgway.]

[p 66]   **RICHARD SMITH JR** and **EBENEZER LARGE** to **JOHN BAKER**

24 March 1750 - Richard Smith Jr of Burlington ... Burlington ... New Jersey, Esqr and Ebenezer Large of Burlington afore Said Merchant ... [sold to] ... John Baker of Northampton ... Burlington ... Yeoman ... [for 240 pounds] ... One ... Tract of Land ... in Northampton ... [Adjacent land owners

BURLINGTON COUNTY DEEDS - BOOK "A"

or names - Henry Cooper, Road from Bridgetown to Eayres Town, Thomas Budd] ... [120 acres] ... [land was purchased from Susanna Dunsdale, Calvert Bonyer, Thomas Boyner, Thomas Dunsdale, Joseph Dunsdale on 28th & 29th of March 1746] ...; [Witnesses - Abrm. Farrington, Thomas Budd.]

[6 March 1775 - A John Burr, Quaker, appeared before Judge Henry Paxson, Burlington, and declared that he knew both Grantors and knew their handwriting.]

[p 70]   **JOSEPH GIBBS to JOHN HUTCHINS**

15 June 1763 - Joseph Gibbs and Mary his wife of Mansfield ... Burlington ... New Jersey ... Yeoman ... [sold to] ... John Hutchins of the same place Shopkeeper ... [for 42 pounds] ... Land ... in Township of Mansfield ... [Adjacent land owners or names - Burlington & Mansfield Road, Road to Mansfield Meeting House, Lyndon Brown, Burlington Road] ... [.5 acres and 12 perches] ...; [Witnesses - Lyndon Brown, Obadiah King; Mary made her mark when signing deed.]

[9 Aug 1763 - Joseph and Mary Gibbs appeared before Judge Robert Smith, Burlington.]

[p 74]   **WILLIAM SYKES to BENJAMIN RANDOLPH**

1 September 1784 - William Sykes ... City of Philadelphia ... Pennsylvania ... Merchant ... [sold to] ... Benjamin Randolph late of the City but now of the City of Burlington ... New Jersey ... Merchant ... [for 600 pounds] ... Land ... in the City of Burlington ... [Adjacent land owners or names - Corner of Fourth St & earl Street, James Verves [?], Delaware River] ... [land is the same lott which Catherine Carey Executrix John Mitchell and John Laurance Executors of ... Will ... of John Carey Esquire Late of ... City of Burlington deceased ... [dated 1 August 1781] ...; [Witnesses - John Redman, Asshton Humphreys.]

[5 September 1785 - William Sykes appeared before Judge Joshua M. Wallace, Burlington Co.]

[p 77]   **BARNT DE KLYNE to HUGH RUNYAN**

30 November 1785 - Barnt De Klyne of Trenton ... Hunterdon ... New Jersey ... Merchant ... to ... Hugh Runyan of Nottingham ... Burlington ... [in consideration of Rents ... agreements in the contract contained in this item] ... Unto the said Hugh Runyan all these three following Farms ... lying & being Contiguous to each other ... All that Farm ... late in possession of Major William Trent deceased known by the name of Barnts [?] place (2) ... Land ... late in possession of Randle Mitchell known by ... Mitchell's place (3d) ... Land ... now or late in possession of the said Barnt De Klyne Known by the name of Meredith place ... the said Runyon and Family shall pass over the Ferries of the said De Klyne Ferriag free ...; [Witnesses - Evan Runyan, Ebenezer Cowell Jn^r.]

BURLINGTON COUNTY DEEDS - BOOK "A"

****

[7 January 1786 - De Klyne appeared before Judge John Cox, Esqr, Burlington; Recorded - 14 January 1785.]

[p 82]   **ISRAEL SMALL to RUTH SMALL**

22 April 1771 - Israel Small ... Township of Evesham ... Burlington ... New Jersey ... Yeoman ... [sold to] ... Ruth Small ... [of the same place] ... Widow ... Whereas John Small Late of ... Evesham aforesaid Yeoman Deceas^d in ... his last Will ... [dated 21 August 1768] ... did give ... Land unto his Sons William and John Small and Robert Small Each Six Acres ... [and the remainder of the tract in Evesham] ... unto his [?] sons Israel Small and Jonas Small ... Now this Indenture Witnesseth ... the sd Israel Small and Ann his Wife for ... [65 pounds, 10 shillings sold unto Ruth Small 1/2 of the remainder of said land devised unto Israel Small in and by the sd Will of his father ... John Small] ...; [Witnesses - Wm Cox, John Cox; Ann Small made her mark when signing.]

[4 January 1786 - John Cox, a Quaker, appeared before Judge Joshua M. Wallace, Burlington Co.]

[p 86]   **GEORGE BOWMAN to JACOB WOLCOTT**

29 July 1785 - George Bowman of the Township of Mansfield ... Burlington ... New Jersey ... Laborer and Mary his wife ...[sold to] ... Jacob Wolcott of the same place Surveyor ... [for 46 pence, 2 shilling] ... Land ... in ... Mansfield ... [Adjacent land owners and names - Mount Pleasant Road, Nathaniel Pope, William Carslake, Joseph Gibbs, Burget Attenger] ... [4 acres, 2 rods, 20 perches] ...; [Witnesses - John Pope, Saly Willas; Mary Bowman made her mark when signing.]

[10 January 1786 - John Pope appeared before Judge Peter Tallman, Burlington Co.]

[1 January 1786 - John Pope ... quit Claimed unto Jacob Wolcott ... [the same property] ... conveyed by George Bowman & Mary his Wife ... [for 5 shillings] ...; [Witnesses - Peter Tallman, Robert White; Recorded - 7 February 1786.]

[p 89]   **JOHN POPE to JOB FOSTER**

27 January 1786 - John Pope Executor ... of Joseph Pope late of Mansfield County of Burlington ... New Jersey deceased ... [sold to] ... Job Foster of the same Place Yeoman ... [for 11 pounds] ... Piece of Cedar Swamp ... [Adjacent land owners or names - middle branch of Wading River, Joseph Pope the Elder, Lot late of late John Aaronson] ... [7 acres, 3 rods and part of a larger Tract of 8 acres, 1 rod and 2 perches] ... located by Joseph Pope the Elder ... [and recorded in Liber L, Page 34] ... as Heir at Law by Joseph Pope the Younger who by his ... Will directed the same to be sold ...;

BURLINGTON COUNTY DEEDS - BOOK "A"

****

[Witnesses - Jacob Vansciver, Joseph Dilworth; 15 February 1786 - John Pope appeared before Judge Joshua M. Wallace, Burlington Co.]

[p 91]   **JOHN POPE to JOSHUA FOSTER**

27 January 1786 - John Pope Executor ... of Joseph Pope late of Mansfield County of Burlington ... New Jersey deceased ... [sold to] ... Joshua Foster of the same Place ... [for 12 pounds] ... piece of Cedar Swamp ... [Adjacent land owners or names - William Pancoast] ... [3 acres, 1 rod, and 10 perches] ... located by Joseph Pope the Elder ... [and recorded in Liber L, Page 34] ... as Heir at Law by Joseph Pope the Younger who by his ... Will directed the same to be sold ...; [Witnesses - Jacob Vansciver, Joseph Dilworth.]

[15 February 1786 - John Pope appeared before Judge Joshua M. Wallace, Burlington Co.]

[p 93]   **JOHN GIBBS to MICHAEL BUFFIN**

8 April 1747 - John Gibbs of the Township of Mansfield ... Burlington ... New Jersey yeoman ... [sold to] ... Michael Buffin ... [of the same place ... Yeoman ... [for 28 pounds] ... Land ... in ... Mansfield ... [Adjacent land owners or names - John Buffin, Thomas Kerlin, Mount Pleasant Road, Lott of Land laid out and Designed for John Hutchins] ... [4 acres being part of Land] ... conveyed to the said John Gibbs by his Brother Richard Gibbs by Deed ... [dated 1 April 1785] ... which ... Richard Gibbs purchased of his Father Isaac Gibbs by Indenture ... [dated 20 January 1720 and recorded in Book E-Page 395] ... and was further conveyed to ... John Gibbs by Deed ... [dated 19 April 1744 by his Father Isaac Gibbs] ...; [Witnesses - Thomas Richards, Thomas Kerlin, Isaac Decounedius [?]; Hannah Gibbs signed as wife of John Gibbs and made her mark when signing.]

[11 November 1773 - John Gibbs appeared before Judge Thomas Rodman, Burlington Co.]

[p 97]   **JOSEPH MULLEN to JOB LIPPINCOTT**

20 January 1786 - Joseph Mullen Esquire late High Sheriff of ... Burlington ... New Jersey ... [sold to] ... Job Lippincott ... Township of Springfield ... Burlington ... New Jersey ... Whereas Job Lippincott late of Springfield ... Dec'd was ... [by deed from Thomas Atkinson dated 13 March 1783] ... Seized of ... Land ... being on the Westerly Side of High Street in Bridgeton ... [the estate of Thomas Shinn Esqr dec'd, North Main Branch of Ancocas [?] Creek, Thomas Atkinson] ... [13 sq perches] ... [And being so Seized made his Will and gave the Estate of which the above Lot was part unto his two sons Joseph and Job Lippincott] ... the said Joseph Lippincott became Seized of one Moiety ... as Tennant in Common And Whereas Thomas Gaskill, Job Rynear, William Pullen and the Executors of Joseph Pancoast Dec'd ... [1784] ... Recovered against the said Joseph Lippincott ... [to recover Certain Debt and Whereas Joseph Mullen, Sheriff, took possession of the property of the

BURLINGTON COUNTY DEEDS - BOOK "A"

aforesaid Joseph Lippincott for want of sufficient funds it and exposed it for sale and Job Lippincott bid 86 pounds with this Indenture] ...; [Witnessed - William Rossell, Jos. Read.]

[23 February 1786 - Joseph Mullen, Esquire, appeared before Judge Joseph Read Esquire, Master of Chancery Court, Burlington Co.]

[p 102]   **JOB LIPPINCOTT to ANNA LIPPINCOTT**

23 February 1786 - Job Lippincott ... Township of Springfield and his Grand Mother Anna Lippincott of Mount Holly ... [both of Burlington Co, New Jersey, sold to] ... Hugh Hollingshead of Mount Holly ... Clock and Watch Maker ... Whereas Job Lippincott party of these Presents by Virtue ... [of an Indenture dated 13 October 1753 regarding] ... Land Situate on the west side of High Street in Mount Holly ... did ... convey Same by Deed to his Mother the afsd Anna Lippincott ... [Job died seized of the property and by his last Will it] ... became the property and Estate his two Sons Joseph Lippincott and the above named Job Lippincott ... Subject to the Life Estate of their said Grand Mother therein And Whereas the said Joseph Lippincotts Estate in the premises ... [was seized and taken in Execution of several writs and delivered to Joseph Mullen Esqr, Sheriff, and was then sold & conveyed unto the above named Job Lippincott the son by deed and sold by Mullen] ... [Adjacent land owners or names - West side of High Street, Samuel Bispham, formerly Thomas Shinn, Esqr, Zachariah Rossell] ... [30 sq perches] ... Now this Indenture Witnesseth that the said Job Lippincott the younger and Anna Lippincott ... in Consideration of ... Hugh Hollingshead and his Wife by Indenture ... Conveying unto ... Anna Lippincott and her Heirs ... [sold] ... Lot of Land in Mount Holly ... Situate ... [by White Street for 131 pounds] ... paid unto Job Lippincott the younger ...; [Witnesses - Joseph Mullen, Jos. Read.]

[23 February 1786 - Job Lippincott and Anna Lippincott appeared before Judge, Joseph Read, Esqr, Burlington Co.]

[23 February 1786 - Samuel Bispham of Mount Holly, Hatter, agreed to Hugh Hollingshead's "Quiet enjoyment of the Dwelling House ... he hath purchased of Job Lippincott ... late in the Tenement of Anna Lippincott Wido ..."; [Witnesses - W. Stretch, Jos. Read.]

[p 108]   **MANUMISSION OF JUDE LAMB**

2 May 1786 - I John Taylor ... Township of Chesterfield ... Burlington ... New Jersey ... do hereby set free from Bondage my negro Wench named Jude Lamb aged about twenty seven years ...; [Witnesses - Isaac Cowgill, Joel Middleton.]

2 May 1786 - John Taylor ... brought before us, two of the Overseers of the Poor ... & two of the Justices of the Peace ... his Slave named Jude Lamb Who ... appears to us to be sound of Mind and

BURLINGTON COUNTY DEEDS - BOOK "A"

not under any bodily Incapacity of obtaining a Support And also is not under twenty One Years of Age nor above thirty five ...; [Tomas Fenimore, Isaac Cowgill - Justices of the Peace; Joel Middleton, Thomas Morr - Overseers of the Poor; Recorded - 10 May 1786 before Judge John Phillips, Clerk of the Peace of Pleas ... Burlington Co.]

[p 110] **JAMES STERLING to RICHARD STOCKTON**

3 November 1785 - James Sterling, Esqr ... City of Burlington ... Burlington ... New Jersey ... Whereas a Certain Plantation ... in the County of Burlington and Township of Springfield was by a Certain Indenture ... December 1761 Mortgaged by Samuel Stockton unto ... James Sterling ... [for 350 pounds] ... which Plantation ... hath become the Estate of Richd Stockton ... Now-know-ye that I ...James Sterling the Mortgagee ... [for 5 shillings] ... paid by ... Richard Stockton do Releases ... Unto the said Richard Stockton ... (the same in his possession now actually being) ... [Adjacent land owners or names - Samuel Stockton, Richard Stockton] ... [25 acres] ...; [Witnesses - James H. Sterling, Jos Reade].

[p 111] **JOSHUA HERITAGE'S POWER OF ATTORNEY**

10 June 1786 - Joshua Heritage late of Township of Chester ... Burlington ... New Jersey ... and now of the Township of Kingwood in ... Hunterdon ... Yeoman ... appoint Reece Edwards Esquire of ... Township of Chester my true and Lawfull Attorney ...; [Witnesses - William Cox, Thomas Stokes.]

[p 113] **JOHN BUDD to WILLIAM CORDEARY**

16 June 1709 - John Budd ... City of Philadelphia ... Pennsylvania ... Brewer ... And William Cordeary of Great Egg Harbour ... Burlington ... New Jersey ... Husbandman ... Witnesseth that ... Jno Budd ... is now ... seized ... of and in the hereafter Granted ... [500 acres] ... Now these Presents ... the said Jno Budd ...[for 5 shillings] ... forever release ... the said Wm Cordeary ... [500 acres] ... on the Sea Coast at Egg Harbour ... [Adjacent land owners or names - Thomas Budd (now possessed by Peter White), the Bay] ...; [Witnessed - Samuel Hoult, John Comius [?], Sarah Morrey.]

[10 October 1786 - John Budd of Mount Holly, Burlington Co, New Jersey, appeared before Judge Joseph Read, Esquire, and said "that he was personally acquainted with his Cousin Jno Budd the Lessor in the within Indenture."]

[From the above item, it would appear that this subject, the John Budd of Philadelphia, signed his name as "John Budd" in an attempt to differentiate himself from his cousin, also named John Budd, but who apparently signed his name as "Jno. Budd".]

BURLINGTON COUNTY DEEDS - BOOK "A"

[p 116] **JAMES STERLING, ESQR to RICHARD STOCKTON**

3 November 1785 - Greetings whereas a certain Plantation and tract of Land in ... County of Burlington ... Township of Springfield was by a certain Indenture ... [dated December 1781] ... Mortgaged by Samuel Stockton unto ... James Sterling for the payment of ... [350 pounds which] ... became the Estate of Richard Stockton ... Now Know ye that I ... James Sterling the mortgagee in the said Mortgage ... [for 5 shillings paid] ... by Richard Stockton do Release ... and forever Quit Claim unto the said Richd Stockton ... a certain part of the ... Mortgaged Premises ... [adjacent land owners or names - [the Division Line between Samuel and Richard Stockton] ... [25 acres] ...; [Signed - James Sterling; witnesses - James H. Sterling, Jos. Reed.]

[p 118] **THOMAS ENGLISH, JUN to JOSEPH ARCHER**

This Indenture ... [dated 28 March 1772] ... Between Thomas English Jr & Ann his Wife of ... Township of Mansfield ... Burlington ... New Jersey ... [sold to] ... Joseph Archer ... [of the same place] ... [for 200 pounds] ... Land Situate ... Township of Mansfield ... which he the s^d Thomas English Jun Purchased of Israel Butler ... [by deed dated 6 May 1771] ... and the said Israel Butler purchased the s^d piece of Land of & from his Father John Butler ... [by deed dated 9 June 1762 and John Butler purchased it from Thomas Shreve by deed on 29 March 1762 and he purchased it from] ... John Shreve Son & Heir of ... Jonathan Shreve dec'd & Hannah Shreve Mother of the s^d John Shreve ... [by deed dated 22 June 1756 & Jonathan Shreve purchased it from James Whitehead by deed dated 15 March 1737, and Whitehead purchased it from William Biddle and Lydia Biddle his wife] ... & William Biddle Junr their Son by deed ... [dated 27 June 1728] ... [Adjacent land owners or names - York Road] ... [14 acres with the Dwelling House] ...; [Witnesses - John Folwell, John Pope Testes [This last word was underlined].

[27 August 1773 - Thomas English, Junr and Ann, his wife, appeared before John Lawrence, Esq, of his Majesty's Council.]

[p 123] **GEORGE GITHENS to JOSEPH GITHENS**

10 June 1782 - George Githens of Cole Town in Evesham ... Burlington ... New Jersey Tanner and Furrier, and Mary his Wife ... [sold to] ... Joseph Githens ... [of the same place] ... Wheelwright ... [for 182 pounds] ... Lot of Ground situate in Colestown ... [Adjacent land owners or names - John Roberts, George Githens] ... [54 sq perches] ... Which Lot ... is part of a larger Lot ... [George Githens purchased from Enoch Allen and Hannah his Wife on 1 March 1782] ...; [Witnesses - Wm Allinson, Saml Allinson.]

[9 April 1783 - George Githens and Mary, his wife, appeared before Judge Saml How, Burlington Co.]

BURLINGTON COUNTY DEEDS - BOOK "A"

[p 126]   **TRETWELL WRIGHT to JONATHAN WRIGHT**

9 March 1785 - Tretwell Wright of Bordentown ... Burlington ... New Jersey and Mary his Wife ... [sold to] ... Jonathan Wright of the Township of New Hanover ... [Burlington Co, NJ] ... Tanner ... Whereas a Certain Thomas Thorn and Jemima his Wife by their Deed ... [dated 6 March 1771 sold] ... a Certain Tract ... in Chesterfield and part in New Hanover ... [Adjacent land owners or names - Patrick Kearness, William Woods Land, Judah Williams] ... [46 acres] ... [for 500 pounds] ... excepting ... A Lot of four Acres of Land Now in the possession ... of William Wright ...; [Witnesses - Altemus Edwards, Jn° Oliver.]

[4 December 1786 - Tretwell Wright and Mary his wife appeared before Judge Israel Shreve, Burlington Co.]

[p 129]   **PETER SHIRAS to AQUILA SHREVE**

4 May 1778 - Peter Shiras of Mount Holly ... Burlington ... New Jersey Merchant and Rebecca his Wife ... [sold to] ... Aquila Shreve of the same Place, Cooper ... Whereas the said Peter Shiras by ... a Certain Indenture ... from Israel Tonkin and Christian his Wife ... [by deed dated 15 April last past] ... became seized ... of Land situate ... on the Western Side of Hight Street in Mount Holly ... [Adjacent land owners or names - Robert Ferrills, William Chew, Lot formerly Sarah Antrame now Solomin Shinns, North Branch of Northampton River (alias Ancocas Creek), John Clark] ... [20 acres, 2 rods, 28 sq perches] ... [for 682 pounds] ...; [Witnesses - Jos Read, Joseph Brearley.]

[20 November 1786 - Joseph Brearley appeared before Judge Joseph Read, Burlington Co.]

[p 133]   **JONATHAN CHESHIRE to THOMAS PLATT**

25 March 1773 - Jonathan Cheshire ... Township of Chesterfield ... Burlington ... New Jersey Farmer ... [sold to] ... Thomas Platt ... Township of New Hanover ... [Burlington Co, NJ] ... Wheelwright ... Whereas Daniel Leeds late of the City of Burlington Dec'd Obtained a Survey ... [of 380 acres] ... of Land in New Hanover ... [by deed dated 4 May 1710 and recorded in Liber BB, folio 424] ... Did Convey ... [300 acres] ... unto Charles Miller & by one other Deed ... [dated 17 March 1711 and recorded in Liber BB, folio 225] ... Conveyed ... [50 acres] ... unto s^d Miller & by one other Deed ... Conveyed the Remaining Ten Acres unto Jonathan Curtis who conveyed the same unto William Dean who by Deed ... [dated 1 May 1710] ... Conveyed the same unto s^d Charles Miller & he being Seized of the Whole ... [380 acres] ... Conveyed the same by his ... Will ... [dated 7 September 1726] ... unto his son Charles Miller & he being so seized whereof Conveyed the same unto John Cheshire by Deed ... [dated 1 September 1728] ... & he being so seized thereof Departed this life and having authorized his Executors to sell the same they to Wit: Jonathan Cheshire & Sarah Cheshire by Deed ... [dated 15 March 1735] ... Conveyed the same unto Benjamin Cheshire & he ... Conveyed the same unto the

BURLINGTON COUNTY DEEDS - BOOK "A"

****

said Jonathan Cheshire by Deed ... [dated - 16 March 1736 & he had it resurveyed] ... after excepting ... 10 acres] ... belonging to Benjamin Jones ... Now this Indenture ... [for 370 pounds] ... sells to Thomas Platt ... [356 acres] ... Being part of said ... [500 acres] ... and also one other piece of ... [14 acres] ... [Adjacent land owners or names - formerly Benjamin Jones] ...; [Witnesses - Robert Kirby, Amey Kirby.]

[22 May 1779 - Robert Kirby appeared before Judge Joseph Borden, Burlington Co.]

[p 136]   **SAMUEL MOORE** to **JONATHAN OLIPHANT**

25 March 1784 - Samuel Moore & Elizabeth his Wife of Evesham Township ... Burlington ... New Jersey ... [sold to] ... Jonathan Oliphant ... [of the same place] ... Wherein Reubin Hains ... City of Philadelphia ...Pennsylvania ... Rightfully Seized of .. Land ... in the Township of Evesham ... [sold by Indenture dated 24 March 1749] ... to Saml Moore Senr ... [who by his last Will, recorded in Liber B, Page 205] ... did bequeath to his Son Samuel Moore the aforesaid Tract ... Now this Indenture ...[for 37 pounds, 10 shillings] ... [sold land in Evesham] ... [Adjacent land owners or names - Near Old Long Bridge on the great Road leading to Foster Town, Rancocus Creek] ... [1 acre, 1 rod, 17 perches] ...; [Witnesses - Thomas Smith, Jesse Haines, John Linch.]

[15 August 1786 - Jesse Haines and "... the said Elizabeth Widow of the s^d Samuel Moore ..." appeared before Judge Thomas Fenimore, Burlington Co.]

[p 140]   **JEREMIAH WALTON** to **ISAAC BOULTON\BOLTON**

1 May 1786 - Jeremiah Walton of the Township of Mansfield ... Burlington ... New Jersey ... [sold to] ... Isaac Boulton (of same place) ... [for 15 pounds, 10 shillings] ... Land ... in ... Mansfield ... [Adjacent land owners or names - Mount Pleasant Road, Isaac Boulton, late John Gibbs, Jeremiah Walton] ... [2 rods, 6 perches] ... & premises is part of a Larger Tract that Jeremiah Walton purchased ... [on 1 December 1785 and Isaac Bolton bought it from Jacob Egly by deed dated 2 January 1775 and "Be it remembered the Punelopah Walton Wife of the said Jeremiah Walton ... quit claimed her Dower rights in this property to Isaac Bolton] ...; [Witnesses - Jacob Wolcott, Israel Shreve; Jeremiah's wife signed as "Penelope".]

[1 November 1786 - Jeremiah & Penelope appeared before Judge Israel Shreve, Burlington Co.]

[p 148]   **BARZILLAI COATE** to **SOLOMON RIDGWAY**

24 March 1773 - Barzillai Coate ... Township of [Springfield is crossed out] Willingboro ... Burlington ... New Jersey Yeoman & Elizabeth his Wife ... [sold to] ... Solomon Ridgway ... Township of Springfield ... [Burlington Co, New Jersey] ... Whereas Thomas Olive by Virtue of two

several deeds Each Dated ... [22nd & 23rd January 1676] ... from Byllinge & Trustees became seized of & in ... [3/4 of One whole Propriety ... of West New Jersey, recorded in Liber B, folio 330/332] ... Thomas Olive being so seized Caused to be surveyed the following Tracts of Land in the Township of Willingboro: [(1)-500 acres, dated 25 April 1682, recorded in Revells Book of Surveys folio 25; (2)-136 acres recorded in s^d Book folio 28, dated 8 July 1682; (3)-139 acres & (4) 200 acres, both dated 1688] ... And being so seized of the ... Land Adjoining to Each other Made his last Will ... [on the 8th day of the ninth month 1692] and therein did Devise ... [860 acres] ... unto his Wife Mary ... who Being so thereof Seized Intermarried with one Robert Eiver of Philadelphia And Whereas Robert Eiver being so seized ... Did together with Mary his Wife by Deed ... [dated 25 March 1697 sell to John Test by deed in Liber B-folio 586] ... And Whereas ... [John Test sold to John Ward on 23 December 1699, Liber AAA, folio 247; and Ward sold it on 1 August 1709 to Hugh Sharp, Liber AAA-folio 269; and Sharp sold it on 11 September 1741 to William Coate, Liber L-folio 23]; And Whereas ... William Coate ... Made his last Will ... 5 December 1749 & therein Devised the said Tract of Land unto His two sons, Israel Coate & Barzillai Coate ... And Whereas The said Israel Coate in behalf of himself & his Brother Barzillai then underage Caused the said Tract of Land to be Resurveyed ... [Recorded Liber O, folio 33] ... And Whereas the said Israel being so seized of the ... half part of the said Tract ... Did by deed ... [dated 15 February 1768] ... Convey the said Moiety unto his Brother Barzillai Coate ... [the Grantor of this deed for 3,000 pounds] ... Land ... in the Township of Willingboro ... [Adjacent land owners or names - Ancocas Creek, William Coxe, Mill Creek, Richard Fenimore, late Joshua Fenimores land, Samuel Newton] ... [850 acres] ...; [Witnesses - Thomas Powell, Daniel Ellis.]

[26 March 1773 - Barzillai Coate & Elizabeth, his wife, appeared before Judge Thomas Rodman, Esqr, Burlington Co.]

[p 150]   DANIEL ELLIS ESQ^R to JOEL MIDDLETON

January 1775 - Daniel Ellis Esqr ... Sheriff ... Burlington ... New Jersey ... [sold to] ... Joel Middleton ... Township of Chesterfield ... Burlington ... Whereas John Emley ... [in May 1774 obtained an order to recover against Abel Middleton 218 pounds plus 3 pounds, 14 shillings, 5 pence in damages] ... [And Whereas Samuel Pleasants, Abel Middleton, Edward Page, and Mason & Hartly recovered against Abel Middleton] ... And Whereas ... Abel Middleton ... was seized ... of Land ... in the Township of Chesterfield ... [Adjacent land owners or names - York Road, Reckeless's Mill] ... [11.5 acres] ... [the Sheriff sold the same at public auction for 404 pounds to "Joel Middleton by Samuel Bunting Bidding"] ...; [Witnesses - Wm Ridgway, Aaron Wills.]

[7 April 1775 - Daniel Ellis, Esqr appeared before Judge Thomas Rodman, Esquire, Burlington Co.]

BURLINGTON COUNTY DEEDS - BOOK "A"

[p 155] **JONATHAN HOUGH ESQ^R to JOHN CROSHAW**

26 May 1770 - Jonathan Hough Esqr of Springfield ... Burlington ... New Jersey & Elizabeth his wife ... [sold to] ... John Croshaw ... [same place] ... Yeoman ... [for 500 pounds] ... Land ... in Springfield ... [lot was granted by Julius Ewan to Ebenezer Antram, to George Rainey and Joseph Wright, formerly Joseph Wrights & Now of Wm Dillwyn] ... 204 acres, 1 rod, 11 pence] ... Which ... the s^d Jonathan Hough purchased of Julius Ewan by Deed ... [dated 29 March 1765] ... and was by the s^d Julius Ewan purchased of his Father John Ewan by Deed ... [dated 25 June 1731] ... and ... [John Ewan purchased it from John Renshaw on 16 May 1720] ...; [Witnesses - John Coate, Daniel Hough, Samuel Hough; Recorded - 26 May 1770.]

[13 January 1787 - Elizabeth Hough appeared before Judge Thos. Reynolds, Burlington Co; Recorded - 27 July 1787.]

[p 159] **THOMAS GILL to BENJAMIN HOLLINSHEAD**

13 July 1756 - Thomas Gill of Chester ... Burlington ... New Jersey Yeoman ... [sold to] ... Benjamin Hollinshead ... City of Philadelphia ... Pennsylvania House Carpenter ... [for 300 pounds] ... all that Dwelling House with the Tract ... in the Township of Chester ... [Adjacent land owners or names - the Heirs of William Hollinshead, Kings Road leading from Burlington to Salem, Benjamin Hollinshead] ... And is the same three acres ... [Thomas Gill bought of Benjamin Hollinshead on 11 April 1752]; [Witnesses - Thomas Bates, Wm Hewlings; Signed - Thomas Gill and Hannah Gill.]

[13 June 1756 (sic) - William Hewlings, a Quaker, appeared before Judge Jacob Hewlings, Esquire, Burlington Co.]

[p 162] **MANUMISSION OF AARON**

24 August 1786 - Know Ye that for Certain good Causes & Consideration Me thereunto Moving I do hereby Manumit & set free my negro slave Aaron aged 32 yr next November ... [Witnesses - John Lacey, Peter Shiras; Signed - Joseph Budd.]

The Manumission of Negro Aaron late a Slave to Joseph Budd is hereby Countersigned by - John Phillips.[Clerk]

22 February 1787 - Clerk of the Peace & Pleas ... Burlington ... We do hereby Certify that on the 24 Day of Augt 1786 Joseph Budd of the Township of Northampton ... Burlington ... before us two of the Overseers of the Poor of said Township & two of the Justices appears to us to be sound in Mind & not under any bodily Incapacity of obtaining a Support And also is above 35 ... [Dated - 24 August

BURLINGTON COUNTY DEEDS - BOOK "A"

****

1786; Witnesses - Aaron Wills, George Budd - Overseers of Poor; Peter Shiras, John Lacey - Justices; Recorded - 22 February 1787.]

[p 163]   **MANUMISSION OF GABRIEL INON [?]**

I do hereby Certify that I have this Day Manumitted & set Free my Negro Lad named Gabriel Inon between the Ages of twenty one Years & Thirty five years of Age Witness my hand & Seal ... [Dated - 24 July 1786; Signed - John Pope.]

We do hereby Certify that on this 24 July 1786 John Pope of the Township of Mansfield ... Burlington brought before us, two of the Overseers of the Poor of s^d Township & two of the Justices of the Peace of s^d County his Slave named Gabriel Inon who on View & Examination appears to us to be sound in Mind & not under any bodily Incapacity of Obtaining a Support & also is not under Twenty one Years of Age nor above Thirty five. [Signed - Joseph Shreve, Abednego Wright - Overseers of the Poor; Thos Fenimore, Israel Shreve - Justices of the Peace.]

[The above Judges certified that Gabriel Inon formerly a Slave to John Pope is Manumitted & set free by his s^d Master by Virtue of a Law passed at Trenton on 2 March 1786; Dated - 13 February 1787.]

[p 164]   **MANUMISSION OF SIP INON**

I do hereby Certify that as Executor to the Estate of my late Mother Mary Pope & also Legatee I do hereby Manumit and Set free my Negro Man named Sip Inon being between the Ages of Twenty one Years & Thirty five years of Age; [Dated - 24 July 1786; Signed - John Pope Exe^r to the Estate of Mary Pope Deceas$^{'d}$.]

[24 July 1786 - John Pope brought "his Negro Man named Sip Inon" before two of the Overseers of the Poor of Mansfield Township & two of the Justices of the Peace of s^d County who on View & Examination found him to be of sound mind and able to obtain support and was not under Twenty one Years of Age nor above Thirty five...; Signed - Tho. Fenimore, Israel Shreve - Justices; Joseph Shreve, Abednego Wright - Overseers of the Poor.]

[The above was sworn to on 13 February 1787 before John Phillips, Peace & Pleas, Burlington Co.]

[p 163]   **MANUMISSION OF ADAM INON**

I do hereby Certify that I have this Day Manumitted & set Free my Negro Lad Named Adam Inon ... [between the Ages of twenty one Years & Thirty five years of Age Witness my hand & Seal ...; Dated - 24 July 1786; Signed - Nathaniel Pope.]

BURLINGTON COUNTY DEEDS - BOOK "A"

[Nathaniel Pope of Mansfield Township, Burlington Co, New Jersey, took his freed slave before Thomas Fenimore and Israel Shreve, two Justices of Peace, and also before Joseph Shreve and Abednego Wright, two Overseers of the Poor; Sworn to before John Phillips on 13 February 1787.]

[p 166]   **MANUMISSION OF GEORGE ROBIN**

I Joshua Bunting ... Township of Chesterfield ... Burlington ... New Jersey ... Manumit & Set free My Negro Man [word "Man" crossed out] Slave Named George Robin ... [under an Act Entitled - To Prevent the Importation of Slaves into New Jersey & to prevent the abuse of Slaves Passed at Trenton March 2^d 1786; [Dated - 1 August 1786; Signed - Joshua Bunting; witnesses - Joel Middleton, Thomas Moore; Burlington Co.]

[Bunting brought his slave before Isaac Cowgill and Israel Shreve, two Justices of Peace and also before Joel Middleton and Thomas Moore, two Overseers of the Poor; Certified and Sworn to before John Phillips on 1 August 1786.]

[p 167]   **MANUMISSION OF SCIPIO**

"... we Abigail Budd William Budd & John Lacy ... Township of Hanover ... Burlington ... New Jersey ... Administrators of the Estate of Joseph Budd late ... [of the same place above] ... dec^d in consideration of a Charge given us by the s^d dec^d while on his death bed and also for other good Considerations ... Grant & Confirm unto Scipio late a Slave to the s^d Budd his Liberty ...; [Dated - 9 October 1786; Signed - Abigail Budd, William Budd, John Lacey.]

[9 October 1786 - Scipio was brought before and examined by Thomas Reynolds and Peter Stretch, Justices, and also before Joseph Lamb Junr and Isaac Bullock, Overseers of the Poor, of New Hanover Township, Burlington Co.]

[Certified before John Phillips, Clerk, Peace & Pleas; Signed - Thomas Reynolds, P. Stretch.]

[p 168]   **REUBEN HAINES to SAMUEL MOORE**

21 March 1749 - Reuben Haines ... City of Philadelphia ... Pennsylvania Brewer ... [sold to] ... Samuel Moore of Evesham ... Burlington ... New Jersey Yeoman ... [for 400 pounds] ... acquit Release & Discharge ... forever One Certain ... Dwelling house ... & Tracts of Land ... lying ... [adjacent land owners or names - Main Branch of Ancosus Creek in Evesham, land Sarah Miller purchased of Reuben Haines, Benjamin Morre Junr] ... [290 acres] ... which the s^d Reuben Haines became lawfully Seized ... by Virtue of the last Wills ... of his Grand Father John Haines & his father Josiah Haines part whereof the s^d Josiah Haines became lawfully Seized by the s^d last Will ... of his father ... [278 acres] ... was surveyed to the s^d John Haines in seven tracts .... & 85 acres ... was

BURLINGTON COUNTY DEEDS - BOOK "A"

surveyed to Thomas Haines ... & was Granted to the s^d John Haines by ... [deed dated 3 November 1695] ... and one other part ... was surveyed to William Haines & Conveyed to Zacharia Prickett who Conveyed 50 acres ... to the s^d John Haines by ... [deed dated 1 February 1705] ...; [Signed - Reuben Haines; witnesses - John Burr, Tim^y Matlack, John Peacock; dated - 30th of ye 4th month 1760 before William Foster, Judge, Burlington Co.]

[p 172]   **MARY WATSON ET AL to JOSHUA M. WALLACE, ET AL**

18 April 1785 - Mary Watson and Daniel Smith Executrix and Executor of the last Will ... of John Watson late of the City of Burlington decd ... [sold to] ... Joshua M. Wallace, Esqr and Frederick Kesselman both of the City of Burlington ... New Jersey ... Whereas Thomas Horten late of the County of Burlington ... became seized ... of and in a Certain Lot of Land ... in the City of Burlington ... [by deed dated 1 May 1737, who sold it to Aaron Lovett late of said City deceased ... And whereas the said Aaron Lovett being so seized died leaving first Made his Last Will, dated 30 September 1740, and did give the said lott of land unto his Son Aaron Lovet - Burlington Book 5-Page 207] ... And Whereas by the ... said Will it appears to be only an Estate for Life therefore the said Aaron Lovet obtained from his Brother Joseph Lovet Sen and Heir of the said Aaron Lovet dec^d a general Release in fee for the said Lot of Land ... [dated 9 September 1758] ... And Whereas the said Aaron Lovet being so thereof seized did by Deed ... [dated 4 October 1758, convey the lot to Frances Giffing of the City of Burlington, who by deed dated 3 September 1762, conveyed it to Isaac Heulings of the said City who I conveyed it by deed, dated 18 May 1764, to Ephraim Phillips, of the City of Burlington, who together with his wife, Elizabeth, conveyed it on 8 June 1777 to John Watson of the City of Burlington and John Watson made his Will, dated 11 March 1782 & appointed his Wife and Daniel Smith above named Executrix and Executor] ... [for 45 pounds] ... Now this Indenture ... [the above Executors sell to the above Grantees all of the above land] ... as Tenants in Common ... purchased by John Watson of Ephraim Phillips aforesaid ... [adjacent land owners or names - Joshua M. Wallace, Frederick Kesselman, formerly James Binghams, Pearl Street] ...; [Signed - Mary Watson Exec^x, Danl Smith Exec^r; witnesses - James Kinsey Junr, Elizabeth Atkinson.]

[20 September 1786 - Daniel Smith appeared before Judge Thomas Fenimore, Burlington Co.]

[p 176]   **PETER WORRAL to JOSHUA M. WALLACE ET AL**

11 March 1785 - Peter Worrall ... City of Burlington ... New Jersey Gentleman ... [sold to] ... Joshua M. Wallace Esqr & Frederick Kesselman both of the City of Burlington ... Whereas the said Peter Worrall by Virtue of two ... Deeds ... [from Daniel Ellis Esqr High Sheriff, dated 1 September 1764 and the other from Ab^m Heulings Esqr, dated 20 August 1764] ... became lawfully seized of & in two Lots of land adjoining each other ... [One Containing 47 feet 11 Inches from on the Delaware River & the other ... 33 feet 4 Inch front on the s^d River, Pearl Street] ... Now this Indenture ... that the s^d Peter Worrall ... [sells for 95 pounds] ... the above mentioned Lotts ... being in the City of Burlington

BURLINGTON COUNTY DEEDS - BOOK "A"

... [adjacent land owners or names - Delaware River, Broad street, lott formerly Thomas Horton now belonging to the Estate of John Watson deceased, the lot formerly of Daniel Cox Esqr, Broad Street or Pearl Street, Lot late of John Watson] ...; [Signed - Peter Worrall; witnesses - Danl Smith, John Cox Junr.]

[20 September 1786 - Daniel Smith "One of the people Called Quakers" appeared before Judge Thomas Fenimore, Esqr, Burlington Co; recorded - 15 March 1787.]

[p 180] SALE OF SLAVE, THOMAS, by GEORGE MITCHELL to SAMUEL SHOEMAKER and FREEDOM FOR THOMAS

26 April 1787 - Whereas in and by a Certain Deed Poll ... [dated 3 April 1787] ... George Mitchell ... City of Burlington ... New Jersey Merch^t ... [for 75 pounds sold to] ... Saml Shoemaker ... City of Burlington ... a Certain Male Negro Slave named Thomas ... Now be it Known ... That I the said Samuel Shoemaker being desirous to restore the said Thomas to his Natural Right of Freedom have absolved from Servitude ... & set free ... said Negro Man Thomas ...; [Witnesses - Thos Fenimore, Joshua M. Wallace.]

[p 180] LIQUOR LICENSE

"... Mr. Okey Hoagland retailer of liquors in the City of Burlington at the Sign of the Blue Anchor the Sum of Six pounds ... full payment for License to sell Wine Beer Porter or Ale for one Year ... ensuing the above date agreeable to Act of Assembly passed at Trenton ... [dated 24 November 1786] ...; [Signed - John Black C. Coll^r; recorded - 1 May 1787.]

[p 181] CERTIFICATION OF SAMUEL SHOWMAKER RE: SLAVE THOMAS

[27 April 1787 - Certification that Samuel Shoemaker Esqr ... City of Burlington ... New Jersey brought Thomas before Abbott Williams and Willm Cooper, Overseers of the Poor, and also before Thos Fenimore and Joshua M. Wallace, Justices of Peace; swore to by Thos Fenimore and Joshua M. Wallace; recorded - 7 May 1787.]

[p 182] MANUMISSION OF BEULAH WATERS

[2 March 1787 - William Wilkins of the Township of Evesham, Burlington Co, New Jersey, brought his Slave named Beulah Waters, over 21 and under 35 years of age, before Enoch Evans and William Evans, Overseers of the Poor, and also before Josiah Foster and Reece Edwards, Justices of Peace, who found Beluah Waters to be of sound mind and able to support herself; Signed - Enoch Evans, Willm Evans, Josiah Foster, Reece Edwards. Wilkins certified the above on the same date. The above was sworn to on the same date before John Phillips, Clerk, Peace and Pleas; recorded - 5 May 1787.]

BURLINGTON COUNTY DEEDS - BOOK "A"

[p 183] MANUMISSION OF PATIENCE PERE/PERO

[2 March 1787 - William Wilkins of the Township of Evesham, Burlington Co, New Jersey, brought his Slave named Patience Pere [or Pero], over 21 and under 35 years of age, before Enoch Evans and William Evans, Overseers of the Poor, and also before Josiah Foster and Reece Edwards, Justices of Peace, who found Patience Pere [or Pero] to be of sound mind and able to support herself; Signed - Enoch Evans, Willm Evans, Josiah Foster, Reece Edwards. Wilkins certified the above on the same date. The above was sworn to on the same date before John Phillips, Clerk, Peace and Pleas; recorded - 5 May 1787.]

[p 184] MANUMISSION OF DINAH

["We do hereby Certify that on ... [17 March 1787] ... William Newbold Esqr of the Township of Springfield ... Burlington Co, New Jersey, brought a Female Slave Named Dinah, over 21 and under 35 years of age, the property of the said William Newbold Esqr before Caleb Earl and Benjamin Hough, Overseers of the Poor, and also before Thomas Reynolds and Peter Stretch, Justices of Peace, who found Dinah to be of sound mind and able to support herself; Signed - Thomas Reynolds and Peter Stretch - Justices of Peace; Caleb Earl and Benj^m Hough - Overseers of the Poor.]

[17 March 1787 - Sworn to by William Newbold at New Mills before John Phillips, Clerk; witnesses - John Lacey, Job Lippincott.]

[p 185] LIQUOR LICENSE

25 May 1787 - James Esdaill Retailer of Liquors ... City of Burlington ... [paid 3 pounds] ... for License to sell Wine on year from 1 May last ...; [Signed - John Black C. Coll^r.]

[p 185] LIQUOR LICENSE

26 June 1787 - Ezra Bake [in pencil is "Baker"] Retailer of spirituous Liquors ... Township of Egg harbour at Clam Town ... [paid 3 pounds] ... to sell ... [from 1 May last] ...; [Signed - John Black C. Coll^r.]

[p 188] EDWARD BLACK ET AL to AQUILA SHINN

20 September 1781 - Edward Black and Jonah Woolman both of the County of Burlington ... New Jersey Executors to the last Will ... of Henry Paxson late of Mount Holly dec^d ... [sold land to Aquila Shinn of the same place] ... [for 700 pounds] ... Dwelling House & piece ... of Land Situate ... in Bridgeton ... North ampton ... Burlington being part of the Estate of Henry Paxson dec^d ... [will dated 9 July 1778 ... [adjacent land owners or names - Corner to John Bispham, Mill Street, formerly

BURLINGTON COUNTY DEEDS - BOOK "A"

corner of Nathaniel Thomas' land, high Street, to Henry Paxson's lott of land, John Clark] ... [52 sq. perches] ... Which said Dwelling House or Piece ... of Land being part of the Estate of Henry Paxson Deceased ... [which Henry Paxson bought of Jacob Pricket by deed, dated 26 June 1760 & Prichet purchased it of Thomas Atkinson (Innholder) by deed, dated 28 January 1748/9, & Atkinson bought of Philo Leeds by deed, dated 25 April 1747 which Leeds bought of Thomas Webster by deed, dated 29 January 1742/3.] ... [Signed - Edward Black, Jonah Woolman; witnesses - Samuel Paxson, William Woolman.]

[6 April 1787 - Henry Paxson and Samuel Allinson, Junr witnessed the payment of the money. Jonah Woolman appeared before Judge Joseph Read Esqr.]

[p 192]   AQUILA SHINN to EDWARD BLACK

28 September 1781 - Aquila Shinn of Mount Holly ... Burlington ... New Jersey ... [sold to] ... Edward Black of the same place ... [for 700 pounds] ... Dwelling House & Land Situate ... in Bridgetown in Northampton ... Burlington ... [adjacent land owners or names - John Bispham, Mill Street, formerly Nathaniel Thomas, Henry Paxson, John Clark] ... [52 sq. perches] ... [this was the same land as described in the above deed] ...; [Signed - Aquila Shinn; witnesses - Henry Paxson, Samuel Allinson, Junr.]

[17 April 1787 - Acquila Shinn appeared before Judge Joseph Read Esqr, Burlington Co, New Jersey.]

[p 195]   MANUMISSION OF HANNAH ACERBY [?]

Hugh and Job Cooperthwaite of Chester Township ... Burlington ... New Jersey do hereby Manumit & set free our Negro Slave Named Hannah Acerby [?]; [Dated - 2 March 1786; signed - Hugh Cooperthwaite, Job Cooperthwaite.]

[The above was brought before Joshua Hunt and John Collins, Overseers of the Poor and also before Josiah Foster and Reece Edwards, Justices of the Peace; certified by Josiah Foster and Reece Edwards before John Phillips, Clerk of the Peace and Pleas; dated - 29 June 1787.]

[p 197]   JOHN HOLLINSHEAD, SHERIFF to JOHN BUTLER

30 June 1787 - John Hollinshead Esqr High Sheriff of ... Burlington ... New Jersey ... [sold to] ... John Butler of Bordentown ... Township of Chesterfield ... Whereas Benjamin Luker ... [obtained a Judgement against Thomas Potts for 157 pounds, 12 shillings for debt and 5 pounds, 13 shillings, and 10 pence for costs of the suit and the Sheriff was ordered to take any goods or chattels of Potts] ... And Whereas, William Potts and Arney Potts by Indenture ... [dated 24 February 1767 did grant unto

BURLINGTON COUNTY DEEDS - BOOK "A"

Thomas Potts] ... All that Lot of Land situate in Chesterfield ... [adjacent land owners or names - Joseph Borden, John Imlay, Lot of land allotted to John Lawrence and Hannah his wife] ... [25 acres and one rod] ... [the Sheriff did seize the above land and sold it to John Butler, being the highest bidder, on 15th of June last for 75 pounds] ...; Dated - MDCCXXXVII; witnesses - John Phillips, John Hous [?], Jacob Wolcott.]

30 June 1787 - John Hollinshead Esquire appeared before Judge Joshua M. Wallace, Burlington Co, New Jersey.]

[p 201] **JOSEPH BLOOMFIELD to BETHANAH HODKINSON**

26 August 1783 - Joseph Bloomfield ... City of Burlington ... New Jersey Esqr and Mary His Wife ... [sold to] ... Bethanah Hodkinson of the same place Cabinet Maker ... [for 150 pounds] ... one Certain Lott ... of Land ... being in the City of Burlington Fronting on Delaware River ... [adjoining land owners or names - corner to the garden of Joseph Bloomfield, River Delaware] ... [130 perches] ... With use ... of a ten foot Alley from the rear of the lot hereby Conveyed Adjoining to Coxes lot into Pearl Street ...; [Signed - Joseph Bloomfield, Mary Bloomfield; witnesses - Daniel Ellis, Gershom Craft.]

[27 September 1786 - Joseph and Mary Bloomfield appeared before Judge Joshua Maddox Wallace Esqr, Burlington Co, New Jersey.]

[p 204] **JOHN BRANIN to CORNELIUS BRANIN**

10 May 1775 - John Brannin and Sarah his Wife of Evesham ... Burlington Yeoman ... [sold to] ... Cornelius Brannin of the same place Yeoman ... Whereas Michael Brannin Father to the Parties of the Within Indenture became seized of ... a Lot ... lying in the Township aforesaid by ... Indenture from Emanuel Stratton and Wife ... [dated 9 July 1748] ... And Whereas Michael Brannin died Intestate John Brannin being eldest Son and Heir at Law became seized of ... all the lands of the said Michael Brannin Which he held at the Time of his Decease Now this Indenture ... John Brannin as well for fulfilling What Was the Intention of his Father as well as for the Love and Affection which he beareth Unto his Brother Cornelius Brannin ... [sells to him for 50 pounds] ... All those ... Parcels of Land ... in the Township aforesaid ... The first Piece ... of Land ... [adjoining land owners or names - by the Creek, Mark Strattons Spring, Daniel Braddock] ... [42 acres] ... The second Piece ... [adjoining land owners or names - East side of the same Creek, Joseph Garwood, John Brannin, Daniel Stratton] ... 14 acres] ... The Third Piece ... [adjoining land owners or names - by the Creek, William Foster, William Brannin] ... [8 acres] ... The fourth and last Piece ... [adjoining land owners or names - by the Spring Corner to Barzillai Branin, Corner to John & Barzillai Branin] ... [2 acres] ...; [Signed - John Branin, Sarah Brannin; witnesses - Charles Read, John Farr[?]; not various spellings of "Branin".]

BURLINGTON COUNTY DEEDS - BOOK "A"

[12 June 1787 - John & Sarah Branin appeared before Judge Israel Shreve, Burlington Co, New Jersey.]

[p 208]   **JOHN HEUSTIS to ISABELLA MATTHESON**

14 September 1787 - John Heustis ... Township of Chester ... Burlington ... New Jersey ... [sold to] ... Isabella Mattheson of the same place Aforesaid ... Whereas ... by a Certain Indenture ... [dated 28 November 1767] ... the Aforesaid John Heustis became seized ... in a Certain lot ... of Land conveyed to him by Joshua Bispham situate in the Township & County Aforesaid ... [43 acres and 28 perches] ... [for 40 pounds] ... [adjoining land owners or names - North side of Salem Road, John Higby, Richard S. Smith, Joshua Hunt, John Huestis, Nathan Middleton] ... [2 acres] ...; [Signed - John Heustis made his mark when signing; witnesses - Reece Edwards, R.S. Smith.]

17 September 1787 - John Huestis appeared before Judge Joseph Read, Esq., Burlington Co, New Jersey.]

[p 211]   **JOHN HOW & DANIEL ELLIS to EZEKIEL JOHNSTON/JOHNSON**

2 September 1785 - John How & Daniel Ellis both of ... City of Burlington ... New Jersey Surviving Executors of the last Will ... of Samuel How late of the City of Burlington ... [City of Burlington with line drawn through it] ... Esqr Deceased ... [sold to] ... Ezekiel Johnston of the Township of Burlington ... Whereas the said Samuel How by Virtue of a Conveyance from ... Isaac Rogers was ... Seized ... in the Lands herein after Described And Whereas ... Samuel How by his last Will ... [dated 12 September 1782] ... did ... devise the said Lands hereinafter Described unto his Son Samuel How and of his said Will Appointed his Wife Hannah his son John & his brother in law Daniel Ellis Executors ... Whereas after the making the Will ... Samuel How by ... Agreement ... [dated 2 June 1783] ... did Contract with the said Ezekiel Johnson for the sale of the said Lands ... [with contract stating to execute a Title before 28 March next] ... And whereas the s^d Samuel How before ... [the above Contract date] ... for Executing the Deed ... Departed this life without making any alteration in the Will ... Whereas the other Devisses of the said Samuel How have released to the use of Said Samuel How the younger all the monies arising by the sale of such of his Estate Devised to his Son Disposed of said the Executing of the will aforesaid And Whereas the said John How & Daniel Ellis as Surviving Executors of Samuel How (the s^d Hannah has Departed this life) ... [they then obtained permission from the Legislature on 27 December 1784 to allow them to execute & convey the land unto Ezekiel Johnston] ... [for 670 pounds] ... [adjoining land owners or names - Mill Creek, William Hewlings, William Deacon] ... Also that 10 acres ... [adjoining land owners or names - William Prosses[?], Samuel How, William Buzby] ...; [Signed - John How, Daniel Ellis; witnesses - John Earl, Abbot Williams.]

BURLINGTON COUNTY DEEDS - BOOK "A"

****

[1 June 1787 - Daniel Ellis Esqr. appeared before Judge Joshua M. Wallace, Burlington Co, New Jersey.]

[p 214]   **EPHRAIM HAINES to JOHN RIELY**

28 April 1783 - Ephraim Haines ... Township of Chesterfield ... Burlington ... New Jersey Yeoman & Hannah his Wife ... [sold to] ... John Riely ... Township of Evesham ... Whereas Francis Hogsett dec'd ... became lawfully seized ... in Sundry Tracts ... Situate in Chester ... Did by his Indenture of ... Release ... [dated 19 or 20 January 1732 in Book E-Page 441] ... Did ... Convey unto Thomas Moore a Certain ... Land situate in Chester ... [33 acres] ... [And Thomas Moore on 31 October 1744 sold 2 acres of the 33 acres to Joshua Humphrey and Moore sold 4 acres on 29th of the second month 1745 unto Charles French & Joshua Humphrey sold the 2 acres on 9 May 1747 to Charles French so French became seized of 6 acres of the 33 acres. And French then sold the 6 acres on 2 April 1773 to Ephraim Haines] ... Now this Indenture ... [sold for 50 pounds] ... to John Reily ... [adjoining land owners or names - Great Road through Moorestown, John Riely, Nathan Middleton] ... [1 acre which is part of the above 6 acres] ...; [Signed - Ephraim Haines, Hannah Haines; witnesses - Joseph Edwards, William Borradaill.]

[Recorded - 17 September 1787 at which time, Hannah Haines, one of the Grantors in the within deed named the Widdow of Ephraim Haines the other Grantor, appeared before Judge Joseph Read, Esqr, Burlington Co, New Jersey.]

[p 217]   **EPHRAIM HAINES to JOHN RYLE**

28 February 1778 - Between Ephraim Haines ... Township of Chester ... Burlington ... New Jersey Yeoman & Hannah his Wife ... [sold to] ... John Ryle ... Township of Evesham ... Shop Keeper ... Whereas Francis Hogsett dec'd ... became lawfully seized ... in Sundry Tracts ... Situate in Chester ... Did by his Indenture of ... Release ... [dated 19 or 20 January 1732 in Book E-Page 441] ... Did ... Convey unto Thomas Moore a Certain ... Land situate in Chester ... [33 acres] ... [And Thomas Moore on 31 October 1744 sold 2 acres of the 33 acres to Joshua Humphrey and Moore sold 4 acres on 29th of the second month 1745 unto Charles French & Joshua Humphrey sold the 2 acres on 9 May 1747 to Charles French so French became seized of 6 acres of the 33 acres. And French then sold the 6 acres on 2 April 1773 to Ephraim Haines] ... Now this Indenture ... Ephraim Haines ... [sold for 70 pounds to] ... John Ryle ... [2 acres] ... [adjoining land owners or names - Great Road leading through Moorestown, Morgan Hollingshead, Ephraim Haines, Nathan Middleton] ...; [Signed - Ephraim Haines, Hannah Haines; witnesses - Samuel Coles sen^r, Jos^a Stokes.]

[17 September 1780 - Hannah Haines, Widdow & Relict of Ephraim Haines, appeared before Judge Joseph Read, Burlington Co, New Jersey.]

BURLINGTON COUNTY DEEDS - BOOK "A"

[p 220]   **MANUMISSION OF NANNY**

I, Nathan Haines ... Township of Evesham ... Burlington ... New Jersey Do hereby Manumit & set free my Negro Slave Named Nanny ... [Dated - 2 March 1787; signed - Nathan Haines; witnesses - Josiah Foster, Reece Edwards.]

[2 March 1787 - Haines brought Nanny before two Overseers of the Poor and two Justices of the Peace, who found her of sound mind & not under any bodily incapacity, not under the age of 21 years nor over the age of 35 years; Signed - Enoch Evans, Wm Evans - Overseers of the Poor; Josiah Foster & Reece Edwards - Justices of the Peace. The above Justices swore to the above before John Phillips, Clerk of the Peace & Pleas, Burlington Co, New Jersey.]

[p 221]   **MANUMISSION OF RONNIA**

I, Nathan Haines ... Township of Evesham ... Burlington ... New Jersey Do hereby Manumit & set free my Negro Slave Named Ronnia ... [Dated - 2 March 1787; signed - Nathan Haines; witnesses - Josiah Foster, Reece Edwards.]

[2 March 1787 - Haines brought Ronnia before two Overseers of the Poor and two Justices of the Peace, who found her of sound mind & not under any bodily incapacity, not under the age of 21 years nor over the age of 35 years; Signed - Enoch Evans, Wm Evans - Overseers of the Poor; Josiah Foster & Reece Edwards - Justices of the Peace. The above Justices swore to the above before John Phillips, Clerk of the Peace & Pleas, Burlington Co, New Jersey.]

[p 222]   **MANUMISSION OF KINGSTON**

I, Nathan Haines ... Township of Evesham ... Burlington ... New Jersey Do hereby Manumit & set free my Negro Slave Named Kingston ... [Dated - 2 March 1787; signed - Nathan Haines; witnesses - Josiah Foster, Reece Edwards.]

[2 March 1787 - Haines brought Kingston before two Overseers of the Poor and two Justices of the Peace, who found him of sound mind & not under any bodily incapacity, not under the age of 21 years nor over the age of 35 years; Signed - Enoch Evans, Wm Evans - Overseers of the Poor; Josiah Foster & Reece Edwards - Justices of the Peace. The above Justices swore to the above before John Phillips, Clerk of the Peace & Pleas, Burlington Co, New Jersey.]

[p 223]   **MANUMISSION OF PHOEBY TONKINS**

We Elizabeth Lippincott & John Lippincott of Evesham Township ... Burlington ... New Jersey ...

BURLINGTON COUNTY DEEDS - BOOK "A"

do hereby Manumitt & set free ... Phoeby Tonkins ...; [Dated - 12 February 1787; signed - Elizabeth Lippincott, John Lippincott; witnesses - Reece Edwards, Josiah Foster.]

[12 February 1787 - Elizabeth & John Lippincott brought Phoeby Tonkins before two Overseers of the Poor and two Justices of the Peace, who found her of sound mind & not under any bodily incapacity, not under the age of 21 years nor over the age of 35 years; Signed - Enoch Evans, Wm Evans - Overseers of the Poor; Josiah Foster & Reece Edwards - Justices of the Peace. The above Justices swore to the above before John Phillips, Clerk of the Peace & Pleas, Burlington Co, New Jersey.]

[p 224]   **MANUMISSION OF MARY WHITE**

Joseph Eves of the Township of Evesham ... Burlington ... New Jersey ... do hereby Manumitt & set free ... Mary White ...; [Dated - 12 February 1787; signed - Joseph Eves; witnesses - Reece Edwards, Josiah Foster.]

[12 February 1787 - Joseph Eves brought Mary White before two Overseers of the Poor and two Justices of the Peace, who found her of sound mind & not under any bodily incapacity, not under the age of 21 years nor over the age of 35 years; Signed - Enoch Evans, Wm Evans - Overseers of the Poor; Josiah Foster & Reece Edwards - Justices of the Peace. The above Justices swore to the above before John Phillips, Clerk of the Peace & Pleas, Burlington Co, New Jersey.]

[p 225]   **MANUMISSION OF SAM WATERS**

Joseph Hackney ... Township of Chester ... Burlington ... New Jersey ... do hereby Manumitt & set free ... Sam Waters ...; [Dated - 2 December 1786; signed - Joseph Hackney; witnesses - Darling Conrow, Reece Edwards.]

[2 December 1786 - Joseph Hackney brought Sam Waters before two Overseers of the Poor and two Justices of the Peace, who found him of sound mind & not under any bodily incapacity, not under the age of 21 years nor over the age of 35 years; Signed - Josiah Hunt, John Collins - Overseers of the Poor; Reece Edwards & Darling Conrow - Justices of the Peace. The above Justices swore to the above before John Phillips, Clerk of the Peace & Pleas, Burlington Co, New Jersey.]

[p 226]   **MANUMISSION OF HANNAH WILLIAMS**

Joseph Hackney ... Township of Chester ... Burlington ... New Jersey ... do hereby Manumitt & set free ... Hannah Williams ...; [Dated - 2 December 1786; signed - Joseph Hackney; witnesses - Darling Conrow, Reece Edwards.]

BURLINGTON COUNTY DEEDS - BOOK "A"

[2 December 1786 - Joseph Hackney brought Hannah Williams before two Overseers of the Poor and two Justices of the Peace, who found her of sound mind & not under any bodily incapacity, not under the age of 21 years nor over the age of 35 years; Signed - Josiah Hunt, John Collins - Overseers of the Poor; Reece Edwards & Darling Conrow - Justices of the Peace. The above Justices swore to the above before John Phillips, Clerk of the Peace & Pleas, Burlington Co, New Jersey.]

[p 227]   **MANUMISSION OF HANNAH MINTUS**

Joseph Eves of the Township of Evesham ... Burlington ... New Jersey ... do hereby Manumitt & set free ... Hannah Mintus ...; [Dated - 12 February 1787; signed - Joseph Eves; witnesses - Reece Edwards, Josiah Foster.]

[12 February 1787 - Joseph Eves brought Hannah Mintus before two Overseers of the Poor and two Justices of the Peace, who found her of sound mind & not under any bodily incapacity, not under the age of 21 years nor over the age of 35 years; Signed - Enoch Evans, Wm Evans - Overseers of the Poor; Josiah Foster & Reece Edwards - Justices of the Peace. The above Justices swore to the above before John Phillips, Clerk of the Peace & Pleas, Burlington Co, New Jersey.]

[p 228]   **MANUMISSION OF LOTT CAREY**

John Cox of the Township of Chester ... Burlington ... New Jersey ... do hereby Manumitt & set free ... Lott Carey ...; [Dated - 19 May 1787; signed - John Cox; witnesses - Reece Edwards, Darling Conrow.]

[19 May 1787 - John Cox brought Lott Carey before two Overseers of the Poor and two Justices of the Peace, who found [the subject] of sound mind & not under any bodily incapacity, not under the age of 21 years nor over the age of 35 years; Signed - Jeremiah Matlack & Reubin Matlack - Overseers of the Poor; Darling Conrow & Reece Edwards - Justices of the Peace. The above Justices swore to the above before John Phillips, Clerk of the Peace & Pleas, Burlington Co, New Jersey.]

[The wording of the manumission indicates that "Lott" was a male.]

[p 229]   **THOMAS BROOKS to HENRY BENNETT**

21 August 1784 - Thomas Brooks of Evesham ... Burlington ... New Jersey ... [sold to] ... Henry Bennett of the same place ... Whereas Thomas Tallman late of Evesham Dec^d was in his life time ... seized of ... a Tract of Land in Evesham ... & being whereof Seized Died Intestate ... Letters of Administration was Granted ... unto Peter Tallman & Hannah Tallman Widow of the said Thomas Tallman ... And Whereas John Cox, Joshua Wright & Joseph Wright Executors of the last Will ... of Richard Satterthwaite ... Recovered against the s^d Peter Tallman, James Buxton & Hannah his Wife

BURLINGTON COUNTY DEEDS - BOOK "A"

****

(late Hannah Tallman) Administrator of the said Thomas Tallman as well as Certain Debt of ... [116 pounds] ... and Whereas John Budd ... Recovered against the said Administration ... a Certain Debt of ... [260 pounds] ... Whereas Elizabeth Hankinson & John Hinchman Executors of the last Will ... of John Hankinson ... [and recovered against the Administration a debt of 92 pounds, 5 shillings, 8 pence and the Sheriff was ordered to seize the possessions of Thomas Tallman deceased to settle the debts] ... Joseph Mullen Esqr Sheriff ... did seize & take in Execution a part of the Plantation late the said Thomas Tallmans ... [advertised and sold to Thomas Brooks the highest bidder and was conveyed to Brooks by deed on the 16 of August instant and Brooks now sells the above land to Henry Bennett for 128 pounds and 14 shillings] ... [adjoining land owners or names - Road leading from Mount Holly to Moorestown, Thomas Brooks, Job Borton] ... [15 acres] ...; [Signed - Thomas Brooks made his mark when signing; witnesses - Samuel Ivins, Edward Darnel.]

[27 June 1887 - Edward Darnell appeared before Judge Israel Shreve, Burlington Co, New Jersey. Although, the deed copy reads 1887, it stands to reason that the date must be 1787 being Edward Darnel would most probably not be alive in 1887.]

[p 233]   **HENRY BENNET to DANIEL DE BRAY**

18 October 1787 - Henry Bennett ... Township of Evesham ... Burlington ... New Jersey & Abigail his Wife ... [sold to] ... Daniel De Bray late of Philadelphia but now of the Township of Chester ... [New Jersey] ... Gentleman ... Whereas Sundry Writs called Fiere Facias Issued ... against the Good Chattels ... of Thomas Tallman late of the Township of Evesham ... dec'd ... [ordered the Sheriff to take into his possession a tract of 50 acres and offered publically at auction and Thomas Brook appearing to be the highest obtained the property by a Sheriff's Deeds dated 16 August 1784; and Brooks then sold 15 of the 50 acres to Henry Bennett the present Grantor] ... Now this Indenture ... [Bennett sold the land in Evesham for 260 pounds to De Bray] ... [adjacent land owners or names - Great Road from Moorestown to Mount Holly Corner, Estate of Thomas Brooks, late sd. Thomas Tallman, Job Barton, "Lands of said Thomas Brooks dec'd now belonging to his son Samuel Brooks"] ... [15 acres] ...; [Signed - Henry Bennet, Abigail Bennet; witnesses - Caleb Austin, Jos. Stokes/Storkes.]

[p 236]   **JOHN HOLLINSHEAD ESQ^R to URIAH WILKINS**

19 September 1787 - John Hollinshead Esqr High Sheriff ... Burlington ... New Jersey ... [sold to] ... Uriah Wilkens ... Township of Evesham ... Whereas Robert Lawrence ... [in Burlington in the November Term of the court recovered against John Barnin a certain debt as recorded in Burlington Book A of Judgements & Executions. The Sheriff was ordered to obtain the Goods and Chattels of one John Branin] ... And Whereas Michael Branin Father of the said John Branin in his life Time became seized ... [of a piece of land in the Township of Evesham of 150 acres] ... "which John Branin became seized as being Heir at Law to his Father Michael Branin" ... [and the Sheriff confiscated the

BURLINGTON COUNTY DEEDS - BOOK "A"

land based upon the Writs from John Branin and exposed it to sale and Uriah Wilkins was the highest bidder] ...; [Signed - Jno. Hollinshead Sheriff; witnesses - John Phillips, Danl Bacon Junr, Thos. Fenimore; recorded - 28 November 1787.]

[p 239]   **JOHN HOLLINSHEAD ESQ^R to SAMUEL ROGERS**

9 October 1787 - John Hollinshead Esqr Sheriff ... Burlington ... New Jersey ... [sold to] ... Samuel Rogers of Bordentown ... Township of Chesterfield ... Whereas John Lee ... [obtained a judgement of debt in the Burlington court in the May 1787 term against] ... James Erdaill Administrator of the Goods & Chattels of John Hind dec^d during the Absence of Mary Hind sold Executrix of the last Will ... of the said John Hind ... And Whereas the said John Hind in his life Time and at the Time of his Death was seized ... [of shares of unlocated land in New Jersey and the Sheriff seized some of this land and set of for auction 300 acres being part of the property rights of Hinds and sold it to the highest bidder] ... The antecedent Chain of Conveyances ... [of the land or rights of John Hind] ... is contained as follows - Edward Byllngee and his Trustees (William Penn, Gawen Lawrie and Nicholas Lucas) by two ... [Indentures dated 12 March 1680 and 29 February 1681 and recorded at New Castle on Delaware, Book B, Pages 46 & 54E, which conveys to John Hind of London Goldsmith (the Ancestor of the aforesaid John Hind) two Whole proprieties in West New Jersey, John Hind against whose Estate the aforesaid Judgement and Execution Was entered ... lawfully claiming under the said John Hind the elder ... [who obtained proof of his claim] ... from the Council of proprietors of West New Jersey ... [on 4 August 1773 & recorded in Burlington in Book AE of deeds giving] ... John Hind the Younger ... [40,000 acres of land] ... The said John Hind the Younger dying seized by his last Will recorded in No. 16 of Wills page 367 dated ... [11 March 1775] ... devise all his Estate ... to his Wife Mary whom he constitutes sole Executor ... Now this Indenture ... John Hollinshead Esqr Sheriff ... [sold to the 300 acres to Samuel Rogers] ...; [Signed - John Hollinshead Sheriff; witnesses - John Phillips, Thos M. Gardiner, Thomas Fenimore; recorded - 28 November 1787.]

[p 242]   **JOHN HOLLINSHEAD ESQR to BENJAMIN PIERSON**

6 November 1787 - John Hollinshead Esqr Sheriff ... Burlington ... New Jersey ... Whereas John Clifford ... [obtained a judgement of debt in Burlington court in the May Term last against Adam Parker] ... And Whereas the said Adam Parker ... [was possessed of land on the East Side of Hight Street ... Burlington ... [adjacent land owners or names - Hannah Kinsey, Ann Odell, Jonathan Guest, Jonathan Odell] ... [.25 acres] ... [the Sheriff confiscated the property, exposed it to sale, and Benjamin Pierson was the highest bidder] ...; [Signed - John Hollinshead Sheriff; witnesses - John Phillips, Danl Bacon Junr, John How, Jos. Read; recorded 29 November 1787.]

[p 244]   **QUIT CLAIM**

Know all Men ... That We Adam Parker and Elizabeth Parker his Wife ... of the City and County of

BURLINGTON COUNTY DEEDS - BOOK "A"

Burlington ... New Jersey have and hereby ... Quit Claim unto Benjamin Pierson ... [of the same place the above .25 acres of land] ...; [Signed - Adam Parker, Elizabeth Parker; witnesses - John Phillips, Danl Bacon Junr, John How.]

[p 245]   **ABRAHAM HEWLINGS to DANIEL KING**

9 April 1779 - Abraham Hewlings ... City of Burlington ... New Jersey ... [sold to] ... Daniel King ... of Burlington County ... [175 pounds] ... All that his House and Lot of Land ... at Crosswicks ... Township of Chesterfield ... Which Lot of Land the said Abraham Hewlings purchased of Thomas Shinn Esq. High Sheriff ... Burlington ... [by deed dated 20 April 1762] ... [adjacent land owners or names - corner of the Grave Yard, land late of Thomas Douglass] ... [23 square perches] ...; [Signed - Abraham Hewlings; witnesses - Eliz^o Hewlings, Danl Ellis.]

[p 247]   **MANUMISSION OF PETER THOM [?]**

Whereas Jonathan Hough late of the Township of Springfield ... Burlington ...   New Jersey dec^d did by his last Will ... Order ... his Executors Daniel Hough and Samuel Hough to liberate ... at his Decease a Mulatto Male Slave Named Peter Thone [Thom?] ...; Dated - 17 March 1787; signed - Jonathan Hough; witnesses - John Lacey, Job Lippincott.]

[27 November 1787 - It was certified that on 17 March 1787, the above named slave was brought before the Overseers of the Poor and the Justices of Peace for Springfield Township who found [the subject] of sound mind & not under any bodily incapacity, not under the age of 21 years nor over the age of 35 years; signed - Thos Reynolds and Peter Stretch - Justices of Peace; Caleb Earl and Benjn Hough - Overseers of the Poor; recorded - before John Phillips, Clerk of the Peace & Pleas on 27 November 1787.]

[p 248]   **MANUMISSION OF PHILLIS**

Know all Men ... that I Samuel Hough ... Township of Springfield ... Burlington ... being at the present time a lawful property ... to a certain Female Slave Named Phillis ... do solemnly liberate the said Phillis ...; [Signed at New Mills]; Samuel Hough; witnesses - John Lacey, Job Lippincott.]

[17 March 1787 - It was certified that the above named slave was brought before the Overseers of the Poor and the Justices of Peace for Springfield Township who found [the subject] of sound mind & not under any bodily incapacity, not under the age of 21 years nor over the age of 35 years; signed - Thomas Reynolds and Peter Stretch - Justices of Peace; Caleb Earl and Benjn Hough - Overseers of the Poor; recorded - before John Phillips, Clerk of the Peace & Pleas on 27 November 1787.]

BURLINGTON COUNTY DEEDS - BOOK "A"

[p 249]   **MEMORANDUM OF AN AGREEMENT**

Memorandum of an Agreement Made ... [14 May 1776] ... Between Joseph Henzey of Philadelphia Turner & Chairmaker ... [regarding the sale to] ... Ellis Lewis of the same place Merchant ... [for 160 pounds] ... One half of the premises and Land Which Joseph Henzey hath lately purchased from Henry Paxson Esqr in Mount Holly ... Burlington ... New Jersey situate between the House occupied by Anna Lippincott and the House occupied by William Chew ...; [Signed - Ellis Lewis, Jo^s Henzey; witnesses - Cha. Read, Jos. Read.]

[3 January 1788 - Joseph Read appeared before Judge Thomas Reynolds, Esqr, of Burlington Co, New Jersey.]

[p 250]   **EDWARD BLACK to ALEXANDER SHIRES**

13 January 1787 - Edward Black ... Township of Galleway ... Gloucester ... New Jersey & Mary his Wife ... [sold to] ... Alexander Shires of Mount Holly ... Burlington ... Merch^t ... [for 750 pounds] ... [adjacent land owners or names - High Street & Mill Street Corner in Mount Holly, John Bispham, formerly of Nathaniel Thomas, Henry Paxson, John Clark] ... [52 square perches] ... [same land was conveyed by Aquila Shinn unto Edward Black by deed dated 28 September 1781, which he became seized by deed from Edward Black & Jonah Woolman Executers of the last Will of Henry Paxson Esquire deceased, who sold it to Aquila Shinn by deed dated 20 September 1786 and is the same land which Henry Paxson Esqr ... purchased with other land of Jacob Pricket by deed dated 26 June 1760] ...; [Signed - Edward Black, Mary Black; witnesses - Saml Read, Jos. Read.]

[p 254]   **TIMOTHY SULLIVAN to ZACHARIAH ROSSELL**

10 September 1776 - Timothy Sullivan of Mount Holly ... Burlington ... New Jersey ... [sold to] ... Zachariah Rossell of the same place ... Whereas the said Timothy Sullivan by ... [two deeds dated the 6th month 26th day 1784 & 5th December 1753 under the seal of Samuel Cripps became seized of two lots in Mount Holly adjoining each other on the Westside of High Street] ... [adjoining land owners or names - Zachariah Rossell, Jacob Webber and Wife, Aquila Shinn, Christopher Shinn & Wife (Daughter & Devisee of said Cripps)] ...; [Signed - Timothy A. Sullivan made his mark when signing; witnesses - Isaac Ward, Aaron Smith, Jo^s Read.]

[p 250]   **TIMOTHY SMITH to NATHANIEL ROBINS**

1 May 1786 - Timothy Smith ... Township of Mansfield ... Burlington ... New Jersey Wheelwright ... [sold to] ... Nathaniel Robins ... [of the same place] Yeoman ... that the said Timothy Smith and Sarah his Wife she remitting all her Right of Dower to her Thirds in her premises ... [for 200 pounds] ... land in Township of Mansfield ... [adjacent land owners or names - Road from black House to the

BURLINGTON COUNTY DEEDS - BOOK "A"
****

Square] ... [61 acres] ... [Being piece of the plantation of William Satterwaite and Jane his Wife by Deed dated 8 February 1783 and is also part of the plantation Satterthwaite purchased of John Hammell Exec^r to his Father John Hammell dec^d which Hammell the elder bought of Caleb Brown by deed 11 M° 13 day old stile 1723 in Deed Book AC-Page 176, Burlington] ...; [Signed - Timothy Smith, Sarah Smith made her mark when she signed; witnesses - Thomas Atkinson, Jesse White.]

[Timothy Smith & wife appeared before Isaac Cowgill on the 16th of April 1788.]

[END OF BOOK "A"]

BURLINGTON COUNTY DEEDS - BOOK "B"

****

[p 1]   **JACOB WEBBER to ZACHARIAH ROSSELL**

31 October 1772 - Jacob Webber ... Town of Derby ... Pennsylvania, Cooper and Ann his Wife one of the Daughters of Nathaniel Cripps formerly of the Township of Northampton ... County of Burlington ... New Jersey ... [sold to] Zachariah Rossell of Mount holley ... county of Burlington ... Whereas ... Nathaniel Cripps ... [was seized of lands near Mount Holly] ... by his Deed Poll ... [dated 11 May 1740] ... did ... grant unto his loving Daughter Ann Crips Now the above named Ann Webber and to her Heirs ... a certain Part thereof ... [by Burlington deed, Book GG-Page 372] ... [adjacent land owners or names - Hight Street, Nathaniel Cripps, Josiah Blackham, Solomon Shinn] ... [5 acres] ... Now this Indenture ... [land was sold for 40 pounds] ... excepting ... two small Lots ... of the North East Corner ... sold to James Mc Clutche and Samuel Haines which Lots are now United in One and said to be the property of Eastwood Allen ...; [Signed - Jacob Webber, Ann Webber; witnesses - Aaron Oakford, Isaac Lloyd..]

[p 5]   **CHRISTOPHER SHUFF to ZACHARIAH ROSSELL**

9 November 1785 - Christopher Shuff, Cooper & Grace his Wife ... [sold to] ... Zachariah Rossell Innkeeper ... both of the Township of Northampton ... Burlington ... New Jersey ... [for 97 pounds, 2 shillings, 8 pence] ... one certain piece of Land ... [adjacent land owners or names - Ancocus Creek, Road from Mount Holly to Burlington, John Lee, Moses Kempton] ... [13 acres, 3 rods, 20 perches] ... And whereas John Cripps of Northampton ... purchased of William Peachy in ... 1677 one Eighth of a Propriety ... which he laid out 350 acres of Land on Ancocus Creek, that afterwards he purchased of Ann Salter one twelfth of a propriety by which he laid out 150 acres ... That Lawrence Morris purchased of said Peachy 100 acres & laid out 50 acres adjoining the said 350 acres and afterwards sold the said 100 to the Said John Cripps, that Thomas Peachy Heir of said William Peachy ... made a Deed to Nathaniel Cripps, who caused a Resurvey ... and whereas ... [John Cripps by his Will devised all the above land to his son Nathaniel Cripps] ... he being so thereof Seized did give a part of Said Tract to his Son Samuel Cripps by Will Dated ... [9 September 1746] ... and the Said Samuel Cripps did give & bequeath unto his Daughter Grace Cripps, now Grace Shuff by Will Dated ... [10 October 1761] ... that part of the above Recited Land lying on the West Side of the Great Road leading from Mount holly to Burlington, adjoining ... Land given to her Sister Hannah by their Said Father Samuel Cripps ... [adjoining land owners or names - Ancocus Creek] ... [13 acres, 3 rods, 20 perches] ...; [Signed - Christopher Shuff, grace made her mark when signing; witnesses - Israel Shreve, Jonah Woolman, Aquila Shinn.]

[p 8]   **JOSEPH MULLEN to JOSEPH RIDGWAY**

21 August 1773 - Joseph Mullen of Mount Holly ... Township of Northampton ... Burlington ... New Jersey Carpenter & Ann his Wife ... [sold to] ... Joseph Ridgway ... Township of Springfield ... Tanner ... [for 107 pounds] ... Two certain lots ... of Land and Meadow ... in the Township of

(37)

BURLINGTON COUNTY DEEDS - BOOK "B"

Northampton ... [5.75 acres] ... & Meadow Ground the other Lott ...   [adjacent land owners or names - James Southwick, Edward Mullen, Abraham Denormandie & Company] ... [9 acres, 2 rods, 10 perches] ... Which first lot ... [was purchased from Henry Paxson & Joseph Hollinshead, Trustees of John Abraham Denormandie And Company ... by deed dated 11 August 1759, Liber x-Page 476] ... the other lot ... purchased of Charles Read Esq. by ... [deed dated 1 February 1770] ... and is part of a larger Parcel ... which ... Read purchased of John Ogbourn by Deed ... dated 1 April 1747] ...; [Signed - Joseph Mullen, Anne Mullen; witnesses - Henry Paxson, John Bispham.]

[p 12]   **JOSEPH BURR to JOSEPH RIDGWAY**

21 August 1773 - Joseph Burr ... Township of Northampton ... Burlington ... New Jersey Farmer ... [sold to] ... Joseph Ridgway ... Township of Springfield ... Farmer ... [147 pounds] ... Two Certain Fields ... on the West Side of the Highway that leads from Barkers Creek to Mount Holly ... [adjoining land owners or names - Estate of Samuel Crips, William Stockton, Abraham Farrington, Thomas Butcher, Ebenezer Large] ... [17 acres, 2 rods, 7 perches] ... the other lot ... [Adjacent land owners or names - Joseph Burr purchased from the Executors of Thomas Shinn, Samuel Cripps, William Stockton] ... [4 acres, 1 rod, 3 perches] ... Which Said Lands the Said Joseph Burr Purchased of his Brother William Burr & Ann his Wife by deed ... [dated 17 August 1772] ... the Said William Burr became Seized ... by .... the last Will ... of his Father Joseph Burr deceased ... [The First piece of land Joseph Burr purchased of Henry Paxson & John Woolman Executors of Thomas Shinn Esq by deed dated 15 July 1754 and which Shinn purchased of Edward Gaskill on 6 January 1740, and the other lot which Joseph Burr bought of Samuel Cripps on 16 July 1754 being part of Land of Samuel Cripps by Will of his Father Nathaniel Cripps] ...; [Signed - Joseph Burr Jun'; witnesses - Henry Paxson, John Bispham.]

[p 15]   **JOHN SLEEPER to JOSEPH RIDGWAY**

29 March 1775 - John Sleeper of Mount Holly ... Township of Northampton ... Burlington ... New Jersey & Hannah his Wife ... [sold to] ... Joseph Ridgway of Northampton ... [90 pounds] ... One certain Lot ... in the Township of Northampton ... [adjacent land owners or names - Main road from Mt Holly to Springfield, Joseph Ridgway, Joseph Burr, Garden Street, William Calvert, John Ridgway, Jasper Moon, John Sleeper, Samuel Cripps] ... [13 acres, 2 rods, 29 perches] ... [land which John Sleeper bought from his brother Jonathan Sleeper by deed on 25 November 1764 and was purchased by Jonathan Sleeper from my brother John Sleeper ... of Ebenzer Large of the City of Burlington Deceased by deed dated 22 August 1759 and was bought by Large from Edward Gaskill by deed dated 12 November 1738, and by Gaskill & Josiah Southwick from Samuel Jennings with other lands by deed dated 14 March 1701 in Book B-Page 708 and was originally surveyed to Jennings for 871 acres ... which land edward Gaskill & Josiah Southwick by deed did release to each other and Gaskill by deed dated 15 April 1737 did obtain "from Edward Gaskill Jun' his Son"] ...; [Signed - John Sleeper, Hannah Sleeper; witnesses - William Calvert, John Bispham.]

BURLINGTON COUNTY DEEDS - BOOK "B"

[p 18]   JOSEPH RIDGWAY to ISAAC HAZELHURST

25 December 1776 - Joseph Ridgway ... Township of Northampton ... Burlington ... New Jersey Gentleman & Mary his Wife ... [sold to] ... Isaac Hazelhurst ... City of Philadelphia ... Pennsylvania ... Merchant ... 700 pounds] ... One Certain ... Plantation & five lots ... within the Township of Northampton ... [Two lots on the West side of road from Barkers Creek to Mount Holly] ... one lot ... [adjoining land owners or names - Samuel Cripps deceased & William Stockton, land of Abraham Farrington now Thomas Butcher, Ebenezer Large] ... [17 acres, 2 rods, 7 perches] ... the other lot ... [adjacent land owners or names - Joseph Burr, Executors of Thomas Shinn, Samuel Cripps, William Stockton] ... [4 acres, 1 rod, 3 perches which Ridgway bought] ... of Joseph Burr Junior (the Son of Joseph Burr aforesaid) by Indenture ... [dated 21 August 1773] ... the same being that part of the Premises whereon the Chirt Building or Mansion House Stands] ... one other of the five lotts ... Joseph Ridgway purchased of John Sleeper & Hannah his Wife ... [on 29 March 1775] ... [adjacent land owners or names - Joseph Ridgway, Joseph Burr, Garden Street, William Calvert, John Ridgway, Jasper Moon] ... the other remaining two ... lots ... Ridgway purchased of Joseph Mullen & Anne his Wife ... [on 21 August 1773] ... the first ... [5.75 acres] ... the other lot ... [adjacent land owners or names - James Southwick, Edward Mullen, Abraham De Normandie & Company] ... [9 acres, 2 rods, 10 perches] ... The whole ... of the five lots ... containing ... [50 acres, 3 rods, 9 perches] ...; [Signed - Jos Ridgway, Mary Ridgway; witnesses - William Budd, Jos. Read.]

[p 23]   JASPER MOON to WILLIAM CALVERT

15 October 1779 - Jasper Moon ... Township of Northampton ... Burlington ... New Jersey Cooper & Martha his Wife ... [sold to] ... William Calvert of Mount Holly ... Merchant ... [for 216 Spanish Milled Dollars] ... One Certain piece or Lot of Wood ... in the Township of Northampton ... [adjacent land owners or names - George Robert, John Ridgway, Isaac Hazelhurst] ... [16 acres, 33 perches] ... [the above land conveyed is Part of the Share ... of the Said Martha Moon in her Father Samuel Cripps' Lands ... by his Will] ...; [Signed - Jasper Moon, Martha Moon; witnesses - Hannah Hooton, Jos. Read.]

[p 25]   RELEASE FOR THE ABOVE LAND

... the within mentioned Lot of Land with other lands are under Mortgage unto me William Smith ... County of Burlington ... New Jersey ... Now know ye that I ... William Smith ... [for 5 shillings] ... paid by William Calvert ... quit claim unto the Said William Calvert ... to the within ... [16 acres, 33 perches] ...; [Signed - William Smith; witnesses -Thomson Neale, Jos. Read.]

[p 26]   WILLIAM CALVERT to ISAAC HAZELHURST

1 November 1779 - William Calvert of Mount holly ... Township of Northampton ... Burlington ...

BURLINGTON COUNTY DEEDS - BOOK "B"

New Jersey Shopkeeper & Martha his Wife ... [sold to] ... Isaac Hazelhurst ... [of the same place] ... Merchant ... [240 Spanish Milled Dollars] ... lot of wood land ... in the Township of Northampton ... [adjacent land owners or names - George Robert, John Ridgway] ... [16 acres, 33 perches] ... [the same land that was conveyed to Martha Moon in her Father Samuel Cripps lands by his Will & divided "among his Daughters"] ...; [Signed - William Calvert, Martha Calvert; witnesses - Ann Read, John Cooper.]

[p 28] **BENAJAH BUTCHER to ISAAC HAZELHURST**

31 December 1787 - Benajah Butcher ... Township of Northampton ... Burlington ... New Jersey Yeoman & Rachel his Wife ... [sold to] ... Isaac Hazelhurst ... of Philadelphia Merchant ... whereas ... Benajah Butcher by ... a certain Indenture ... [by the Executor of the Will of his Father Thomas Butcher (deceased), dated 9 March 1787] ... became Seized ... in a lot of Land ... in the Township of Northampton ... [16 acres] ... it being a part of the Plantation whereon the Said Benajah Butcher now lives & which his Father ... Thomas Butcher ... bargained for with George Roberts of Philadelphia Merchant ... but no Conveyance was Executed ... untill after the Death of Said Thomas Butcher to wit ... [on 25 March 1786] ... the Said George Roberts & Thomasine his Wife executed a Deed therefore unto Sarah Butcher Mary Butcher & Joseph Ridgeway Executors of ... Thomas Butcher's Will ... which Plantation ... [George Roberts bought of Joseph Gaskill & Sarah his Wife by deed dated 19 November 1776 & the 16 acres is also a part of Cripps' Survey & was conveyed by Cripps to Joseph Gaskill the Uncle of the Said Joseph Gaskill ... by deed dated 11 September 1750] ... Now this Indenture ... [for 154 pounds, 15 shillings, for the 16 acres lot] ... [adjacent land owners or names - Isaac Hazelhurst, Benjamin Brian, Abel Harker, William Calvert] ... [15.25 acres, 35 perches] ...; [Signed - Benajah Butcher, Rachel Butcher; witnesses - Abel Harker, Jos. Read; witnesses for payment of above - Phillip Bochm, Junr and John Wilcocks Junr.]

[p 31] **COMMISSIONERS OF LOAN OFFICE to JOSEPH WATSON**

4 March 1788 - Commissioners of the Loan Office ... County of Burlington ... [sold to] ... Joseph Watson of Nottingham ... Burlington ... [400 pounds] ... All that ... Tract of Meadow Land ... in Nottingham .... [adjacent land owners or names - John Watson, William Watson] ... [9 acres] ...; [Signed - Soloman Ridgway, R. Strettell Jones, John Black; witnesses - John Abbot, John Taylor.]

[p 33] **RECEIPT**

19 March 1788 - Received from Henry Hayes ... [154 pounds, 8 shillings, 6 pence] ... which was by him tendered on ... 18 March 1788] ... to William Smith Esqr ... City of Burlington in the Presence of William Hayes and Barnaby VanSciver at the House of Daniel Ellis Esqr in full Discharge of a certain Bond & Mortgage given by Henry Hayes to William Smith Esqr ... [on 1 January 1875] ... Conditioned for the payment of ... [496 pounds] ... and the Said William Smith Esqr refusing to

BURLINGTON COUNTY DEEDS - BOOK "B"

receive the same as is Said the Said Henry Hayes hath lodg'd the Said Monies or so much thereof in my hands to be delivered to the Said William Smith ... In Witness Whereof I the Subscriber Clerk of the Peace and Pleas ... [Burlington] ...; [Signed - John Phillips; received - 25 March 1788; the foregoing money was received by Wm Smith ... who delivered up the Obligations ...; Signed - Phillips Clk.]

[p 34] **BOUNDARY SETTLEMENT**

To all that it may concern, Know ye that We ... Taunton Earl, Samuel Smith & Abigail Smith of the Township of Springfield ... Burlington ... New Jersey do hereby Certify that we have this ... [15 April 1788] ... mutually agreed upon and fixed a Line between our Plantations Situate in Said Township of Springfield aforesaid ... [adjacent land owners or names - Joseph Biddle, Samuel & Abigail Smith, Taunton Earl, Samuel Haigh] ...; [Signed - Taunton Earl, Samuel Smith, Abigail Smith; witnesses - Caleb Wright, Caleb Earl, John Black; recorded - 18 April 1788.]

[p 35] **ABRAHAM WINNER to JOHN WINNER**

28 May 1787 - Abraham Winner ... Township of Burlington ... New Jersey and Mary his Wife ... [sold to] ... John Winner of Great Egg Harbour ... Gloucester ... Whereas the Said Abraham Winner ... [by deed from Joseph Butterworth and Sarah his Wife dated 29 May 1780 and from Samuel Shinn dated 1 February 1776 became seized of two certain parcels of land in the Township of Northampton ... [for 260 pounds] ... All these his two ... Parcels ... of Land ... [adjacent land owners or names - Jacob Hilliard, Edward Hilliard, Edward Andrew, Nathan Gaskill, Cripps Estate] ... [3 acres, 2 rods, 23 perches] ... The other Piece ... [adjacent land owners or names - Side of the Great Road called Gaskill's Lane, Hannah Belcher, Johanna Brown] ... [7 acres, 7 perches].

Memorandum - [Before the execution of the above deed, Abraham Winner excepts two Small Pieces, the one sold by him to Abel Harker and the other to Isaiah Bishop Which is Within the above bounds] ...; [Signed - Abraham Winner, Mary Winner; witnesses - Charles Ellis, Daniel Ellis.]

[p 39] **WILLIAM SMITH to JOHN WINNER**

William Smith ... City of Burlington ... New Jersey Esquire (To whom the tenements and Premises within Mentioned ... are Mortgaged) Send Greetings Know ye that the Said William Smith ... [for 170 pounds] ... paid by John Winner Grantee in the Within Indenture Named ... forever Quit claimed ... unto ... John Winner ... to the two Pieces of Land ...; [Dated - 26 June 1787; signed - William Smith; witnesses - Charles Ellis, Daniel Ellis.]

BURLINGTON COUNTY DEEDS - BOOK "B"

****

[p 41]   JOSIAH WHITE to JOSIAH GASKILL JUN[R]

28 August 1753 - Josiah White of Bridgetown in Northampton ... Burlington ... New Jersey (Clothier) being the only Surviving Executor of the last Will ... of Thomas Budd of Bridgetown aforesaid Cooper, Dec[d] ... [sold to] ... Josiah Gaskill Jun[r] of Northampton ... (Yeoman) ... Whereas the aforesaid Thomas Budd ... at the time of his Death ... [was seized in one certain piece of land in Northampton & being so seized put in his Will dated 7 July 1751 and named Benjamin Bispham & Josiah White sole Executors and under the hands of Thomas Budd dated 9 January 1748 ... it appears that Budd was bound unto Josiah Gaskill Jun[r] for ...[240 pounds, 12 shillings, 10 pence] ... shall execute a deed unto Josiah Gaskill for Land in the Township of Northampton ... [adjacent land owners or names - Indian Run, James Budd, Josiah Gaskill] ... [202 acres] ... Now this Indenture Witnesseth that Josiah White ... [sold for 200 pounds paid unto him the above] ...; [Signed - Josiah White; witnesses - Rebekah Budd, Saml Atkinson Cooper, John Burr Junr, Absalom Ewan.]

[17 August 1765 - Josiah White acknowledged the same before Judge Henry Paxson, Burlington Co.]

[p 45]   SAMUEL GASKILL to WILLIAM SHINN JUN[R]

21 May 1765 - Samuel Gaskill & Lucretia his Wife Both of the Township of New Hanover ... Burlington ... New Jersey ... [sold to] ... William Shinn Jun[r] ... Township of Springfield ... [2 pounds, 5 shillings] ... two certain tracts ... of Land One of which is ... in the Township of New Hanover ... [adjacent land owners or names - Absalom Ewans, James Budd, Josiah Gaskill] ... [61 acres] ...; [Signed - Samuel Gaskill, Lucretia Gaskill; witnesses - Henry Reeves, Rachel Reeves, Joseph Gaskill.]

[p 48]   WILLIAM LOVET SMITH ESQ[R] to JO[S] SHINN

1 February 1787 - William Lovet Smith Esq[r] ... Township of Springfield ... Burlington ... New Jersey ... [sold to] ... Jo[s] Shinn ... Township of Northampton Yeoman ... Witnesseth that ... [William Lovet Smith Sells unto Joseph Shinn a piece of Cedar swamp] ... on a Branch of Joseph Burr's Sawmill Creek above a Cedar Swamp called the great Swamp ... [18 acres] ... [which piece was bought by Smith and Mary his Wife & William Shinn joint partners, which is nine Acres to each ... from Sheriff Joseph Emley in January 1767] ... [18 acres] ... of which Levi Briggs became seized by ... [last Will of his Father George Briggs, late of Northampton ... deceased who bought it from Joseph Burr, Junr on 26 January 1753, And Whereas the Sheriff took possession of the Goods of Levi Briggs & put them out to auction on 24 December 1786 & William Lovet Smith & William Shinn bought the land] ... Now this Indenture ... [the land is sold for 22 pounds, 12 shillings, 6 pence] ...; [Signed - William Lovet Smith Esq[r], Mary Smith; witnesses - Sam. Shinn, Anne Smith.]

BURLINGTON COUNTY DEEDS - BOOK "B"

[p 51] **THOMAS ENGLISH to ISAAC ENGLISH**

... I Thomas English ... Township of Mansfield ... Burlington ... New Jersey Yeoman do send Greetings Know ye, I the Said Thomas English ... for & in the consideration of the Love good will & affection which I have & do bear toward my loving & dutiful Son Isaac English ... [of the same place] ... do ... Grant unto ... Isaac English my son ... all the Plantation where I now dwell to him ... Provided ... [he] ... shall ... pay yearly ... [70 pounds until the debts against the Estate are paid] ... Note further that the true intent of my mind is that this Place or tract of Land ... Shall be reserved for Thomas English the Son of Isaac English, my Grandson after his the Said Isaac English my son's decease ... [150 acres] ... [adjacent land owners or names - Thomas Biddle, John Sutton] ... Reserving half an acre for a Meeting House about the place where the old Meeting House now stands ... I also Reserve the House for his Son Thomas after his Decease ...; [Dated 9 March 1776; signed - Thomas English; witnesses - Henry Clarke, Fretwell Warren.]

[17 April 1788 - Joseph English, one of the People called Quakers, appeared before Judge Thomas Rodman of Burlington Co.]

Note - There was a note that read: "Delivered Original Deed to Saml Woolman Adm^n of Thos English Agst 25th 1791."]

[p 52] **JOSEPH MULLEN to JOSEPH ENGLISH**

1 November 1785 - Joseph Mullen Esqr late High Sheriff ... Burlington ... New Jersey ... [sold to] ... Joseph English of Mansfield ... Burlington ... Whereas Isaac English ... Township of Mansfield ... Burlington was by Virtue of a Deed of Gift, from under the hand & Seal of his Father Thomas English, bearing date ... [9 March 1775] ... seized in a Certain Plantation ... in ... Township of Mansfield on which the Said Thomas English then dwelt which tract of Land is Bounded on the River Delaware & on the Land formerly William English, now the Land of Joseph English Minor (Son of Joseph English the Elder) as also of & in one other tract of Land ... [in the same place] ... [150 acres] ... [adjacent land owners or names - Thomas Biddle, John Sutton] ... And Whereas the Said Isaac English being so seized, the Said Joseph Mullen ... [by a Writ re: a suit of Jacob Phillips did seize a part of the last mentioned tract & on the remainder of the tract of 76 acres, & did expose the same for sale] ... [the 76 acres was sold to Joseph Bloomfield Esqr] ... and whereas one Abraham Hewling ... [in 1782 recovered against Isaac English as well as another debt which John Imlay esqr, Daniel Ellis Esqr, Joshua Foster, Abel Tomas & Henry Drinker recovered against said English] ... [And because there was insufficient funds to cover the debts, the Sheriff] ... did seize ... the aforesaid Plantation, whereon the Said Thomas English decease'd did Dwell, as also the Remainder of the Said ... [150 acres which was sold on 30 July 1783 for 460 pounds] ...; [Signed - Joseph Mullen late Sheriff; witnesses - Jacob Austin, Daniel Ellis.]

BURLINGTON COUNTY DEEDS - BOOK "B"

****

[7 April 1788 - Joseph Mullen appeared before Judge Daniel Ellis of Burlington Co.]

Note - There was a note also at the end that read: "Delivered Original Deed to Saml Woolman Adm^n of Thos English Agst 25th 1791."]

[p 57]   **MANUMISSION OF ANDREW CARY**

I Joshua Bispham ... Township of Evesham ... Burlington ... New Jersey ... do hereby Manumit & Set free my Negroe Slave named Andrew Cary ...; [Dated - 10 December 1787; signed - Joshua Bispham.]

We do hereby Certify ... [10 December 1787] ... Joshua Bispham ... brought before us, two of the overseers of the Poor ... & two of the Justices of the Peace ... his Slave named Andrew Cary who ... appears ... to be Sound in mind & not under any Bodily incapacity ... & also is not under Twenty one Years of Age nor above thirty five ...; [Dated - 10 December 1787; signed - James Wilkins, Joshua Borton - Overseers of the Poor; Reece Edwards, Darling Conrow - Justices of the Peace.]

We the ... two ... Justices of the Peace ... do hereby Certify that the Bearer Andrew Cary is Manumitted & Set Free by his Master Joshua Bispham ...; [Dated -10 December 1787; signed - Reece Edwards, Darling Conrow - Justices of the Peace; John Phillips, Clerk of Pleas, Burlington Co.]

[p 58]   **INCORPORATION OF THE METHODIST EPISCOPAL CHURCH ... HANOVER**

This is to certify ... [re: a law passed at Trenton on 16 March 1786 to incorporate ... persons ... in every religious society] ... thereof A Meeting was called and held ... at the Methodist Episcopal Church in Hanover Township, Burlington County ... New Jersey on ... [14 April 1788] ... When and Where we the Subscribers were elected and chosen by plurality of Voices ... as Trustees of said ... [church] ... As Witness hereof we set our Hand & Seals - William Budd, Isaac Budd, George Kemble, Andrew Heisler (his name in Dutch), Jonathan Budd, John King, Samuel Budd.

[The above subjects then swore they hold no Allegiance to the King of great Britain and then swore Allegiance to the Government established in this State; recorded - 17 May 1788.]

[p 60]   **THOMAS WEBSTER to PHILO LEEDS**

The following Note was written by the Clerk - "This Deed at the time of being brought for Recording had the Beginning corner torn off which is the Reason of the many Blanks on this and the following Page - Phillips Clk."

BURLINGTON COUNTY DEEDS - BOOK "B"

***

29 January 1743 - [Thomas Webster ... New Jersey Yeoman ... [sold to] ... Philo Leeds of Bridg. Town ... Burlington ... New Jersey ... [57 pounds, 10 shillings] ... Lot of Land ... in Bridge - town ... [adjoining land owners or names - John Adams, Henry Maccolloah, Mill Street, Philo Leeds, High Street, Thomas Shinn] ... [58.5 square perches] ... Lot of Land was ... purchased part of Oddy Brock by Deed ... [dated 2 April 1733] ... and part of the above Granted Premises was ... purchased of Thomas Shinn Esqr by Deed ... [8 January 1743] ...; [Signed - Thomas Webster; witnesses - Saml Scattergood, Ben Bard, Benjn Brian.]

[12 February 1788 - Joseph Hollinshead, one of the People called Quakers, appeared before Judge Joseph Read, Esqr, and swore that he personally acquainted with all of the above subjects and witnesses.]

[p 65]   WILLIAM STOCKTON to JAMES SHREVE

29 January 1763 - William Stockton of Springfield ... Burlington, Sole Executor of the last Will ... of Benjamin Braman late of New Hanover ... Burlington ... New Jersey late deceas'd ... [sold to] ... James Shreve of New Hanover ... Burlington ... Yeoman ... Whereas ... Benjamin Braman did by his last Will ... [direct his land to be sold] ... Now these presents Witnesseth that ... William Stockton ... [for 43 pounds, 11 shillings sells to Shreve] ... all that piece of Swamp and upland ... [6 acres, 2 perches] ... [which Benjamin Braman purchased of William Duckworth and is the third and last piece mentioned in a Deed ... by Duckworth to Braman on 3 November 1740 and was purchased by Duckworth from Jacob Ong by Deed dated 6 July 1740] ...; Signed - William Stockton; witnesses - John Stephens, John Robinson.]

29 January 1763 - Know all Men ... that I Elizabeth Braman Widow of the within named Benjamin Braman ... [quit claimed to James Shreve all Dower rights] ...; [Signed - Elizabeth Bramam who made her mark when signing; witnesses - John Stephens, John Robinson.]

[24 June 1788 - Samuel Stockton Son of William Stockton dec^d appeared before Judge Thomas Fenimore, Burlington Co, and testified that he was well acquainted with his Father's handwriting which was on the above deed.]

[p 67]   EDWARD TONKIN to ZACHARIAH ROSSELL JUN^R

28 October 1758 - Edward Tonkin of Springfield & Henry Cooper of Northampton both in the County of Burlington ... New Jersey (Yeoman) Executors of the last Will ... of Thomas Atkinson of Northampton aforesaid late dec^d ... [sold to] ... Zachariah Rossell Junr of Northampton afores^d (Inn holder) ... [for 250 pounds] ... One certain ... lot of Land ... on the West Side of high Street in Bridgetown in Northampton ... [adjoining land owners or names - Ancocus Creek, John Hatkinson, High Street, Job Lippincott Junr] ... [26 square perches] ... Which ... Land the Said Thomas Atkinson purchased of Benjamin Bispham by Deed ... [dated 21 July 1749] ... being part of a larger lot of land

BURLINGTON COUNTY DEEDS - BOOK "B"

which [Bispham bought of Thomas Shinn Esq' by deed dated 5 September 1748, & which Shinn bought of edward Gaskill & in part of Andrew Conrow] ...; [Signed - Edward Tonkin, Henry Cooper; witnesses - Tho' Lawrance, John Burr Jun'.]

[3 January 1788 - John Burr, witness and one of the People called Quakers, appeared before Judge Joseph Read, Burlington Co.]

[p 71]   **MANUMISSION OF CHLOE**

I Nathan Haines ... Township of Evesham ... Burlington ... New Jersey ... do hereby Manumit & Set free my Negroe Slave named Chloe ...; [Dated - 19 June 1787; signed - Nathan Haines.]

We do hereby Certify ... [19 June 1787] ... Nathan Haines ... brought before us, two of the overseers of the Poor ... & two of the Justices of the Peace ... his Slave named Chloe who ... appears ... to be Sound in mind & not under any Bodily incapacity ... & also is not under Twenty one Years of Age nor above thirty five ...; [Dated - 19 June 1787; signed - Isaiah Haines, Joshua Borton - Overseers of the Poor; Reece Edwards, Josiah Foster - Justices of the Peace.]

We the ... two ... Justices of the Peace ... do hereby Certify that the Bearer Chloe is Manumitted & Set Free by his Master Nathan Haines ...; [Dated -19 June 1787; signed - Reece Edwards, Josiah Foster - Justices of the Peace.]

[21 May 1788 - Recorded before John Phillips, Clerk of Pleas, Burlington Co.]

[p 72]   **MANUMISSION OF CATO HAMMEY**

I John Hinchman Esq' ... Township of Evesham ... Burlington ... New Jersey ... do hereby Manumit & Set free my Negroe Slave named Cato Hammey ...; [Dated - 16 September 1788; signed - John Hinchman, Esq'.]

We do hereby Certify ... [16 September 1788] ... John Hinchman, Esq' ... brought before us, two of the overseers of the Poor ... & two of the Justices of the Peace ... his Slave named Cato Hammey who ... appears ... to be Sound in mind & not under any Bodily incapacity ... & also is not under Twenty one Years of Age nor above thirty five ...; [Dated - 16 September 1788; signed - Joshua Lippincott, Thomas Dudley - Overseers of the Poor; Peter Shiras, Reece Edwards - Justices of the Peace.]

We the ... two ... Justices of the Peace ... do hereby Certify that the Bearer Cato Hammey is Manumitted & Set Free by his Master John Hinchman, Esq' ...; [Dated 10 December 1787; signed

BURLINGTON COUNTY DEEDS - BOOK "B"

****

- Peter Shiras, Reece Edwards - Justices of the Peace; John Phillips, Clerk of Pleas, Burlington Co.; 16 September 1788 - Recorded before John Phillips, Clerk of Pleas, Burlington Co.]

[p 73]   **MANUMISSION OF Mc INTOSH HAMMEY**

I John Hinchman Esqr ... Township of Evesham ... Burlington ... New Jersey ... do hereby Manumit & Set free my Negroe Slave named Mc Intosh Hammey ...; [Dated - 16 September 1788; signed - John Hinchman, Esqr.]

We do hereby Certify ... [16 September 1788] ... John Hinchman, Esqr ... brought before us, two of the overseers of the Poor ... & two of the Justices of the Peace ... his Slave named Mc Intosh Hammey who ... appears ... to be Sound in mind & not under any Bodily incapacity ... & also is not under Twenty one Years of Age nor above thirty five ...; [Dated - 16 September 1788; signed - Joshua Lippincott, Thomas Dudley - Overseers of the Poor; Peter Shiras, Reece Edwards - Justices of the Peace.]

We the ... two ... Justices of the Peace ... do hereby Certify that the Bearer Mc Intosh Hammey is Manumitted & Set Free by his Master John Hinchman, Esqr ...; [Dated 10 December 1787; signed - Peter Shiras, Reece Edwards - Justices of the Peace; John Phillips, Clerk of Pleas, Burlington Co.]

[16 September 1788 - Recorded before John Phillips, Clerk of Pleas, Burlington Co.]

[p 74]   **THOMAS FENIMORE, AGENT to JAMES GREGSON**

... I Thomas Fenimore Esquire, agent for taking charge of forfeited Estates in the County of Burlington ... New Jersey ... [did advertise on 26 September 1786 for sale] ... Lot of Land and the Barracks thereon ... [in Burlington City] ... [and sold it to James Gregson of Said City, Brewer, for 1,200 pounds] ... [adjacent land owners or names - south side of Broad Street, Assisconck Creek in the City of Burlington, William White] ... [1 acre] ... being the same lot of Land and Premises which William White of the City of Burlington ... [sold by deed on 3 June 1758 to] ... Honorable Andrews Johnson, James Hude, and Richd Salter Esquires and Robert Lawrence, Charles Read, William Morris, John Johnson, Ebenezer Miller and Richard Smith trustees appointed by ... New Jersey ... for Building of Barracks within the Colony ... [Liber O, Page 290-294] ...; [Dated - 8 November 1786; signed - Thomas Fenimore Agent; witnesses - Israel Shreve, Joseph Bloomfield, Joseph Mc Ilvaine, J^r.]

[p 80]   **JAMES GREGSON to JOSEPH BLOOMFIELD**

8 November 1786 - James Gregson ... City of Burlington ... Burlington ... New Jersey, Brewer and Mary, his Wife ... [sold to] ... Joseph Bloomfield of the same place Esquire, Counsellor at Law ... [for

BURLINGTON COUNTY DEEDS - BOOK "B"

City of Burlington ... [adjoining land owners or names - William White, Broad Street] ... [1 acre] ... which Thomas Fenimore ... Agent of Confiscated Estates ... [by deed dated 8 November 1786 conveyed to James Gregson] ...; [Signed - James Gregson, Mary Gregson; witnesses - Hester Hodkinson, Thos Fenimore.]

[p 83]   JOSEPH BLOOMFIELD to WILLIAM COXE, JUNIOR

1 November 1788 - Joseph Bloomfield ... City of Burlington ... New Jersey Counsellor at Law and Mary his Wife ... [sold to] ... William Coxe Junior ... City of Philadelphia Merhcant ... [the same land 1 acre of land as noted in the above deed for 1,000 pounds] ... ; [Signed - J. Bloomfield, Mary Bloomfield; witnesses - Jo^s Mc Ilvaine, Fra Bullus, Jno M White.]

[p 87]   WILLIAM CALVERT to ISAAC HAZELHURST

26 December 1776 - William Calvert of Mount Holly ... Burlington ... New Jersey Merchant and Martha his Wife ... [sold to] ... Isaac Hazelhurst ... City of Philadelphia ... Pennsylvania Merchant ... [for 325 pounds] ... Two certain Lotts of Land adjoining to each other on the northerly side of the new Street called Garden STREET in Mount Holly ... being part of a larger tract which the said William Calvert purchased of John Sleeper and Hannah his Wife ... [by deed dated 29 March 1775] ... [adjoining land owners or names - Garden Street, Calvert's other land, John Ridgway, being a line formerly settled between Samuel Cripps and John Sleeper, Joseph Ridgway] ... [13 acres] ... And whereas John Shields and Margaret his Wife by ... [deed dated previous to this deed did sell to Isaac Hazelhurst 3.5 acres of land in Mount Holly which John Shields became seized of from William Calvert and Martha his wife] ...; [Signed - Wm Calvert, Martha Calvert; witnesses - Samuel Atkinson, Jos. Read.]

[31 October 1788 - Samuel Atkinson, one of the People called Quakers, appeared before Judge Joseph Read, Esquire, Burlington Co.]

[p 91]   ABRAHAM FARRINGTON to BENJAMIN BRYANT

21 May 1740 - Abraham Farrington ... Township of Northampton ... Burlington ... New Jersey Yeoman ... [sold to] ... Benjamin Bryant (of the same place) ...Yeoman ... Whereas Penn. Gawen Lawry, Nicholas Lucas and Edward Billings did ... [on the 22nd or 23rd of January 1676 sell unto] ... Richard Mew, Percival Fowle, Peter Hayles, Thomas Martin, Nicholas Bell and Richard Clayton one full equal and undivided hundreth part of all that tract of Land called west new Jersey ... And whereas the said Richard Clayton ... bearing date 20 or 21 September 1678 did sell his 1/6 part of the above unto Benjamin Antrobus and Antrobus on the 1st or 2nd of May 1683 sold it to Richard Mew, and Mew on the 18th or 19th of June 1683 sold it to Robert Hopper, and Hopper sold it on 9 November 1693 to William Crossley] ... [500 acres ... who laid out and surveyed ... [482 acres] ...

BURLINGTON COUNTY DEEDS - BOOK "B"

on the north side of northampton river in the township of Northampton ... And whereas John Crosby Son and heir at Law of him the said William Crosby together with Frances the Widow of him the said William Crosby by their ... [deed dated 13 May 1685 sold it to James Budd of Burlington and Budd by deed sold it on 8 April 1686 to John Rodman of Rhode Island Surgeon recorded in Liber B, Page 102 and John Rodman sold the 492 acres of 13 March 1723 to his Son Thomas Rodman of New York] ... and whereas the said Thomas Rodman by his lawful Attorney John Rodman ... [sold it on 20 May 1740 to Abraham Farrington] ... Now this Indenture ... [for 181 pounds sells one tract of 492 acres] ... [adjoining land owners or names - John Estaugh, Josiah Southwick, where Oddy Brock now dwells] ... [amounting to 100 acres] ...; [Signed - Abr^m Farrington; witnesses - James Lippincott, Samuel Scattergood, Jos. Scattergood.]

[p 100] **JAMES STERLING to WILLIAM NORCROSS**

13 November 1788 - James Sterling ... City of Burlington ... New Jersey Merchant and Rebecca his Wife ... [sold to] ... William Norcross ... [of the same place] ... Merchant ... [for 1,500 pounds] ... All that certain ... Land ... [in the City of Burlington ... late the Estate of Thomas Wetherill deceased ... [as described in a Deed by John Irick and Mary his Wife to James Sterling on 18 August 1788 in Liber AP-Page 314] ... Noe this INdenture ... [sells to Norcross ... All those three ... Lots of Ground ... Within the Island of Burlington ... known by the Name of the Wetherill Place or Estate ... containing ... [45 acres, 10 perches] ...; [Signed - James Sterling; witnesses - Herbert Mc Elroy, William Cummings.]

[p 102] **BENJAMIN MOORE ET AL to THOMAS & BENJAMIN WILKINS**

7 August 1780 - Benjamin Moore, Joseph Moore, John Moore, Bethuel Moore and William Wilkins all of Evesham ... Burlington ... New Jersey Farmers ... [sold to] ... Thomas and Benjamin Wilkins of Evesham ... [whereas the above are possessed of Land near water called Bread & Cheese Run being one of the branches of the South Main Branch of Ancocus Creek, with part of the land in Northampton and part in Evesham and known as Haine's Mill Tract] ... Now this Indenture ... [sells one part of the tract of land] ... [adjoining land owners or names - Road from Charles Reads to Coloxing Pond, John Brannin, Bethuel Moore, John Moore, Cold Water Run] ... [848 acres] ...; [Signed - Benjamin Moore made his mark, Joseph Moore made his mark, John Moore, Bethuel Moore, William Wilkins; witnesses - William Foster, Josiah Foster.]

[28 March 1788 - Josiah Foster, Esqr, one of the People called Quakers, appeared before Judge Joseph Read, Burlington Co.]

[p 106] **BENJAMIN WILKINS to THOMAS WILKINS**

4 March 1788 - Benjamin Wilkins ... Township of Evesham ... Burlington ... New Jersey (Farmer)

BURLINGTON COUNTY DEEDS - BOOK "B"

... [sold to] ... Thomas Wilkins of the same place (Farmer) ... [The above Benjamin & Thomas became seized of a parcel of Land by a deed of Partition dated 7 August 1780 from Benjamin Moore, Joseph Moore, John Moore, Bethuel Moore, and William Wilkins for 848 acres of land and for this Indenture sold one half equal share of the land for One deed of Partition] ... [adjoining land owners or names - Part of the land in Northampton & part in Evesham, Jabez Buzby, Benjamin Wilkins, John Branin, Bethuel Moore, John Moore] ... [amounting to 415 acres] ...; [Signed - Benjamin Wilkins; witnesses - Uriah Wilkins, Josiah Foster.]

[p 109] **MONEY RECEIPT**

10 March 1789 - George Jobs of Bucks County ... Pennsylvania ... [3 pounds, 10 shillings] ... [paid the above sum to Lewis Evans on 9 March 1789 of Nottingham Township ... Burlington] ... in the presence of George Beatty of the Township of Trenton ... Hunterdon ... in full Discharge of an Account containing all Debts ... against him the Said George Jobs ... the Said George Jobs hath lodg'd the Said Money ... in my Hands to be delivered to ... Lewis Evans ...; [Signed - John Phillips; witnesses - Francis Wm Shippen; recorded - 10 March 1789.]

Note - 13 June 1788 - The aforesaid Seventy Shillings was withdrawn from Me by an Order in favor of George Jobs Senr given George Jobs Junr & the Orig^l & delivered upon payment of the Money in presence of T. M. Gardiner - Phillips.

[p 110] **MANUMISSION OF PHILIP STILL**

I, Esther Wilkins .... township of Evesham ... Burlington ... New Jersey ... do hereby manumit and Set free my Negro Slave named Philip Still ...; [Dated - 12 February 1787; signed - Esther Wilkins; witnesses -Enoch Evans, Joseph Thornton.]

Esther Wilkins ... brought before us, two of the overseers of the Poor ... & two of the Justices of the Peace ... the Slave named Philip Still who ... appears ... to be Sound in mind & not under any Bodily incapacity ... & also is not under Twenty one Years of Age nor above thirty five ...; [Dated - 12 February 1787; signed - Enoch Evans, William Evans - Overseers of the Poor; Josiah Foster, Reece Edwards - Justices of the Peace.]

We the ... two ... Justices of the Peace ... do hereby Certify that the Bearer Philip Still is Manumitted & Set Free by ... Esther Wilkins ...; [Dated - 2 March 1787; signed - Josiah Foster, Reece Edwards - Justices of the Peace; John Phillips, Clerk of Pleas, Burlington Co.]

[Recorded before John Phillips, Clerk of Pleas, Burlington Co.]

BURLINGTON COUNTY DEEDS - BOOK "B"

[p 111] **MANUMISSION OF HOPE STILL**

I, Esther Wilkins .... township of Evesham ... Burlington ... New Jersey ... do hereby manumit and Set free my Negro Slave named Hope Still ...; Dated - 12 February 1787; signed - Esther Wilkins; witnesses -Enoch Evans, Joseph Thornton.]

Esther Wilkins ... brought before us, two of the overseers of the Poor ... & two of the Justices of the Peace ... the Slave named Hope Still who ... appears ... to be Sound in mind & not under any Bodily incapacity ... & also is not under Twenty one Years of Age nor above thirty five ...; [Dated - 12 February 1787; signed - Enoch Evans, William Evans - Overseers of the Poor; Josiah Foster, Reece Edwards - Justices of the Peace.]

We the ... two ... Justices of the Peace ... do hereby Certify that the Bearer Hope Still is Manumitted & Set Free by ... Esther Wilkins ...; [Dated - 2 March 1787; signed - Josiah Foster, Reece Edwards - Justices of the Peace; John Phillips, Clerk of Pleas, Burlington Co.]

[Recorded before John Phillips, Clerk of Pleas, Burlington Co.]

[p 112] **MANUMISSION OF CANDAS STILL**

I, Thomas Wilkins .... township of Evesham ... Burlington ... New Jersey ... do hereby manumit and Set free my Negro Slave named Candas Still ...; Dated - 2 March 1787; signed - Thomas Wilkins made his mark when signing; witnesses -Thomas Lippincott, Job Lippincott.]

Thomas Wilkins ... brought before us, two of the overseers of the Poor ... & two of the Justices of the Peace ... the Slave named Candas Still who ... appears ... to be Sound in mind & not under any Bodily incapacity ... & also is not under Twenty one Years of Age nor above thirty five ...; [Dated - 2 March 1787; signed - Enoch Evans, Wm Evans - Overseers of the Poor; Josiah Foster, Reece Edwards - Justices of the Peace.]

We the ... two ... Justices of the Peace ... do hereby Certify that the Bearer Candas Still is Manumitted & Set Free by ... Thomas Wilkins ...; [Dated - 2 March 1787; signed - Josiah Foster, Reece Edwards - Justices of the Peace; John Phillips, Clerk of Pleas, Burlington Co.]

[Recorded before John Phillips, Clerk of Pleas, Burlington Co.]

[p 113] **MANUMISSION OF DARCUS PEER**

I, Abraham Stockton ... Burlington ... New Jersey ... Set free my female Negro Slave called Darcus Peer Wife of Michael Peer, and lately called Darcus Elton: which Said Darcus was formerly the

BURLINGTON COUNTY DEEDS - BOOK "B"

property of Samuel Kemble of the County of Burlington now deceased ...; [Dated - 6 November 1788; signed - Abraham Stockton; witness - John Phillips.]

Abraham Stockton ... [of the City of Burlington] ... brought before us, two of the overseers of the Poor ... & two of the Justices of the Peace ... the Slave named Darcus Peer who ... appears ... to be Sound in mind & not under any Bodily incapacity ... & also is not under Twenty one Years of Age nor above thirty five ...; [Dated - 6 November 1788; signed - William Cooper, John Elton - Overseers of the Poor; Isaac Cowgill, Josiah Foster - Justices of the Peace.]

We the ... two ... Justices of the Peace ... do hereby Certify that the Bearer Darcus Peer is Manumitted & Set Free by ... Abraham Stockton ...; [Dated - 6 November 1788; signed - Isaac Cowgill, Josiah Foster - Justices of the Peace; John Phillips, Clerk of Pleas, Burlington Co.]

[Recorded before John Phillips, Clerk of Pleas, Burlington Co.]

[p 114] MANUMISSION OF DAVID

I, William Lovet Smith of Springfield ... Burlington ... New Jersey ... free my Negro man David ...; [Dated - 6 February 1789.]

William Lovet Smith ... brought before us, two of the overseers of the Poor ... & two of the Justices of the Peace ... the Slave named David who ... appears ... to be Sound in mind & not under any Bodily incapacity ... & also is not under Twenty one Years of Age nor above thirty five ...; [Dated - 6 February 1789; signed - Henry Ridgway, Caleb Earl - Overseers of the Poor; Thomas Fenimore, Asher Gaunt - Justices of the Peace.]

We the ... two ... Justices of the Peace ... do hereby Certify that the Bearer David is Manumitted & Set Free by ... William Lovet Smith ...; [Dated - 6 February 1789; signed - Thomas Ridgway, Asher Gaunt - Justices of the Peace; John Phillips, Clerk of Pleas, Burlington Co.]

[Recorded before John Phillips, Clerk of Pleas, Burlington Co.]

[p 115] MANUMISSION OF GEORGE MINTUS

... We Daniel Hough and Samuel Hough ... Township of Springfield ... Burlington ... New Jersey: the lawful Executors of the last Will ... of Jonathan Hough of the Same place deceased ... Set free a certain Negro Man late the property of the Said deceased Named George Mintus. We ... do therefore give grant and Confirm unto the Said George Mintus late a Slave of the Said deceased his Liberty ...; [Dated - 3 January 1789; signed - Daniel Hough, Samuel Hough.]

BURLINGTON COUNTY DEEDS - BOOK "B"

[Daniel Hough and Samuel Hough] ... brought before us, two of the overseers of the Poor ... & two of the Justices of the Peace ... the Slave named George Mintus who ... appears ... to be Sound in mind & not under any Bodily incapacity ... & also is not under Twenty one Years of Age nor above thirty five ...; [Dated - 1789; signed - Henry Ridgway, Caleb Earl - Overseers of the Poor; Peter Stretch, John Lacey - Justices of the Peace.]

We the ... two ... Justices of the Peace ... do hereby Certify that the Bearer George Mintus is Manumitted & Set Free by ... David and Samuel Hough ...; [Dated - 1789; signed - P. Stretch, John Lacey - Justices of the Peace; John Phillips, Clerk of Pleas, Burlington Co.]

[Recorded before John Phillips, Clerk of Pleas, Burlington Co.]

[p 116]   **JOHN TALMAN to BANJAMIN TALMAN**

2 December 1727 - John Talman of Flushing on Long Island, Gen^t ... [sold to] ... Benjamin Talman, late of the aforesaid Long Island but now of the Township of Mansfield ... Burlington ... West Jersey Yeoman ... [for 100 pounds] ... One certain piece ... of Land ... in the Township of Mansfield ... Burlington ... [250 acres] ... it being the One Moiety or half part of that ... [500 acres] ... of Land known by the Name of Springhill being formerly laid forth and Surveyed for John Underhill and is divided from the other part ... as follows ... [adjoining land owners or names - Joseph Talman, Isaac Gibbs, Job Talman, Henry Thomson's House, Jonathan Shreves, Land formerly Saml Andries now John Hammell.] ...; [Signed - John Talman; witnesses - Joseph Shreve, Jonathan Shreve, Tho. Scattergood, James Talman, Samuel Scattergood.]

[9 January 1747 - Jonathan Shreve appeared before Judge John Allen Esqr, Burlington Co.]

[p 120]   **JOSEPH MULLEN, LATE SHERIFF to SAMUEL BLOOMFIELD**

6 February 1786 - Joseph Mullen Esqr late high Sheriff ... Burlington ... New Jersey ... [sold to] ... Samuel Bloomfield ... Township of Mansfield Burlington Practitioner of Physic and Surgery ... Whereas Peter Talman of Mansfield ... Burlington Esqr was by Virtue of some good Conveyance ... Seized ... in a certain Plantation and Tract of Land ... in the Township of Mansfield ... Burlington ... [adjoining land owners or names - Barzillai Forman, Joseph Tallman, Thomas Smith, Annis Thomson, Thomas Aaronson, Benjamin Aaronson, Spring-hill Brook, Richard Gibbs, Thomas Bunting] ... [253.5 acres] ... And Whereas [Jacob Phillips, Luke Morris and Elizabeth Tallman recovered against the said Peter Tallman] ... And Whereas certain Writts ... [directed the Sheriff to recover the good and chattels of Peter Tallman and the Sheriff seized the above] ... Tract of Land and premises ... [and offered the same for sale on 19 May 1785 and continued until the 13th of January last] ... when Colonel Joseph Ellis ... on the behalf of the above mentioned Samuel Bloomfield ... [bid 910 pounds] ... Now this Indenture Witnesseth that ... [the Sheriff deeded the property to Bloomfield] ...; [Signed

BURLINGTON COUNTY DEEDS - BOOK "B"

****

- Joseph Mullen late Sheriff of Burlington; witnesses - Isreal Shreeve, Jos. Read, James Tate, Jos. Bloomfield.]

[29 April 1786 - Joseph Mullen appeared before Judge Joseph Read, Burlington Co.]

[p 121]   SAMUEL BLOOMFIELD to JOSEPH BLOOMFIELD

3 June 1786 - Samuel Bloomfield ... Township of Mansfield ... Burlington ... New Jersey Practitioner of Physic and Surgery and Abagail his Wife ... [sold to] ... Joseph Bloomfield of the City of Burlington, County and State aforesaid Esqr Counsellor at Law ... [for 1,210 pounds] ... all that certain Plantation & tract of Land in the Township of Mansfield ... [this is the same piece of property in the above deed] ...; [Signed - Samuel Bloomfield, Abigail Bloomfield; witnesses - John Pope, Caleb Shreeve, Thomas Curtis.]

[3 June 1786 - Both Samuel and Abigail Bloomfield appeared before Judge Isreal Shreve, Burlington Co.]

[p 130]   JOHN HAMMELL to WILLIAM SATTERTHWAITE

29 December 1770 - John Hammell son & Executor of John Hammell of Mansfield Deceas'd of the Township of Winsor ... Middlesex ... New Jersey Yeoman ... [sold to] ... William Satterthwaite ... Township of Chesterfield Burlington ... New Jersey ... Witnesseth that whereas the last Named John Hammell aforesaid ... [was lawfully seized of land in the] ... Township of Mansfield ... Burlington ... [by a deed from Caleb Brown dated 13 January 1723] ... and the said Caleb Brown became Seized ... by one other Indenture ... from his Brother Preserve Brown ... [dated 4 November 1710; Burl. Deed - Liber BB-folio 451-453] ... Relation being thereunto had the Several recited conveyances from William Biddle to Samuel Andrews and from Samuel Andrews to his Son Edward Andrews and from Edward Andrews to the aforementioned Preserve Brown ... And Whereas the said John Hammell ... made his Last Will ...[dated 13 March 1765] ... did appoint his Eldest Son John Hammell to be his sole and only Executor ... Now this Indenture ... [sells for 340 pounds unto William Satterthwaite 159 acres] ... [adjacent land owners or names - at the branches of the Water below the lands formerly called Spring Hill Which was Surveyed to John Underhill Now the property of Joseph & Benjamin Tallman, John Falwill, land late of John Rockhill, John Areson, land formerly Johnathan Shreeves Now the property of Peter Tallman, Benjamin Areson] ...; [Signed - John Hammell Exe; witnesses - John Linton, Martha Linton, Gervas Pharo.]

[5 January 1771 - John Hammell appeared before Judge Joseph Borden, Burlington Co.]

BURLINGTON COUNTY DEEDS - BOOK "B"

[p 137]   **WILLIAM SATTERTHWAITE to TIMOTHY SMITH**

8 February 1783 - William Satterthwaite ... Township of Chesterfield ... Burlington ... New Jersey Yeoman ... [sold to] ... Timothy Smith of Mansfield ... Wheelwright ... [for 500 pounds] ...to them the said William Satterthwaite and Jane his Wife ... Land ... in the Township of Mansfield ... [adjacent land owners or names - at the fork of the run of water below the Land formerly called Spring Hill, late John Folwill, the Great Road that leads through the Plantation, Land late John Rockhill Now Nathan Robins, to a lot Satterthwaite sold to Thomas Scattergood, Benjamin Arionson, Tallman Land] ... [165 acres being the same land] ... John Hammill the Elder bought of Caleb Brown ... [on the 11th month, 13th day, 1723 in Book AC-Page 176] ...; [Signed - William Satterthwaite, Jane Satterthwaite; witnesses - Joseph Satterthwaite, Gervas Pharo.]

[14 May 1788 - William & Jane Satterthwaite appeared before Judge Isreal Shreeve, Burlington Co.]

[p 144]   **RECEIPT**

11 May 1789 - Received from Saml Lippincott ... Township of Chester the Sum of ... [157 pounds, 4 shillings, 9 pence] ... Said Money the Said Samuel Lippincott was by him tendered on this day to John Lippincott of the City of Burlington (late of the Township of Chester) in Presence of John Warrington and John Chambers both of the Township of Chesterfield in full Discharge of a certain Bond ... [dated 11 May 1786] ...; [Witness - John Phillips, Clerk of the peace & pleas; recorded - 11 May 1789.]

[The af'd Money received by John Lippincott 18 May 1789 at the House of Isreal Tonkin in presence of Ab^m Stockton.]

[p 145]   **JOHN COX to PAUL CRISPIN**

24 November 1778 - John Cox of the Township of Chester ... Burlington ... New Jersey Inn Keeper and Abigail his Wife ... [sold to] ... Paul Crispin of Willingborough ... Burlington ... Wheel-wright ... Whereas Frances Hogsett, deceas'd ... became possessed of divers Lands within the Township of Chester ... by his Indenture ... dated 19th or 20th of January 1732, Burl. Deeds, Book E-Page 441, sold to] ... Thomas Moore a certain Tract ... of Land ... in the ... Township of Chester ... [33 acres] ... And ... Thomas Moore by Indenture ... [dated 8 April 1754, sold to Charles French of Waterford, Gloucester Co, New Jersey, 13 acres] ... it being part of the ... [33 acres] ... above mentioned And ... Charles French ... by one certain Indenture ... [dated 8 April 1772, sold it to Richard Fleming of Moorestown ... Township of Chester, amounting to 4 acres, 3 rods, and 8 perch] ... it being part of the Thirteen acres above mentioned. And the said Richard Fleming ... by ... Indenture ... [dated 18 October 1777, sold to John Shields of the City of Philadelphia, the 4 acres, 3 rods, and 8 perch] ... and ... [Shields sold 4 acres of the above, on 6 November 1778, to] ... John Cox, Party of these

(55)

BURLINGTON COUNTY DEEDS - BOOK "B"

Present ... Now this Indenture ... John Cox and Abigail his Wife ... [sell for 700 pounds to Paul Crispin] ... All the aforementioned 4 acres, 3 rods, and 8 perch ... [adjoining land owners or names - Thomas Morton on Salem Road Moorestown, Michael Linch, Edward French] ...; [Signed - John Cox, Abigail Cox; witnesses - Moses Kempton, Thos Matlack, Joshua Dudley.]

9 April 1783 - John Cox appeared before Judge Samuel How, Esqr, Burlington Co; recorded 9 April 1783.]

[p 150]   **ARBITRATION AGREEMENT**

Nehemiah Matthis, Job Matthis Junr, & Nehemiah Matthis Junr of Little Egg Harbour ... Burlington ... New Jersey are ... firmly bound ... unto Micajah Matthis of the same place ... [for 500 pounds] ...; [Dated - 22 August 1786.]

The Conditions of the above Obligation is such that if the above bound ... shall Arbitrate final End ... of John Leek, Joseph Biddle and David Anderson arbitrators indifferently ... elected ... on ... behalf of them ... [the above named Matthis individuals] ...as of him the said Micajah Matthis to settle ... disputes Relative to the Boundaries of their Lands & damages done by cutting of Timber ... before ...[the next September 1st] ...; [Signed - Nehemiah Matthis, Job Matthis, Nehemiah Matthis, Junr; witnesses - Amos Pharo, William Weatherby.]

[29 November 1788 - Amos Pharo appeared before Judge Ebenezer Tucker, Esq.]

[p 152]   **AGREEMENT**

To All Persons ... Know ye that whereas Micajah Matthis of Little Egg Harbour ... Burlington ... New Jersey ... of the one part ... and Nehemiah Matthis, Job Matthis Junr, Nehemiah Matthis Junr of the same place, of the other part ... [entered into the above agreement with John Leek & Joseph Biddle & David Anderson] ... Do order and determine that the Line of Partition between the Lands of said Parties shall begin at ... [adjoining land owners and names - Daniel Matthis, Oak Island Bridge] ... and order that they ... [Nehemiah Matthis Senr, Job Matthis Junr, and Nehemiah Matthis Junr] ... pay unto ... Micajah Matthis ... [10 shillings] ... within one Month for damages of cutting timber] ...; [Dated - 24 August 1786; signed - John Leek, Joseph Biddle, and David Anderson.]

[29 January 1789 - Captain John Leek testified before Judge Ebenezer Tucker that he signed and delivered the within award with Biddle & Anderson to Micajah Mathis.]

[p 154]   **JAMES PEMBERTON to JOHN CLAPP**

25 March 1788 - James Pemberton ... City of Philadelphia ... Pennsylvania Merchant and Phebe his

BURLINGTON COUNTY DEEDS - BOOK "B"

****

Wife ... [sold to] ... John Clapp and Martha Clapp wife ... of the Township of ...[left blank] ... Burlington ... New Jersey ... Whereas Daniel Smith late of the City of Burlington deceased ... [was seized of land in Burlington County, part in the Township of New Hanover and part in Northampton at New Mills, and by his Will dated 24 November 1768, proved in Burlington on 28 March 1769] ... devised the Same with other real Estate to his daughter Sarah the then Wife of James Pemberton aforesaid ... Which Land ... James Pemberton and Sarah his Wife ... [sold by deed, dated 1 January 1770, Burlington Deeds - Book AD, Page 104] ... conveyed to Peter Reeve who by his Deed ... [dated 2 January 1770 sold it to James Pemberton] ... Now this Indenture ... [Pemberton and his wife for the payment of Rent] ... hereinafter mentioned on the Part of the said John Clapp and Martha his Wife ... [sell to John Clapp and Martha] ... all that Lot ... [marked #5 on Pemberton's map in] ... the Village called New Mills ... [adjoining land owners or names - Main St or County road, Pemberton St, Jervis St] ... [part of 10 acres conveyed to] ... Danl Smith aforesaid by a deed from Robert Smith ... [dated 13 May 1757] ... [with first payment due on 1 March 1789 & they shall build on the ground a substantial] ... Dwelling House of Brick Stone Frame or Plank with a Brick Chimney within One Year from the date hereof ... [The rest of the deed is filled with various contract language and penalties, etc.] ... claiming under the aforesaid Sarah the late Wife of the said James Pemberton or under Daniel Smith aforesaid ...; [Signed - James Pemberton, Phebe Pemberton; witnesses - Cha. Jervis, R.R.[?] Smith.]

[3 March 1789 - James and Phebe Pemberton appeared before Judge John Lacey, Burlington Co.]

[p 161]   **URIAH WILKINS to WILLIAM THOMSON**

3 January 1789 - Uriah Wilkins ... Township of Evesham ... Burlington ... New Jersey Yeoman ... [sold to] ... William Thomson of the same Township ... Hammer Man ... Whereas ... Uriah Wilkins by ... a certain Indenture ... [from the sheriff John Hollinshead on 19 September 1787 became seized of a plantation near Evesham near the Road leading from Bearhead to Indian Town] ... [160 acres which was the late property of John Branin lost by a judgement on behalf of Robert Lawrence where John Branin became seized as being eldest Son and Heir of his Father Michael Branin deceased] ... Now this Indenture ... [sells the same to Wilkins for 112 pounds] ...; [Signed - Uriah Wilkins; witnesses - Henry Shinn, Jos. Read.]

[p 164]   **MANUMISSION OF CATO**

To John Lacey and peter Stretch Esq and to John Rogers and Thomas Earl, Overseers of the Poor of New hanover ... Burlington ... New Jersey Greeting - You are hereby required to Manumit and Set free my Negro Man named Cato Mac lane, now aged 24 years and 4 months ...; [Dated - 10 January 1789; Signed - Richd Potts; witness - Dennis Carty.]

BURLINGTON COUNTY DEEDS - BOOK "B"

We, the subscribers two of the Justices assigned to keep peace ... and the two lawful Overseers of the Poor of the Township of New hanover ... do certify that on ... [10 January 1789] ... Richard Potts of Said Township ... brought his Negro Slave named Cato Mc lane and requested us by Writing ... to Manumit and set free the said Slave and on Examination it appears to Us on View and Examination of Said Slave that he is sound in body & Mind and that he is above 21 Years of Age, and Under the Age of thirty five ...; [Signed - Peter Stretch, John Lacey - Justices of Peace; Thomas Earl Junr, John Rogers - Overseers of the Poor of New hanover.]

We the Subscribers two of the Justices ... do certify that the Bearer Cato Mc lane is Manumitted and Set free by his Master Richard Potts of the township of New hanover; [Signed at New Mills ... 10 January 1789 - P. Stretch, John Lacey - Justice of the Peace; countersigned - John Phillips, Clk of the peace and pleas for the County of Burlington.]

[p 165]   DANIEL HARVEY to TIMOTHY SMITH

23 December 1782 - Daniel Harvey and Sarah his Wife of Mansfield Township ... Burlington ... Western ... New Jersey ... [sold to] ... Timothy Smith Yeoman of the same place ... [for 22 pounds, 10 shillings] ... A certain Lot or piece of Meadow ... in ... Mansfield Township ... [adjoining land owners or names - Harvey and Abner Page, Folwell's Run] ... [1.75 acres] ... which said piece of Land is part of a larger Tract that John Folwell Father of the said Sarah Harvey late dec^d did in ... his last Will ... [dated 24 February 1782] ... give and devise unto his said Daughter Sarah Harvey ...; [Daniel Harvey, Sarah Harvey; witnesses - Thomas Atkinson, Abner Page, Jno. Black]

[p 168]   TIMOTHY SMITH to JOSEPH BLOOMFIELD

17 May 1788 - Timothy Smith ... Township of Mansfield ... Burlington ... New Jersey, Carpenter and Sarah his Wife ... [sold to] ... Joseph Bloomfield Esquire ... City of Burlington ... Counsellor at Law ... [for 350 pounds] ... All that ... piece of Meadow Ground ... in the Township of Mansfield ... [adjoining land owners or names - Abner Page, Folwell's Run] ... [1.75 acres] ... being the same Lot ... which Daniel Harvey and Sarah Harvey his Wife ... [sold on 23 December 1782] ... Also ... Land ... in the Township of Mansfield ... [adjoining land owners or names - Spring hill, Folwell's Run, Abner Page, Daniel Harvey (both formerly John Folwell's land), Thomas Aiken, Nathan Robins, the Road leading towards Bordentown, Thomas Scattergood, Benjamin Aaronson, Joseph Bloomfield, Joseph Talman] ... [102 acres] ... it being the same Tract ... which William Satterthwaite and Jane his Wife by their Deed ... [dated 8 February 1783] ... conveyed to ... Timothy Smith and Sarah his Wife ... [who on 1 May 1786 it was] ... conveyed to the said Nathan Robins ...; [Signed - Timothy Smith, Sarah Smith made her mark when signing; witnesses - Israel Shreve, Joseph Talman, Benjamin Aaronson, John Shreve.]

BURLINGTON COUNTY DEEDS - BOOK "B"

[p 172]   **JOSEPH BLOOMFIELD to DAVID RIDGWAY**

27 August 1788 - Joseph Bloomfield ... City of Burlington ... New Jersey Esquire Counsellor at Law ... [sold to] ... David Ridgway ... Township of Springfield ... Burlington ... New Jersey ... Farmer ... [for 1,500 pounds] ... All those two certain Plantations ... in ... Township of Mansfield ... [adjoining land owners or names - Barzillai Forman, Joseph Talman, Thomas Smith, Annis Thompson, Thomas Aaronson, Benjamin Aaronson, Spring Hill Brook, Richard Gibb's land, Thomas Bunting] ... [253.5 acres] ... It being the Same ... Land which Doctor Samuel Bloomfield and Abigail his Wife by Deed ... [on 3 June 1786 conveyed to] ... the said Joseph Bloomfield ... The Second ... [adjoining land owners or names - Springhill, Folwell's Run, Abner Page, Daniel Harvey, John Folwell, Thomas Atkinson, Nathan Robins, Road leading towards Bordentown, Thomas Scattergood] ... [102.5 acres] ... And also all that certain Lot ... of Meadow ... in the Township of Mansfield ... [adjoining land owners or names - Abner Page, Folwell's Run] ... [1.75 acres] ... [being bought from Timothy Smith & wife Sarah] ... excepting ... the Incumberance of a ... Mortgage ... [dated 17 March 1786] ... given by Said Doctor Samuel Bloomfield to Elizabeth Rogers of Philadelphia ...; [Signed - J. Bloomfield, Mary Bloomfield; witnesses - Thomas Rodman, Robert Pearson Jun', James Giles, J. McIlvaine.]

[p 178]   **JOHN EVENS to JAMES ELDRIDGE**

18 October 1765 - John Evens ... Township of Evesham ... Burlington ... New Jersey Yeoman ... [sold to] ... James Eldridge of the same Town ... Wheelwright ... [for 146 pounds] ... a certain ... Tract of Land ... In the Township of Evesham ... [adjoining land owners or names - Benjamin Haines, William Rogers, near the bridge] ... [68 acres, 2 rods] ... part ... of ... [1,050 acres] ... purchased by Thomas Middleton of Evesham ... Yeoman of John Engle of the same place Yeoman together with other Lands and was conveyed by the said Thomas Middletown who by his last Will ... devised the one Moiety thereof unto his Son Timothy Middleton ... forever but by an accident of Fire as well the conveyance from ... John Engle to the said Thomas Middleton as the conveyance from ... Thomas Middleton to the Said William Middleton was consumed and destroyed by reason where the Fee in the Said ... [150 acres] ... was apparently vested in Robert Engle Son and Heir at Law of the Said John Engle who by his Indenture ... [dated 15 January 1742/3] ... did convey unto the said Timothy Middleton the one Moiety of the ... Tract ... and ... [Timothy Middleton sold it on 14 October 1754 to Samuel Clement, who then sold it on 3 May 1765 to John Evans] ...; [Signed - John Evens, Martha Evens; witnesses - Benjamin Haines, Abel Lippincott, Abraham Allen.]

[p 182]   **DANIEL HOPEWELL to JOHN WEST**

18 December 1759 - Daniel Hopewell Yeoman ... [sold to] ... John West Sadler of Mount Holley in Burlington County ... Western ... New Jersey ... [for 110 pounds] ... One certain Dwelling house and two Lots ... in Mount Holley ... The First ... [adjoining land owners or names - north side of the street that leads from the Bridge near the house that formerly belonged to Nathaniel Thomas towards the

BURLINGTON COUNTY DEEDS - BOOK "B"

Saw mill fronting on the said Street, Henery Paxson, Thomas Shinn deceased, by the House and Lot lately belonging to Benjamin Moore] ... The other Lot ... [adjoining land owners or names - by Mill Street, Thomas Shinn deceased, Henry Paxson] ... [13.5 square perches] ... In which said Lot an old Shop lately stood ... [claimed by Hopewell by a deed from Sheriff William Smith, it being lately the estate of Enoch Stratten dated 28 October 1775, Liber M, folio 443]...; [Signed - Daniel Hopewell, Mary Hopewell; witnesses - Ebenez^r Dotey, Chichester Reynolds.]

[7 April 1761- Daniel Hopewell and wife appeared before Judge Revell Elton Esquire and acknowledged the deed.]

[11 December 1787 - I Mary Eldridge Widow of Jabez Eldridge deceas'd formerly Mary Hopewell the Wife of Daniel Hopewell the Grantor acknowledged the above deed and gave her release of her Dower rights ...; [Signed - Mary Eldridge; witnesses - Joseph Read, Maj. Cur. Canc^a.]

[p 185] **JOHN WEST to RICHARD COX**

15 December 1787 - John West ... Township of Northampton ... Burlington ... New Jersey and Beulah his Wife ... [sold to] ... Richard Cox of Mount Holly ... Merchant ... Whereas Daniel Hopewell late of the County ... yeoman ... of a certain Indenture ... [dated 28 October 1755 for a certain tenement and two lots of land in the Township of Mount Holly being the property in the same deed listed above] ... Now this Indenture ... [West and wife sell it for 260 pounds to Richard Cox] ...; [Signed - John West, Beulah West made her mark when signing; witnesses - John Lacey, Jos. Read.]

[p 187] **AGREEMENT TO PARTITION AND SET LINES OF LAND**

9 March 1789 - ...William Shin late of the County of Burlington Deceased the Father of us the subscribers ... by his last Will ... [gave land] ... unto us to be equally divided between us ... do Acknowledge that the following lines are and shall be & remain the lines of Partition between us ... [adjoining land owners or names - Aaron Shinn, Joseph Shin, Arney Lippincott, Indian Run, Ancocas Creek, William Shin] ...; [Signed - Joseph Shinn, Aaron Shinn; witnesses - John Goldy, Junr, Joseph Biddle.]

[p 188] **CHRISTOPHER WETHERILL to ISAAC WETHERILL**

11 June 1781 - ...Whereas Elizabeth Johnson ... City of Burlington ... New Jersey ... by her last Will ... [dated 12 November 1780] ... did give to Isaac Wetherill Son of Christopher Wetherill ... [10 acres] ... of land adjoining his fathers Land ... [adjoining land owners or names - Robert Moon, the road leading to Elnathan Stevenson, Christopher Wetherill] ... And, Whereas the said Isaac Wetherill pursuant to the Said Will caused the same to be surveyed as ... [adjoining land owners or names - road to Christopher Wetherill, Joseph Wetherill, Abigail Bishop, William Hewling] ... [10 acres] ...

BURLINGTON COUNTY DEEDS - BOOK "B"

Now know ye that Christopher Wetherill ... City of Burlington heir at Law to the said Elizabeth Johnson doth for and in Consideration of Removing Doubts in Regard to the Devisee of said Isaac Wetherills ten Acres as well as in Consideration of the Naturaul Love and Affection which he hath and beareth to the Said Isaac Wetherill his Son ...; [Signed - Chris^{er} Wetherill; witnesses - Edward Collins, Wm. Heulings.]

[30 July 1784 - Christopher Wetherill acknowledged the above deed before Judge Peter Tallman.]

[p 191]   JOHN HOLLINSHEAD, SHERIFF to BARZILLAI BRADDOCK

10 March 1790 - John Hollinshead Esq. Late High Sheriff ... [sold to] ... Barzilai Braddock ... Township of Evesham ... Whereas ... [Robert Lawrence won a Judgement aghainst John Branin] ... And Whereas ... [John Brannin as heir of his Father Michael Branin was seized of Land in the Township of Evesham] ... [adjoining land owners or names - Barzillai Braddock, Peter Anders, Thomas Shinn] ... [2 acres, 3 rods, 23 perches] ... [And the Sheriff seized the property, offered it for sale on 20 February 1790 at the House of Joseph Hammett Innkeeper and Braddock was the high bidder] ...; [Signed - Jno Hollinshead; witness - John Phillips, Tho. M. Gardiner.]

[p 195]   MANUMISSION OF RICHARD ALEXANDER

24 March 1790 - ...I Joseph Bloomfield ... Township of Burlington ... Burlington ... New Jersey do by these Presents Manumit & Set free my Negro called Richard Alexander ...; [Signed - Joseph Bloomfield; witnesses - Gershom Craft, John Moore White.]

[p 195]   MANUMISSION OF THE CHILDREN OF RICHARD ALEXANDER

24 March 1790 - ... I Joseph Bloomfield ... Township of Burlington ... Burlington ... New Jersey do by these Presents Manumit & Set free, Negroes Mary being in her 6th Year, Charles being in his 3^d Year & Ann an Infant of about 8 months the ... Children of my Servants Richard Alexander & Sarah his Wife and they are all hereby Manumitted & Set at Liberty from my Service forever ...; [Signed - Joseph Bloomfield.]

[Certified by Gershom Craft Jn^r, Moore White - Burlington County, on 24 March 1790 that he set free his Slave named Richard Alexander, who is not under 21 or over 35 years of age ...; Signed - Wm Smith Junr, Israel Tonkin- Overseers of the Poor; Jonah Foster, Robt Shettell Jones - Justices of the Peace; Countersigned - John Phillips.]

[p 196]   MANUMISSION OF SARAH ALEXANDER

24 March 1790 - ... I Joseph Bloomfield ... Township of Burlington ... Burlington ... New Jersey do

BURLINGTON COUNTY DEEDS - BOOK "B"

by these Presents Manumit & Set free my Negro Woman called Sarah Alexander Wife of Richard Alexander ...; [Signed - Joseph Bloomfield; witnesses - Gershom Craft, John Moore White.]

[Certified by Gershom Craft Jn', Moore White - Burlington County, on 24 March 1790 that he set free his Slave named Sarah Alexander, who is not under 21 or over 35 years of age ...; Signed - W'm Smith Jun', Israel Tonkin- Overseers of the Poor; Jonah Foster, Rob' Shettell Jones - Justices of the Peace; Countersigned - John Phillips.]

[p 197] WILLIAM COXE JUNIOR to JOHN BLOOMFIELD

1 February 1790 - William Coxe Junior ... City of Burlington ... New Jersey Gentleman and Rachel his Wife ... [sold to] ... John Bloomfield of the same place Nailor and Ann his Wife ... Whereas Joseph Bloomfield Esquire by two ... Indentures ... [one dated 28 August 1788 to John Bloomfield and the other dated 1 November 1788 to Coxe] ... did convey to each of them ... a moiety or undivided half part of all that Certain Lot ... on the South side of Broad Street ... adjoining Assinkunk Creek in the City of Burlington ... [adjoining land owners or names - William White, Broad Street, William Coxe] ... [now this deed is to partition the land] ...; [Signed - W'm Coxe Jun', Rachel Coxe, Jn° Bloomfield, Ann Bloomfield; witnesses - Joseph McIlvaine, Francis Bullus.]

[p 202] HUMPHREY WALL to JOSEPH WALL

5 January 1785 - Humphrey Wall ... Township of Nottingham ... Burlington ... New Jersey ... [sold to] ... Joseph Wall of the same place Whereas Samuel Stevenson of the same Place by his deed of sale ... [dated 21 January 1775] ... Did convey unto Humphrey Wall ... Land in said Township ... [Now by this Indenture sells it for 2,045 pounds] ... Land ... [in Nottingham] ... [adjoining land owners or names - Doctor Creek, Abraham Tilton, Isaiah Robins] ... [409 acres & 5 perches] ...; [Signed - Humphrey Wall; witnesses - Cornelius Dern, Richard Herbert.]

[11 April 1786 - Humphrey Wall acknowledged the deed before Judge George Anderson.]

[28 May 1788 - Cornelius Dorn acknowledged the deed before Judge Hendrick Hendrickson; Signed - Cornelius Doorn, Hendrick Hendrickson.]

[23 September 1788 - Cornelius Dorn & Richard Herbert acknowledged the deed before Judge Hendrick Hendrickson; recorded - 27 April 1790.]

[p 206] JOHN HOLLINSHEAD, SHERIFF to BENJAMIN BELL

1 December 1789 - John Hollinshead Esquire, late Sheriff ... Burlington ... New Jersey ... [sold to] ... Benjamin Bell son of John Bell alias John Crane of the Township of Evesham ... [Robert Lawrence

BURLINGTON COUNTY DEEDS - BOOK "B"

recovered against John Branen and the Sheriff confiscated land and sold it to Stephen Cunningham to and for the said Benjamin Bell for 8 pounds] ... [adjoining land owners or names - road leading to the Indian and near a large Pond of Water, William Thompson, Jonathan Crispan] ... [85 acres] ... which ... [John Branin became seized of as heir at Law to his Father Michael Branin deceas'd] ... [Signed - John Hollinshead; witnesses - Hosea Eayre, Abram Hewlings, Junr.]

[p 211]   **WILLIAM WOOD to JOHN BURR JUN^R**

15 May 1789 - William Wood of Northampton ... Burlington ... Western ... New Jersey (Windsor Chair Maker) and Sophia his Wife (late Sophia Burr) ... [sold to] ... John Burr Junr ... [of the same place] ... (Farmer) ... [100 pounds] ... one certain ... Dwelling House and Wharf Lott ... on the East Side of Water Street between Market Street and Chestnut Street, Philadelphia and also the Ground Rents ... out of one other Lott ... on the West Side of fifth Street now or late in the Occupation of Samuel Clark and also that Dwelling House and ... [3 acres] ... adjoining land late of John Hillier dec'd at Eayres Town in Northampton ... which Said Moiety ... the Said Sophia became seized of as being one of the Daughters ... of her Mother Mary Burr dec'd which the said Mary became Seized of by ... the last Will of her Grandfather William Freedson [?] dec'd ... [while the Dwelling house and 3 acres where purchased by Sophia from Thomas Eayre dec'd] ...; [Signed - William Wood, Sophia Wood; witnesses - Phinehas Kirkbride, Michael Rush.]

[p 213]   **PROPERTY LINE OF PETER CHEVALIER and HENRY BURR**

26 August 1790 - We ... do hereby certify ... the lower line of 100 acres of Cedar Swamp Surveyed for Peter Chevalier adjoining to Land late Henry Burr dec'd is as follows: ... [adjoining land owners or names - Mullicas Cedar Swamp, the House on Said Burr's Survey now occupied by Abel Gale] ...; [Signed by "John Burr for himself and Brothers with the consent of Uriah Woolman Guardian to Henry Burr a Minor"; Signed - Lewis Darnell, John Burr, Junr; witnesses - Uriah Woolman, Joseph Biddle.]

[26 August 1790 - Memorandum - John Burr, Junr acknowledged that he signed the deed for purposes of establishing a Division Line between "Lewis Darnell and Henry Burr Sons & Grantus..."]

[p 214]   **HENRY BURR to HIS DAUGHTERS**

20 December 1783 - ...I Henry Burr of Kitts Run in Northampton ... Burlington ... Western New Jersey Farmer, for and in Consideration of the natural Love and Natural Affection which I have & do bear towards my two Daughters Elizabeth the Wife of Abraham Hewlings Junr and Priscilla the Wife of Thomas Kemble as well as for other good Causes ... do fully freely clearly and give ... unto ... Elizabeth Hewlings and Priscilla Kemble ... to be divided between them ... all that my Tract ... of Land ... [adjoining land owners or names - Little Egg harbour River in the County of Gloucester ...

BURLINGTON COUNTY DEEDS - BOOK "B"

at Landing Creek and Teel Creek] ... which ... was Surveyed unto me ... and Recorded ...; [Signed - Henry Burr Senr; witnesses - John Burr, Junr, Thomas Burr, Henry Burr, Rebekah Cook.]

[10 January 1786 - John Burr, Junr and Rebecca Cook appeared before Judge Joshua M. Wallace and acknowledged the deed.]

[p 216]   JOSEPH WOODMANSEE to JOHN WOODMANSEE

16 August 1783 - ... Know ye that Joseph Woodmansee of Nottingham ... Burlington ... Western New Jersey, Yeoman ... [for 100 pounds] ... quit claim ... unto John Woodmansee of Upper Freehold ... Monmouth ... Eastern New Jersey ... Land ... Eastward of Crosswix Creek ... [adjoining land owners or names - Crosswicks Creek, John Leonard, William Bustisee, Peter Sexton] ... [103 acres] ... that the Said Joseph Woodmansee and John Woodmansee bought in Partnership of William Bourtis it being a Tract of Land that Richard Bourtis gave his Son John Bourtis and after his Decease it was sold by his Executors to Joseph Bullock & Thomas Thorn to William Bourtis ...; [Signed - Joseph Woddmansee; witnesses - Daniel Woodmansee, Samuel Rogers.]

[1 September 1783 - Joseph Woodmansee acknowledged the deed before Monmouth Judge Elisha Lawrence.]

[p 218]   MANUMISSION OF AARON WILLIAMS

... I Mary Mitchell ... do hereby Manumit & Set free my Negro Man Aaron commonly called Aaron Williams ...; [Dated - 21 October 1790; signed - Mary Mitchell; witnesses - Isaac Cowgill, Geo. Anderson.

We do hereby certify on ... [21 October 1790] ... Mary Mitchell of the Township of Nottingham ... Burlington ... New Jersey brought before us ... her Slave named Aaron ... [not under 21 or over 35 years of age] ...; [Signed - Isaac Cowgill, George Anderson - Justices; Ely Anderson, Joseph Disbrow - Overseers of the Poor.]

[Certified the same day that "Mrs Mary Mitchell ... brought her Slave Aaron ... before us & set him free; Signed - Isaac Cowgill, Geo. Anderson; Countersigned - Jno Phillips, Clerk of the Peace.]

[p 219]   MANUMISSION OF CLOE & HER UNBORN CHILDREN

... I Mary Mitchell ... do hereby Manumit & Set free my Negro Woman Cloe and all her Porterity hereafter to be born and all her Goods, Chattels ...; [Dated - 21 October 1790; signed - Mary Mitchell; witnesses - Isaac Cowgill, Geo. Anderson.]

BURLINGTON COUNTY DEEDS - BOOK "B"

We do hereby certify on ... [21 October 1790] ... Mary Mitchell of the Township of Nottingham ... Burlington ... New Jersey brought before us ... her Slave named Cloe ... [not under 21 or over 35 years of age] ...; [Signed - Isaac Cowgill, George Anderson - Justices; Ely Anderson, Joseph Disbrow - Overseers of the Poor.]

[Certified the same day that "Mrs Mary Mitchell ... brought her Slave Cloe ... before us & set her free; Signed - Isaac Cowgill, Geo. Anderson; Countersigned - Jn° Phillips, Clerk of the Peace.]

[p 220]   **MANUMISSION OF JOHN SOBERS**

I Abraham Matlock ... Township of Evesham ... Burlington ... New Jersey do hereby Manumit and Set Free my Negro Slave Named John Sobers ...; [Dated - 13 October 1790; signed - Abraham Matlock; witnesses - Josiah Foster, Reece Edwards.]

We do hereby certify on ... [30 October 1790] ... Abraham Matlock of the Township of Evesham ... Burlington ... New Jersey brought before us ... his Slave named John Sobers ... [not under 21 or over 35 years of age] ...; [Signed - Josiah Foster, Reece Edwards - Justices; William Vinicomb, Thomas Evans - Overseers of the Poor.]

[Certified the same day that Abraham Matlock ... brought his Slave John Sobers ... before us & set him free; Signed - Josiah Foster, Reece Edwards; Countersigned - Jn° Phillips, Clerk of the Peace.]

[p 222]   **MANUMISSION OF MARY**

To Peter Stretch and Asher Gaunt Esqr ... Justices of Peace ... and to Joseph Biddle and Caleb Earl ... Overseers of the Poor ... We the Subscribers of this Township being at this time Seized and possessed of a female Negro Slave named Mary ... [under 35 and over 21 years of age] ... being desirous the She Should be Manumitted ...; [Signed at Job Town in Springfield the 18th June 1790; Mary Stockton, Samuel Stockton; witnesses - Elihu Gaunt, Adin Antrum; Signed - Joseph Biddle, Caleb Earl - Overseers of the Poor; P. Stretch, Asher Gaunt - Justices of Peace.]

[p 223]   **MANUMISSION OF ARGULUS**

To Peter Stretch and Asher Gaunt Esqr ... Justices of Peace ... and to Joseph Biddle and Caleb Earl ... Overseers of the Poor ... We the Subscribers of this Township being at this time Seized and possessed of Male Negro Slave named ... Argulus ... [under 35 and over 21 years of age] ... being desirous the She Should be Manumitted ...; [Signed at Job Town in Springfield the 18th June 1790; Mary Stockton, Samuel Stockton; witnesses - Elihu Gaunt, Adin Antrum; Signed - Joseph Biddle, Caleb Earl - Overseers of the Poor; P. Stretch, Asher Gaunt - Justices of Peace.]

BURLINGTON COUNTY DEEDS - BOOK "B"

[p 224]   MANUMISSION OF PHEBE

To Peter Stretch and Asher Gaunt Esq' ... Justices of Peace ... and to Joseph Biddle and Caleb Earl ... Overseers of the Poor ... We the Subscribers of this Township being at this time Seized and possessed of a female Negro Slave named Phebe ... [under 35 and over 21 years of age] ... being desirous the She Should be Manumitted ...; [Signed at Job Town in Springfield the 18th June 1790; Mary Stockton, Samuel Stockton; witnesses - Elihu Gaunt, Adin Antrum; Signed - Joseph Biddle, Caleb Earl - Overseers of the Poor; P. Stretch, Asher Gaunt - Justices of Peace.]

[p 225]   MANUMISSION OF JACK

... I William Wood ... Township of Chesterfield ... have Manumitted & Set free ... my Mulotto Slave named Jack ...; [Dated - 9 September 1789; signed - William Wood.]

[9 September 1789 - It was certified that Wood brought Jack before Isaac Cowgill, Geo. Anderson - Justices of the Peace; George Apelgate, Joel Middletown - Overseers of the Poor and set him free.]

[p 226]   MANUMISSION OF SIRO

... I William Wood ... Township of Chesterfield ... have Manumitted & Set free ... my Mulotto Slave named Siro ...; [Dated - 9 September 1789; signed - William Wood.]

[9 September 1789 - It was certified that Wood brought Siro before Isaac Cowgill, Geo. Anderson - Justices of the Peace; George Apelgate, Joel Middleton - Overseers of the Poor and set him free.]

[p 227]   MANUMISSION OF GEORGE WATERFORD

[Before Peter Stretch and Asher Gaunt Esqr, Justices of the Peace and Joseph Biddle and Caleb Earl, Overseers of the Poor]; ... This is to Certify that I have a Negro Slave named George Waterford (aged 27 years) who I purchased of Joseph Pearson I request that you may manumitt him ...; [Dated 26 January 1791; Signed - Henry Chambers.]

[26 January 1791 - It was certified that Chambers brought George Waterford before Peter Stretch and Asher Gaunt Esqr, Justices of the Peace and Joseph Biddle and Caleb Earl, Overseers of the Poor; recorded before Phillips, Clerk.]

[p 229]   SARAH BUTCHER, WIDOW to ISAAC HAZELHURST

1 January 1791 - Sarah Butcher widow of Thomas Butcher late of Northampton ... Burlington deceased, Joseph Ridgway of Springfield in the same county, Joseph Morgan Junior of Chester in the

BURLINGTON COUNTY DEEDS - BOOK "B"

same County and Mary his Wife all of Western ... New Jersey, which same Sarah Butcher, Joseph Ridgway, and Mary Morgan formerly Mary Butcher, are Executors of the last Will ... of the aforesaid Thomas Butcher deceased ... [sold to] ... Isaac Hazel hurst ... Philadelphia ... Pennsylvania Merchant ... Whereas ... Thomas Butcher ... Became seized ... of Land ... in the said Township of Northampton ... [and was sold to Hazelhurst by the above Executors on 20 February 1789, Burlington Co, Book C-Page 1] ... [and since the writing on his Will] ... Mary hath Intermarried with the Said Joseph Morgan Junior ... Now this Indenture ... [sells to Hazelhurst for 199 pounds, 15 shillings] ... Two Certain Lotts ... of Land being part of the above mentioned Plantation formerly of Thomas Butcher's ... adjoining ... Land here to fore purchased by the Land of Isaac Hazelhurst ... [adjoining land owners or names - Land Isaac Hazelhurst purchased of the Said Executors of Late Thomas Butcher now in the possession of his Son Thomas Butcher Junr, Daniel Gaskill] ... [12 acres, 18 sq. Perches] ... The other part to the Southward ... [of the above land] ... [adjoining land owners or names - land late John Comforts now Samuel Stocktons, William Lovet Smith's line, the Road leading to Mount Holly] ... [15 acres, 2 rods, 38 sq. Perches] ... [with the sale based upon] ... So as the Land Grantors be not compelled to travel above Seven Miles from their respective places of Abode for the doing thereof ...; [Signed - Sarah Butcher, Jos. Ridgway, Sarah Morgan, Mary Morgan; witnesses - John Butcher, Benaiah Butcher, John Hatkinson.]

[10 January 1791 - Joseph Ridgway and Sarah Butcher acknowledged the deed before Judge Joseph Read ... "and at the Same Time John Butcher one of the Witnesses ... being of the people called Quaker ... declared that he was present and saw his Mother Sarah Butcher and the Said Joseph Ridgway" sign the deed.]

[19 February 1791 - Quaker, John Hatkinson, affirmed and acknowledged the deed.]

[p 236]   **NOTICE OF INFORMATION**

To all whom these Presents shall Come John Ross Collector of the Port of Burlington Sendeth Greetings Whereas John Phillips Esqr lately my Deputy at the said Port ... hath received sundry duties & Tonnage and a Ballance remained in his hands at the Time of his Death. [No date was on this item but the following was written under it - "Mistake Vide Liber".]

[p 236]   **MANUMISSION OF PHILLIS SELSEY**

We Alice Curtis, Thomas Curtis and Asa Curtis administrators to the Estate of Thomas deceased ... Township of Mansfield ... Burlington ... Western New Jersey, having obtained the Consent of all parties ... do hereby set free from bondage a Negro (or black) Woman named Phillis Selsey belonging to the said Estate now about ... [24 years old] ...; [Dated - 26 January 1795; Signed - Alice Curtis, Thos. Curtis, Asa Curtis; witnesses - Nathan Wright, William Black, William Newbold.]

[The above was certified on the same above date before Caleb Scattergood the only Overseer of the Poor for Mansfield and Jacob Wolcott and A. Gaunt - Justices of the Peace.]

[p 238] **MANUMISSION OF SARAH NURSLEY**

... Whereas Sarah a Mulatto Slave now the wife of John Nursley a free Mulatto Man in the Township of Northampton, previous to her Marriage was a Slave to Samuel Stockton of the said Township, and he the said Samuel Stockton a Considerable time past did ... Sell all his Right ... in said Slave Sarah unto Henry Burr junior of the same place And the said Henry Burr did Contract and agreed to with the Said Samuel Stockton in the Space of four years thereafter to manumit and Set free the said Slave Sarah ... And the said Mulatto Slave Sarah now being above the age of ... [21 and under 35 years] ... We the said Samuel Stockton and Henry Burr Junr in Consideration of the premises and in order to free the Said Sarah from Slavery ... do manumit ... and Set at Liberty ... Sarah Nursley ...; [Dated 12 December 1795; signed - Samuel Stockton, Henry Burr Junr; witnesses - Jos. Read, Wm Rossell.]

[The above was certified on the same date before Jos. Read, Wm Rossell - Justices of the Peace and Joseph Bennit, John Ridgway - Overseers of the Poor; received - 31 December 1795; countersigned by Lawrence, Clk of the Pleas and Peace.]

[END OF BOOK "B"]

BURLINGTON COUNTY DEEDS - BOOK "C"

****

[p 1]   **EXECUTORS OF THOMAS BUTCHER to ISAAC HAZELHURST**

20 February 1780 - Sarah Butcher, Mary Butcher and Joseph Ridgeway Executors of the last Will ... of Thomas Butcher late of the Township of Northampton ... Burlington , New Jersey, Yeoman, deceased ... [sold to] ... Isaac Hazelhurst of ... Philadelphia ... Pennsylvania Merchant ... Whereas James Budd of the Township of Northampton ... [was seized of a certain Plantation and Tract of Land in the Township of Northampton and by a certain deed dated February 1686 did] ... Convey ... unto [missing] Rodman ... And Whereas the said John Rodman ... by a ... Deed poll ... [dated 13 January 1723] ... did convey the Same unto his Son Thomas Rodman ... and Whereas ... Thomas Rodman being then an Inhabitant of Long Island in the province (now State) of New York ... [on 19 November 1739] ... did empower his Brother John Rodman ... And Whereas ... John Rodman ... by ... Power of Attorney ... [dated 20 March 1740 sold it to Abraham Farrington who by his last Will proved on 25 May 1756 devised it to his son Samuel Farrington] ... And Whereas ... Samuel Farrington ... [sold it by deed dated 16 August 1770 unto Thomas Butcher] ... And Whereas Ebenezer Large of the City of Burlington ... became seized ... of a certain Tract of Land adjoining the Plantation ... above ... and by his last Will ... devised his Estate to his Grandsons Thomas, Joseph and Samuel Pryor, and the Children of his Daughter Jane Burling ... And by his Will ... directed that his Legatees shall apply to the Monthly Meeting of Friends at Burlington who are thereby empowered to appoint a Committee of Six Men to divide the Said Estate ... And Whereas the aforesaid Joseph Pryor being thus entitled to a Share in the Said Ebenezer Large's Estate ... [did Convey his right on 30 November 1763 - Book T, Page 156] ... to his brothers Thomas and Samuel Pryor ... And Whereas a Committee ... [divided it on 13 January 1764 - Book T, Page 196] ... And Whereas ... Thomas Pryor and Hannah his Wife ... [sold on 21 April 1772, 72 acres unto John Moore, who with his wife Hannah, sold it by deed dated 19 June 1772 to Earl Shinn, and Shinn and his wife Rebecca sold 35 acres by deed dated 20 June 177- to Thomas Butcher] ... And Whereas ... Samuel Pryor being ... so seized of his ... Share, he and Elizabeth his Wife ... [by deed dated 7 September 1768-Book Y, P 364, sold to Charles West, 2.75 acres of his Share, and West, by deed dated 25 April 1772 conveyed it to John Comfort] ... And Whereas Thomas Butcher and John Comfort ... did exchange a part of their ... Tracts of Land with each other ... And ... John comfort and Mary his Wife ... [by deed dated 17 September 1772 conveyed 8 acres and 20 perches unto Thomas Butcher] ... And Whereas Thomas Butcher ... [being so seized by his Will dated June 1775, did appoint his Wife Sarah Butcher, his Daughter Mary Butcher and Joseph Ridgway Executors and the said Premises Butcher died seized] ... And Whereas ... [John and Mary Comfort, since Butcher's decease did on 12 January 1786 convey a small piece of land to the Executors] ...

Now this Indenture ... [the executors for 6 pounds, 15 shillings by the acre sold to Isaac Hazelhurst a certain Part of the said Plantation] ... consisting of a farm called Clover Hill ... [adjacent land owners or names - Road leading from Mount Holly into Gaskills Lane, Isaac Hazelhurst, old corner of Cripps Survey, Thomas Butcher, Daniel Gaskill, William Smith, Doughty, John Comfort, Jabez

BURLINGTON COUNTY DEEDS - BOOK "C"

Woolston] ... [137 acres, 3 rods, 31 perches] ...; [Signed - Sarah Butcher, Mary Butcher, Jo^s Ridgway; witnesses - Moses Kempton, Saml Reed, Jos. Read.]

[p 9] **DIVISION OF LAND**

... Whereas Christopher Wetherill ... City of Burlington ... New Jersey ... [by his last Will dated 27 March 1786 devised to] ... his son Isaac a certain ... [20 acres] ... and the Remainder of his lands in the City of Burlington and lying in the Counties of Hunterdon, Morris and Sussex ... New Jersey and elsewhere ... unto his three Sons Samuel Wetherill, Joseph Wetherill and Isaac Wetherill, and his Daughter Anna and Sarah Wetherill to be divided among them ... Now ... [by] ... these Presents ... that the said Samuel Wetherill, Joseph Wetherill, Isaac Wetherill, Anna Wetherill and Sarah Wetherill have mutually agreed on a Division ...

Isaac Wetherill and Anna and Sarah Wetherill in Consideration of the Lands and Premises herein Released to them ... by Samuel Wetherill and Joseph Wetherill ... confirm unto ... [Samuel and Joseph Wetherill land in the Township of Amwell ... Hunterdon ... [281 acres] ... now in Possession of Jeremiah King ... [adjacent land owners or names - Thomas Wetherill, Amos Shettle, Isaac De Cou, Thomas Wetherill Junr, Robert Pearson and William Penn] ... Secondly ... [Samuel, Joseph, Anna and Sarah Wetherill in consideration of lands from Isaac Wetherill in the City of Burlington] ... being all those lands late of the Said Christopher Wetherill and now ... occupied by the said Isaac Wetherill ... neat Popes Run including ... [20 acres] ... devised ... to him ... [adjacent land owners or names - Mount Holly Road, John Rogers, Elizabeth Johnson, Isaac Wetherill, William Hewlings] ... [84 acres] ... Also all that ... Ground ... Broad Street ... devised by Thomas Wetherill to his Son ... Christopher Wetherill ... Thirdly ... [Samuel, Joseph, and Isaac Wetherill in consideration of lands from Anna & Sarah Wetherill confirm to Anna & Sarah interest in the lot of Ground] .... where they now live ... [adjacent land owners or names - High Street, Abigail Bishop, James Smith, Daniel Ellis, York Street, Samuel Wetherill, Isaac Wetherill, Friends School, Joseph Wetherill] ...; [Dated - 9 September 1789; signed - Saml Wetherill, Junr, Joseph Wetherill, Isaac Wetherill, Anna Wetherill, Sarah Wetherill; witnesses - Danl Smith, Nathaniel Coleman.]

[p 12] **JOHN HOLLINSHEAD, SHERIFF to THOMAS REYNOLDS**

15 August 1789 - John Hollinshead Esq. Late High Sheriff ... Burlington ... New Jersey ... [sold to] ... Thomas Reynolds ... Township of New Hanover ... and Richard Edwards Esq ... Whereas Thomas Mayberry ... [won a Judgement against George Hastings in 1788 and Benjamin Morgan also obtained a Judgement and the Sheriff confiscated property and offered it to public sale] ... And whereas ... George Hastings ... became possessed of the land and premises on 14 July 1785 from Thomas Mayberry and Mary his wife; to wit] ... All that Forge Furnace and ... Land commonly called ... Tanton situate in the Township of Evesham ... And also ... one undivided eighth part of a Certain Saw Mill And then acres of Land being the Mill Seat in Evesham ... And also ... Two Tracts of Land ...

BURLINGTON COUNTY DEEDS - BOOK "C"

contiguous to the said Iron Works and Saw Mill. The Tanton Tract was Formerly the property of Charles Read Esq[r] the elder ... The other lands and Mill Tract was formerly the property of Francis Austin now deceased ... [the following are former owners and present owners of adjacent property - Charles Read, David Oliphant's Mill Pond called Meadow Run, John Wilkins, Benjamin Thomas, Absalom Thomas, John Pricket, Benjamin Haines, Michael Branin, Jonathan Haines, Emanuel Stratton, Prickett Mill or Atsion Pond, Kettle Run, Solomon Haines, Thomas Mayberry, Prickets or Haines' Mill Company, Borton's Road, Enoch Evans] ... [the high bidders for the property were Thomas Reynolds Esq[r] and Richard Edwards as Tenants in Common who bid 530 pounds and bought the property] ...; [Signed - John Hollinshead; witnesses - John Phillips, Daniel Ellis.]

[p 20]   **JOHN HOLLINSHEAD ESQ[R], SHERIFF to ELISHA LAWRENCE, ESQ[R]**

25 November 1788 - John Hollinshead, Esq[r] ... High Sheriff ... Burlington ... [sold to] ... Elisha Lawrence Esq[r] ... Monmouth ... New Jersey ... [Whereas Elisah Lawrence won a Judgement against Ezekiel Groom and the Sheriff confiscated and exposed for sale the property] ... And Whereas Joseph Imlay Esq[r], Sheriff of Burlington ... dated 18 December 1767 did Convey unto John Groom of Chesterfield ... Land ... in the Said Township of Chesterfield and the Said Ezekiel Groom being Heir at Law to the Said John Groom, and at his Death became ... Seized of the above Mentioned ... Land ... [adjoining land owners or names - the road that goes to Reckless Mills] ... [1 acres] ... [and Elisha Lawrence Esq[r] bid 50 pounds for the property] ...; [Signed - John Hollinshead; witnesses - John Thompson, John Phillips, Jacob Wolcott.]

[p 24]   **MANUMISSION OF PHILIP BITTO**

I Thomas Thorn ... Township of Chesterfield ... Burlington ... have Manumitted and set free my Negro Slave named Philip Bitto ...; [Dated 14 April 1790; signed - Thomas Thorn; witnesses - John Pope, Isaac Cowgill.]

[Bitto was brought before John Pope and Isaac Cowgill, Justices and John Thorn and John Middleton, Jun[r] - Overseers of the Poor. It was confirmed before John Pope and Isaac Cowgill.]

[p 25]   **MANUMISSION OF PHILLIS DILLON**

... Joseph Woodward ... Township of Chesterfield ... Burlington ... have Manumitted and set free my Negro Slave named Phillis Dillon ...; [Dated - 14 April 1790; signed - Joseph Woodward; witnesses - John Pope, Isaac Cowgill.]

[Phillis Dillon was brought before John Pope and Isaac Cowgill, Justices and John Thorn and John Middleton, Jun[r] - Overseers of the Poor. It was confirmed before John Pope and Isaac Cowgill.]

BURLINGTON COUNTY DEEDS - BOOK "C"

****

[p 26] MANUMISSION OF BRUTUS

... Samuel Rogers ... Township of Chesterfield ... Burlington ... have manumitted my Negro Slave named Brutus ...; [Dated 14 April 1790; signed - Samuel Rogers.]

[Brutus was brought before John Pope and Isaac Cowgill, Justices and John Thorn and John Middleton, Jun[r] - Overseers of the Poor. It was confirmed before John Pope and Isaac Cowgill.]

[p 27] MANUMISSION OF GRACE

... Joseph Kirkbride ... [of Chesterfield Township, Burlington] ... have manumitted or set free my Negro or Mulatto Woman named Grace aged about twenty seven years ...; [Dated - 8 June 1789; signed - Jos. Kirkbride.]

[Grace was brought before John Pope and Isaac Cowgill, Justices of Peace and Joel Middleton and George Apelgate, Overseers of the Poor.]

[p 28] ROBERT PARRISH to WILLIAM CLARK

21 November 1785 - Robert Parrish late of Philadelphia ... Pennsylvania Merchant and Mary his Wife ... [sold to] ... William Clark of ... the Town of Mount Holly ... Burlington ... New Jersey Carpenter ... [for 17 pounds] ... All that ... Land ... in Mount Holly ... [adjoining land owners or names - Garden Street, land purchased of Aquilla Shinn, lands now of Buddell Shinn, Joseph Grice] ... land is part of ... purchased of Rev'd John Brainard and Elizabeth his Wife by deed dated ... [14 December 1776] ...; [Signed - Robert Parrish; witnesses - Jon Hall, Jos. Hugg.]

[p 31] RHUBEN HAINS to SOLOMON HAINS

14 April 1786 - ... whereas Rhuben Hains of ... Philadelphia ... Pennsylvania being seized of ... Land in Evesham Township ... Burlington ... New Jersey ... [sold by deed dated 24 March 1749 part of the land] ... Said to contain ... [150 acres] ... unto Sarah Mills, widow living in said Township which said Plantation is now by Virtue of his Marriage with Sarah Mills Daughter of the afsd Sarah Mills Widow in the Possession of Daniel Coate and whereas it appears probable ... a certain Piece of Meadow Ground said to be two acres ... may be a large Quantity which ... was given off of said Tract when in the Possession of Jonathan Hains who devised same to his Son Job by his last Will ... who sold the same to Carlile Hains the Father of Solomon. Now know ye that for ... [3 pounds] ... Rhuben Hains ... Quit Claim unto the said Solomon Hains (in his full and peacible possession ... thereof now being) ... [adjoining land owners or names - Daniel Coates, John Hains] ...; [Dated - 14 April 1786; signed - Rhuben Hains; witnesses - L.M. Morris, Casper W. Haines.]

BURLINGTON COUNTY DEEDS - BOOK "C"

[20 March 1789- Caspar Wistar Haines, "who being one of the People called Quakers" ... appeared before Judge Joseph Read Esqr and "declared that he was present and saw his Father Rhuben Haines" sign same.]

[p 33] **MANUMISSION OF PETER HILL**

... I do hereby for myself ... Manumit and set free my Negro or Mulatto Man Peter Hill aged twenty Seven years the 19th of July 1794 ... whereof I have hereunto Set my Hand & Seal at Burlington the place of my dwelling the 16th day of April 1795 ...; [Signed - Joe Hollinshead; witness - John Thompson.

[We do ... certify that on 1 May 1795 Joseph Hollinshead of the Township of Burlington ... brought before Nathl Fitz and Saml. Stockton, Overseers of the Poor & Wm. Coxe Junr & Thos. Adams, Justices of Peace.]

[p 34] **SAMUEL BORTON to BENJAMIN BORTON**

1 August 1782 - Samuel Borton ... Township of Evesham ... Burlington ... West New Jersey ... [sold to] ... his Brother Benjamin Borton ... [of the same place] ... whereas John Borton Grandfather to the above named Parties did by ... [deed dated 3 May 1738 sell to] ... his son Obadiah Borton Father to the Parties above mentioned ... [and the said Obadiah Borton being so Seized did by his last Will dated ... [28 June 1761 and] therein conveyed to his Sons ... Now this Indenture ... [for 50 pounds sells] ... one certain Piece ... of Land it being Meadow Ground ... [adjoining land owners or names - Samuel Borton] ... [5 acres] ...; [Signed - Samuel Borton and Rhoda his Wife as a Confirmation of her Release of Dower ...; witnesses - John Borton, Abr^m Woolman.]

[5 January 1790 - Samuel and Rhoda Borton appeared before Judge Joseph Read Esqr and acknowledged the above deed.]

[p 37] **JOSEPH ENGLISH to WILLIAM WRIGHT**

15 April 1788 - Joseph English ... Town and County of Burlington ... New Jersey yeoman & Ann his Wife ... [sold to] ... William Wright of the same place yeoman ... Whereas Thomas English late of Mansfield afsd dec^d was ... seized ... of certain plantations & Tracts of Land ... in the Township of Mansfield ... [and by a deed of gift dated 9 March 1776 granted to his Son Isaac English] ... the Plantation whereon the Said Thomas English then lived & also ... [150 acres] ... adjoining lands of Thomas Biddle & John Sutton & Samuel Bullus and the said Isaac English being so ... seized Joseph Mullen Esqr high Sheriff ... Burlington ... [by several writs did seize the same on 1 October 1785 and expose the same for sale & Joseph English was the high bidder] ... [adjoining land owners or names -

BURLINGTON COUNTY DEEDS - BOOK "C"

corner standing near the old School house, John Sutton, Samuel Bullus, Thomas Biddle, William Wright] ... [100 acres] ...; [Signed - Joseph English; witnesses - Charles Ellis, Jacob Wolcott.]

[Daniel Ellis Esqr ... City of Burlington ... New Jersey to whom the Premises within mentioned and granted are mortgaged ... Know ye that the said Daniel Ellis ... for ... [300 pounds] ... paid by William Wright ... Hath ... forever quit claim ... unto the said William Wright ... [the lands in the above Indenture] ...; [Dated - 17 April 1788; signed - Danl Ellis; witnesses - Charles Ellis, Jacob Wolcott.]

[p 42]   **DANIEL DE BRAY to WILLIAM BROWN**

5 January 1791 - Daniel De Bray late of the Township of Chester ... Burlington ... New Jersey but now of the City of Philadelphia Gentleman ... [sold to] ... William Brown of the said City Merchant ... [Whereas writs against the lands, etc of] ... Thomas Tallman late of the Township of Evesham ... deceased ... [And Joseph Mullen Esqr High Sheriff seized the land & exposed 50 acres for sale and sold it to Thomas Brooks on 6 August 1784, and Brooks sold 15 acres of it on 21 August 1784 to Henry Bennett; and Bennett sold the 15 acres to Daniel De Bray on 18 October 1787] ... Now this Indenture ... [De Bray for 300 pounds sells to William Brown the 15 acres in Evesham] ... [adjoining land owners or names - the Great Road leading from Moor's Town to Mount Holly, land of the estate of Thomas Brooks dec'd, land late of Thomas Tallman, land Thomas Brooks sold to Job Borton, by lands of Thomas Brooks deceased now belonging to his Son Samuel Brooks] ...; [Signed - Daniel De Bray; witnesses - Da^l Beveridge, Jno Patton ... both of Philadelphia.]

[p 46]   **RICHARD STOCKTON to JAMES ASH**

19 January 1791 - Richard Stockton of the City of Philadelphia ... Pennsylvania Gentleman ... [sold to] ... James Ash of the same place Esqr ... [for 72 pounds, 10 shillings] ... Land ... in Northampton Township ... Burlington ... New Jersey ... [adjoining land owners or names - Benjamin Stockton, land purchased by George Kimble] ... [3 acres, 30 perches] ... [Being the same lot & premises which Benjamin Stockton & Hannah his Wife & Samuel Stockton & Ann his Wife by Indenture dated 6 January 1791, granted to Richard Stockton & is part of a tract of 58 acres] ... which William Stockton by his Will ... [dated 8 April 1780] ... devised to his three Sons the said Benjamin, Samuel & Richard Stockton ...; [Signed - Richard Stockton; witnesses - Wm Hartung, Joshua M. Wallace.]

[Rec'd on the above date from James Ash ... 72 pounds, 10 shillings; Signed - Richard Stockton; witnesses - Jona^n Sergeant, Wm Hartung.]

[p 48]   **MISTAKE**

... John Ross Collector of the Port of Burlington senth Greeting - Whereas John Phillips Esqr my late Deputy at the same Port ... hath Received sundry duties & Tonage & a Ballance remained in his

BURLINGTON COUNTY DEEDS - BOOK "C"

****

Hands at the time of his Death of ...[$130.20] ... which have to be paid ... unto the Treasury of the United States Now I the said John Ross ... do transfer ... unto the United States the said Ballance ...; [Dated - 17 February 1791; signed - Jnº Ross Collector; witnesses - Zach. R. Reed[?], Jos. Read.]

[p 49]   **BENJAMIN STOCKTON ET AL to RICHARD STOCKTON**

6 January 1791 - Benjamin Stockton yeoman & Hannah his Wife ... Township of Northampton ... Burlington ... New Jersey & Samuel Stockton yeoman & Ann his Wife ... Township of Springfield ... [of the same place, sold to] ... Richard Stockton ... City of Philadelphia ... Whereas Vincent Leeds by a warrant ... [dated 20 June 1748] ... did locate & survey a Tract of ... [50 acres in Burlington County] ... at the lower end of the North Branch of Willis Cedar Swamp & Leeds conveyed same by deed dated 12 December 1748 to William Stockton of the Town of Burlington, And Stockton] ... on surveying the sd Land & finding overplus of ... [8 acres, 2 rods on 24 October 1763 & Stockton became seized of all 58 acres & 2 rods & by his last Will dated 8 April 1780] ... did devise the same unto his three Sons the s^d Benjamin, Samuel & Richard Stockton ... Now this Indenture ... the sd Benjamin Stockton and Hannah his Wife & Samuel Stockton & Ann his Wife ... [for timber and rails & 5 pounds] ... release ... unto ... Richard Stockton ... [adjoining land owners or names - Benjamin Stockton, cedar swamp purchased of George Kimble] ... [3 acres, 30 perches] ...; [Signed - Benjamin Stockton, Hannah Stockton, Samuel Stockton, Ann Stockton; witnesses - Mary Cowperthwaite, William Cowperthwaite, William Cowperthwaite, Junr.]

[Res'd upon the Execu^n of this Deed five pounds ...; signed - Samuel Stockton, Benjamin Stockton; witnesses Wm Cowperthwaite, Wm Cowperthwaite, Junr.]

[p 53]   **JAMES BUNTING to THOMAS NEWBOLD**

9 May 1791 - James Bunting of Chesterfield ... Burlington ... New Jersey Farmer and Mary his Wife ... [sold to] ... Thomas Newbold of the same place Farmer ... Whereas John Bunting Father of the s^d James Bunting became lawfully Seized ... [in 495 acres, 2 rods] ... of Land ... in Chesterfield ... [Liber K-Page 293] ... And Whereas the same John Bunting by Deed of Gift dated ... [25 April 1763] ... convey to his Son James Bunting ... [174 acres, 3 rods] ... being part of the afsd ...[495 plus acres] ... [adjoining land owners or names - Benjamin Field, Joshua Bunting, Aaron Bunting, Peter Tilton, Joseph Thorn] ... [174 acres, 3 rods] ... And Whereas the same James Bunting ... [by Deed Liber AP, Page 481] ... Became ... seized ... in the same 174.75 acres ... [did convey] ... a part thereof to Humphrey Walsh ... [22 acres, 3 rods, 20 perches] ... also one other piece of Land ... to Isaac Field ... [2 acres, 1 rod, 5 perches] ... Now this Indenture ... [for 730 pounds sells to] ... Thomas Newbold ...; [Signed - James Bunting and Mary Bunting both made their marks when signing; witnesses - Michael Taylor, Jnº Oliver.]

BURLINGTON COUNTY DEEDS - BOOK "C"

****

[p 57]   **THOMAS ASHMORE to PHILLIP FISHER**

15 January 1788 - Thomas Ashmore ... Township of Nottingham ... Burlington ... New Jersey and Elenor his Wife ... [sold to] ... Phillip Fisher ... [of the same place] ... Merchant ... [for 8 pence, 15 shilling] ... a certain Lot of Land No 15 ... in the Township of Nottingham ... [adjoining land owners or names - the road from Trenton to Crosswicks] ... .25 acres] ... together with Lot #14 that Thomas Ashmore purchased of John Hollinshead Esqr High Sheriff ... by Deed dated ... [6 December 1787] ...; [Signed - Thomas & Eleanor Ashmore; witnesses - Roland Hall, George Anderson.]

[22 April 1789 - Thomas Ashmore and Nelti his Wife acknowledged the above deed in court.]

[p 59]   **THOMAS MOORE to PHILLIP FESTER**

19 August 1775 - Thomas Moore of Springfield Township ... Chester ... Pennsylvania Cordwainer and Elizabeth his Wife ... [sold to] ... Phillip Fester of Kingsbury Hill near Trenton ... Burlington ... New Jersey Yeoman ... [for 13 pounds, 10 shilling] ... a certain Tract ... of Land ... on Kingsberry Hill on ... south eastwardly side of Broad Street ... [adjoining land owners or names - John Brandt, George Jobes' land] ... [.25 acres] ... which s^d Premises Robert Letter[?] Hooper of Trenton Esqr by Indenture ... [dated 20 June 1770] ... granted to s^d Thomas Moore ...; [Signed - Thomas Moore; witnesses - Jacob Ehernzeller, John Knight.]

[11 November 1790 - Jacob Ehrenzeller acknowledged the above deed before Edward Shippen Esqr.]

[p 63]   **RENSSALAER WILLIAMS to PHILLIP FISTER**

20 May 1773 - Renssalaer Williams of Nottingham ... Burlington ... New Jersey and Catherine his Wife ... [sold to] ... Phillip Fister of the same place ... Whereas ... Williams ... recovered against Robert Lettiu[?] Hooper Esqr ... [and the Sheriff confiscated & sold his property] ... two lotts in ... Nottingham ... [which Williams bought from the Sheriff on 3 March 1772 for 34 pounds, 15 shillings] ... Now the Indenture sells for ... [38 pounds] ... to Fister ... [James Paxton, Broad Street, Thomas Moors Lott] ... [.25 acres] ...; [Signed - Renssel^r Williams, Catherine Williams; witnesses - Thomas Bends, Andover Wilson.]

[p 68]   **JOSEPH CARSON to THOMAS REED**

18 March 1783 - Joseph Carson ... City of Philadelphia ... Pennsylvania Merchant and Mary his Wife ... [sold to] ... Thomas Reed ... [of the same place] ... Mariner ... [for 800 pounds] ... All that ... Lot ... in Bordentown ... New Jersey ... [House of Edward Wheatcraft, Second Street, Main Street] ... [1 acre] ... The said Lot being half of a two Acre Lot sold by Joseph Borden to Daniel Farnsworth and bequeathed by the s^d ... Farnsworth to John Edwards by his last Will ... [dated 24 May 1747] ...

BURLINGTON COUNTY DEEDS - BOOK "C"

****

Which said Lot ... the s^d John Edwards & Letitia his Wife ... [sold on 7 August 1764 to] ... John Imlay ... and which ... [John Imlay and Catharine his Wife erected] ... the Messuage thereon ... [and sold the above by deed dated 20 November 1777 to Joseph Carson above] ...; [Signed - Joseph Carson, Mary Carson; witnesses - Robert McCleary, Wm Webb.]

[7 May 1791 - McCleary acknowledged the above deed in Court on this date.]

[p 70]   **SAMUEL DOWNING to PHILLIP FESTER**

20 June 1788 - Samuel Downing of Trenton Township ... Hunterdon ... New Jersey and Martha his Wife ... [sold to] ... Phillip Fester of Nottingham Township ... Burlington ... [for 17 pounds, 5 shillings] ... two Lots of Land which George Anderson, Hugh Runyon and Phillip Fester Auditors of Hugh Smith conveyed to Samuel Downing ... by a Deed ... [as lots #16 & 17 in a draft made by John Watson Surveyor] ... [adjoining land owners or names - the road from trenton to Crosswicks, Ferry Lane, Colonel Mitchell's] ... [.5 acres] ... purchased of Hugh Runyon and Sarah his Wife by a deed ... to Hugh Smith ...; [Signed - Saml Downing, Martha Downing; witnesses - John Flekey, Thom^s Janney.]

[15 March 1791 - Both Samuel and Martha Downing acknowledged the above deed in court.]

[p 73]   **WILLIAM SATTERTHWAITE to PHILIP FISTER**

12 July 1790 - ... William Satterthwaite ... Township of Chesterfield ... Burlington ... New Jersey and Meribah his Wife ... [sold to] ... Philip Fister ... Township of Nottingham ... Whereas Robert Lettiu[?] Hooper ... [29 November 1766] ... sells unto David Satterthwaite ... [of 1 acre] ... in Kingsbury ... and the afs^d William Satterthwaite being sole heir at Law to the s^d David Satterthwaite ... [the property descended to him] ... sells it for 20 pounds] ... a certain Lot ... in Nottingham Township ... [adjoining land owners or names - Broad Street, Jeremiah Warden, Abbot's Lot, John Cox Esqr] ... [.25 acres] ...; [Signed - William Satterthwaite, Meribah Satterthwaite; witnesses - Jam^s Ewing, Joseph Disbrow, Jno Dougherty.]

[p 76]   **JOHN CURLEY to PHILIP FISTER**

31 March 1789 - John Curley and Elinor his Wife ... Township of Nottingham ... Burlington ... New Jersey ... [sold to] ... Philip Fister of the same place ... [for 32 pounds, 10 shillings] ... two ... Lots ... No 18 & No 19 ... [in the same place as above] ... [adjoining land owners or names - the road from trenton to Crosswicks, John Stevens] ... [.5 acres] ...; [Signed - Both John Curley and Elinor Curley made their marks when signing; witnesses - Geo. Anderson, James Coalman.]

BURLINGTON COUNTY DEEDS - BOOK "C"

[p 79] LEVINA BISHOP to SAMUEL BISHOP

20 June 1791 - Levina Bishop Relict of William Bishop late of the Township of Northampton ... Burlington ... New Jersey ... [sold to] ... Samuel Bishop the son of the s^d William Bishop ... And whereas the s^d Levina Bishop is now pregnant with Child some oversight ... no provision hath been made in the Will of the s^d William Bishop And Whereas an agreement hath taken place between the s^d Levina Bishop and Samuel Bishop ... if the s^d Child ... shall hereafter appear to be a male and attain ... [the age of 21] ... he is to receive out of his Father's Estate ... [150 pounds] ... if the s^d Child shuld prove to be a female and ... attain the age of ... [18 years] ... it shall be intitled to receive ... [100 pounds] ... and if the s^d Child should happen to die before the ages ... specified ... the s^d Samuel Bishop & his Heirs shall be exonerated ... Now this Indenture ... [for the above promises and 5 shillings releases Dower to Samuel Bishop] ...; [Signed Levinah Bishop, Samuel Bishop; witnesses - Hudson Burr, Joseph Budd.]

[5 June 1791 - Hudson Burr ... (he being of the People called Quakers) acknowledged that he knew the above parties.]

[p 83] WILLIAM FOSTER to DANIEL HAMMITT

30 March 1790 - William Foster ... Township of Chester ... Burlington ... New Jersey Cordwainer and Anna his Wife ... [sold to] ... Daniel Hammitt ... [of the same place] ... Taylor ... Whereas Reece Edwards ... [by Indenture of 26 February 1783 bought the property from Ephraim Haines & Hannah his wife who sold 5 acres in Moorestown ... Township of Chester] ... And Reece Edwards and Sarah his Wife ... [sold the property by Deed, dated 1 March 1783, to Richard Edwards, who with his wife, Abigail, sold two acres and 2 rods of the property to William Foster on 2 September 1789] ... Now this Indenture ... [sells land being part of the 2 acres and 2 rods for 37 pounds] ... [adjoining land owners or names - William Bonadails, Salem Road, William Foster, John Haines] ... [amounting to 3 rods and 24 perches] ...; [Signed - William Foster, Junr, Anna Foster; witnesses - Thos. Stokes, John Cox.]

[p 86] CYRUS STILL to WILLIAM HAINES

15 August 1791 - ... I Cyrus Still of Northampton ... Burlington do justly owe unto William Haines of the same place ... [for 40 pounds] ... Now Know ye that I the said ... Still ... To secure payment ... unto ... Haines plus 5 shillings ... [sells unto] ... Haines ... one Brown Horse, one Brindle Cow and Calf, one bedstead Bed and Bedding, one Table, one Doughtrough, two chairs, one cupboard, two pine Chests, one Iron Pot, one ax & three Hoes ... [to pay and satisfy for the money owed] ...; [Signed - Cyrus Still made his mark when signing; witness - Saml Read.]

BURLINGTON COUNTY DEEDS - BOOK "C"

[p 87]   **JOSHUA NEWBOLD to CALEB HAINES**

25 March 1787 - Joshua Newbold and Rebeckah his Wife of Mount Holly ... Township of Northampton ... Burlington ... New Jersey Blacksmith ... [sold to] ... Caleb Haines ... farmer ... whereas John Pancoast by Deed ... [dated 28 October 1680] ... caused ... [162 acres to be surveyed on 4 April 1682 in the Township of Mansfield and by his Will devised] ... same to son William Pancoast and Whereas John Antram ... [caused 150 acres to be surveyed in September 1683 joining the above survey and by deed ... [dated 19 November 1698 conveyed] ... the same to the above s^d William Pancoast and being ... seized of ... [312 acres] ... did by his last Will ... devise to his Son Aden Pancoast ... [214 acres] ... and the s^d Aden Pancoast by deed ... [dated 25 March 1769] ... conveyed the same ... [214 acres] ... unto Jacob Ridgway ... [who by deed sold 196 acres on 20 March 1784 to Joshua Newbold] ... Now this Indenture ... [for 1,440 pounds sells] ... Land ... in the Township of Mansfield ... [adjoining land owners of names - John Hervey, Peter Ellis, Jonathan Barton, John Watson, John Tonkins, Hepzibah Tonkin] ... [194.25 acres] ...; [Signed - Joshua Newbold, Rebekah Newbold; witnesses - Mahlon Atkinson, Ebenezer Collins.]

[March 1788 - Received of Caleb Haines 1,400 pounds ...; signed - Joshua Newbold; witnesses - Robert Blair, Jacob Keeler.]

[p 92]   **AGREEMENT ON LAND DIVISION**

1 June 1791 - ... David Davis & Japhiet[?] Garwood ... confirmed the fourth Line on said David Davis Land to be the true Division Line between our Lands lying in Evesham ... [adjoining land owners or names - Corner to Davis' & Garwood's Land, road from Newbold's Mill to Ayre's Town, Barzillai Brannens] ...; [Signed - David Davis, Japieth[?] Garwood; witnesses - Jonathan Crispin, Josiah Foster; recorded - 18 October 1792.]

[p 93]   **WILLIAMS HEWLINGS to JOSEPH BIDDLE JUN^R**

2 May 1770 - William Hewlings ... City of Burlington ... New Jersey Esqr ... [sold to] ... Joseph Biddle Junr of Springfield ... Burlington ... Surveyor ... [for 10 pounds] ... [78 acres] ... of ... Land ... Surveyed for ... Joseph Biddle ... and in part of a Warrant Granted ... unto the said William Hewlings for the Surveying of ... [273.2 acres dated 3 November 1768] and also One[?] Two Tirtieth part of a Propriety ... of One Equal Undivided Ninieth part in One hundred parts ... of West New Jersey ... [which was purchased by Hewlings of Samuel Budd on 9 February 1765] ... which descended to him the said Samuel Budd as only Son and heir at Law to his father George Budd late of Anapolis in ... Maryland Sadler which said George Budd was lawfully seized of ... [1/3 part] ... of all the Rights and Shares of Propriety late George Hutchinson's as will appear by the above recited Indenture from ... Samuel Budd ... [Liber X-Folio 43] ...; [Signed - Wm Hewlings; witnesses - John Shaw, Amos Pharo.]

BURLINGTON COUNTY DEEDS - BOOK "C"

****

[p 95]   **LETTER OF ATTORNEY**

24 November 1791 - ... Tench Coxe ... City of Philadelphia Esqr and Rebecca his wife ... appoint Joshua Maddox Wallace and William Cox Junior of ... City of Burlington ... their true and Lawfull Attornies ... to acknowledge their due Execution of a Certain Deed to Nathaniel Fitz. Of the same place sadler for a Lot of Land on Pearl Street ... City of Burlington and the Building thereon Being the same which was formerly owned by John Baslie and purchased by Tench Coxe from Joshua Maddox Wallace Esqr ...; [Signed - Tench Coxe Esqr, Rebecca Coxe; witnesses - Margaret Shippen, Sarah Lee [both of Pennsylvania.]

[p 97]   **ORDER TO PARTITION THE ESTATE OF JOHN SHARP**

James Kinsey Esquire Chief Justice ... Supreme Court ... New Jersey to William Rogers & Samuel Evans ... Township of Evesham and Moses Kempton ... Township of Northampton ... Burlington ... concerned in Interest in the tracts of Land ... Whereas John Sharp of Evesham ... deceased was ... seized ... of Land ... one tract known by the name of the homestead Place the ... Remainder of his land ... in the will ... of the same John Sharp ... also a Lot of Cedar ... [per the Will dated 5 July 1788] ... [adjoining land owners or names - Samuel Sharp Junr, Thos. Sharp, Amos Sharp, John Sharp, Isaac Sharp, Samuel Ballinger, Barzillia Sharp] ... [150 acres] ... now in possession of Dinah Sharp the Widow of the same John Sharp deceased ... And Whereas since the Decease of the same John Sharp ... [1790] ... Mahlon Sharp died under age intestate and without issue by means ... [the rights of Mahlon Sharp descended to] ... his Surviving Brothers & Sisters to wit John Sharp, Amos Sharp, Isaac Sharp, Samuel Sharp, Ann Sharp, Deborah Sharp, Hannah Sharp, Mary Sharp, and Priscilla Sharp ... And Whereas on ... [5 April] ... I did nominate ... William Rogers, Samuel Evans & Moses Kempton ... to make a partition of the Lands afs^d ... Now know Ye by ... [an act of the General Assembly of New Jersey the above three subjects were appointed to partition the land] ...; [Signed - James Kinsey, Ch. Just.]

[The next 46 pages in Book "C" deal with the division of the James Sharp property amongst the his heirs by the NJ Supreme Court. This material is primarily each heir's lot or lots with their metes and bounds. Due to the similarity involved in these lots and material, it has not been abstracted in detail. Originally included with this material was a detailed map that had been glued into Book "C". At this time, the map is missing and only the glue spots show where it was once located.

To divide this property, the Commissioners put 13 tickets into a box with the name of the 4 brothers and 5 sisters of Mahlon Sharp and children of John Sharp. The boys were to receive 2/13ths and the girls to receive 1/13th each of the estate. The tickets were put into the box with each ticket having the child's name and the number of shares; i.e. - John 2, Amos 2, Samuel 2, Isaac 2, Ann 1, Deborah 1, Hannah 1, Mary 1, and Priscilla 1. The Commissioners then put

BURLINGTON COUNTY DEEDS - BOOK "C"

13 other tickets with numbers 1-13, corresponding to the 13 lot divisions on their map, into another box. They then first drew the child's name from the one box and then a ticket with a number from the other box. In this fashion, the Sharp property was divided amongst the heirs of John Sharp deceased. The person responsible for drawing the tickets for the lottery was Zachariah Rossell of the Township of Northampton.]

[p 102]   **ACTUAL PARTITION OF THE SHARP PROPERTY**

18 August 1791 - James Kinsey Esqr Chief Justice of the Supreme Court ... New Jersey And ... William Rogers and Samuel Evans ... Township of Evesham & Moses Kempton ... Township of Northampton Commissioners ... [appointed to divide & survey the land's late of John Sharp deceased regarding his heirs including that of Mahlon Sharp, deceased, who died intestate] ... and without Issue one of the Sons of John Sharp of Evesham ... deceased which same John Sharp by his last Will ... [dated 5 July 1788] ... did devise unto the same Mahlon part of his real Estate by the name of his Homestead place ... [and amongst the Brother & Sisters] ... of the same Mahlon Sharp ... [adjoining land owners or names to the 13 parcels of property - John Sharp, Samuel Sharp, Samuel Sharp Junr, Isaac Sharp, Saml Ballenger, Tho. Sharp, Wm Bishop, Barzillai Sharp, Jno Horner, Amos Sharp] ...; [Signed - Wm Rogers, Saml Evans, Moses Kempton; James Kinsey - Chief Justice signed on 24 September 1791; recorded - Lawrence, Clerk.]

[p 146]   **RECEIPT**

[This receipt was another entry regarding Item #16 above, dated 17 February 1791, by John Ross Collector of the Port of Burlington.]

[p 147]   **WILLIAM SHARP to ISAAC HAZELHURST**

27 December 1791 - William Sharp ... Township of Evesham ... Burlington ... West New Jersey Husbandman & Elizabeth his Wife ... [sold to] ... Isaac Hazelhurst ... City of Philadelphia ... Pennsylvania Merchant ... Whereas Robert Bradock by one certain Indenture ... [by Mary & Joseph Burley Executors of the Will of William Burley deceased dated 14 February 1761 did purchase a Certain piece of Land in the Township of Evesham and] ... Robert Braddock by Virtue of a Warrant ... [dated 6 April 1761 did Survey a piece of Land and Cedar Swamp which Robert Braddock then gave by his Will] ... unto his Son Barzillai Braddock And whereas the sd Barzillai Braddock ... [sold it to William Sharp on 13 August 1789] ... Now this Indenture ... [sells the property to Hazlehurst for 35 pounds] ... [adjoining land owners or names - Edge of Pellock Swamp, David Davis] ... [11 acres, 2 rods, 30 perches] ... of Cedar Swamp & Pine Land ...; [Signed - William Sharp, Elizabeth Sharp; witnesses - Thomas Shinn, William Sharp Junr.]

BURLINGTON COUNTY DEEDS - BOOK "C"

****

[p 151]   **JOSHUA BISPHAM to JOHN HUESTIS**

28 November 1767 - Joshua Bispham of Moorestown ... Township of Chester ... Burlington ... West New Jersey Merchant ... [sold to] ... John Huestis ... Township of Evesham ... Whereas John Rodman ... [sold on 10 June 1691 in Liber B-folio 484, 475 acres of land in Chester to John Adams Dec^d] ... and Adames gave on ... [27 January 1696 one half of the above 475 acres unto his Son James Adams Dec^d who in his last Will gave the ½ unto Esther his Wife also dec^d, who by her last Will gave power to her Executors Thomas French & Judah Allen since dec^d] ... And the Executors together with Jedidiah Adams eldest Son and Heir unto the said James Adams and Esther his Wife ... conveyed the Same unto Nathan Allen dec^d who by one Indenture ... [on 23 March 1723 sold it unto Jedidiah Adames Dec^d, who on 4 April 1726 conveyed same to the Commissioners of the Loan Office for Burlington & they sold it to Thomas Ford dec^d. And Ford & his wife Elizabeth ... [sold 160 acres on 21 July 1729 to Joshua Granger, and Granger & Elizabeth his Wife on 17 November 1731 sold same unto Robert Davis, and Davis on 22 November 1731 with other lands sold the parcel to Lancelet Brown, whereupon Brown sold it on 21 April 1737 to Nehemiah Haines since dec^d and Haines on 11 February 1742/3 sold 1 acre and 2 rods of land to Lancelet Brown filed in Liber EF-folio 328, 329. And Brown sold the above 1 acre and 2 rods of land on 20 February 1743/4 to Joshua Bispham] ... one of the Parties of these Presents - And whereas the Said Nehemiah Haines ... [on 7 August 1744 sold a small piece of the land to Joshua Bispham adjoining the above mentioned Lot] ... And whereas Ephraim Haines Son and Heir at Law to the said Nehemiah Haines ... [sold on 1 July 1761 another small piece to Joshua Bispham] ... adjoining the last mentioned Lot conveyed by his Father containing in the whole ... [2 acres, 6 perches] ... And whereas Clark Rodman of the Collony of Rhode Island ... became legally vested ... in the Sundry Lands ... within the Division aforesaid and who by his Indenture of Lease and Release ... [on 12 and 13 October 1730 sold unto Francis Hogsett deceased 300 acres of Land in the Township of Chester And Hogsett ... on 14 November 1733 sold to Lancelet Brown 36 acres of the before mentioned which last recited Indenture is in Book E-page 165 and Brown then sold the aforementioned 36 acres to Thomas Moore dec^d] ... And Whereas ... [Hogsett on 19 and 20 January 1732 sold to Thomas Moore 33 acres of the aforesaid 300 acres] ... And the said Thomas Moore and Elizabeth his Wife ... [on 29 April 1745 sold 1 acres and 2 rods of the last mentioned 33 acres to John Manes (sic) and Means and Jane his Wife sold on 18 July 1747 the above to Joshua Bispham] ... And ... Thomas Moore and Elizabeth his Wife on 10 August 1747 sold to Joshua Bispham the aforesaid ... [36 acres together with part of the aforesaid 33 acres] ... making in the last mentioned Purchase 39 acres, 3 rods and 19 perches] ... Now this Indenture ... Bispham and Ruth his Wife ... [for 1200 pounds sell to] ... John Heustis ... all that the above mentioned five lots ... the first Lott is ... the Same purchased of Lancelet Brown whereon the Mantion House of the Said Bispham now Standeth ... [adjoining land owners or names - North side of Salem Road, John Cox] ... [1 acre and 2 rods] ... [#2] ... purchased of Nehemiah Haines ... [adjoining land owners or names - Salem Road, John Cox, lands of Nehemiah Haines deceased] ... [1 rod] ... [#3} ... purchased of Ephraim Haines ... adjoining ... the last mentioned Lot on which the Stone House now Standeth ... [adjoining land owners or names - North side of Salem Road, Ephraim Haines, Bispham's other

BURLINGTON COUNTY DEEDS - BOOK "C"

lands] ... [9 perches] ... [#4] ... purchased of John Means ... [adjoining land owners or names -line late of Joshua Humphries, north side of Salem Road, John Risdon's land, line of Nathan Middleton's land, lands then of Thomas Moores] ... [1 acre, 2 rods] ... [#5} ... purchased of thomas Moore ... [which he bought of Lancelet Brown and part of Francis Hogsett] ... [adjoining land owners or names - William Hooton's land, land late Joshua Humpries, Ephraim Haines, north side of Salem road corner to the Meeting House lands, lands late of Nathan Middleton dec^d, lot purchased of John Means] ... [39 acres, 3 rods, 19 perches] ...; [Signed - Jos^a Bispham, Ruth Bispham; witnesses - Thos Morton, John Cox, Abigail Cox.]

[p 161] **DEED OF TRUST**

10 October 1791 - Joseph Kimble of Mount Holly ... Township of Northampton ... Burlington ... West New Jersey Skipper and Martha his wife ... [granted to] ... Thomas Haines ... [of the same place] ... Husbandsman and Thomas Rogers ... Township of Burlington ... Husbandsman (two of the Creditors of the said Joseph Kimble) ... Whereas [Kimble is indebted unto Thomas Haines and Thomas Rogers ... and Kimble at a meeting with his other creditors sold his land to Haines & Rogers in Trust in order to be disposed of] ... Now this Indenture ... Joseph Kimble and Martha his wife ... [sold for 5 shillings] ... all that Messuage, Stable & Lots of Land in Mount Holly ... containing ... [1.25 acres] ... bounded by the land of several deeds made to Kimble ... [including land from Abraham Prickett on 3 October 1772 and John Budd on 16 November 1772] ... Also all Bonds, Bills, Notes and Book debts whatsoever due and owing unto the said Joseph Kimble ...; [Signed - Joseph Kimble made his mark when signing, Martha Kimble, Thomas Haines, Thomas Rogers Junr; witnesses - Peter Sbiras [?], Moses Kempton; recorded - 2 June 1792 by Lawrence, Clerk.]

[p 166] **WILLIAM KIMBLE ET AL to JOSEPH READ, ESQ^R**

24 October 1788 - William Kimble and Ruth his Wife, Samuel Kimble and Mary his Wife, all of the County of Burlington ... New Jersey which William and Samuel are acting Executors of the last Will ... of their Father Samuel Kimble deceased ... [sold to] ... Joseph Read Esqr of Mount Holly ... Attorney at Law ... Whereas Abel Pearson late of the said County deceased ... [sold on 11 November 1763] ... the Tract of Land herein after described with other lands unto Joshua Fenimore ... [And Pearson claimed right by a Conveyance from his Father James Pearson on 10 March 1755 in Liber L-folio 428 and which James Pearson purchased of John Fenimore by deed 9 October 1731 and which Fenimore had right to by last Will of his Father William Fenimore dated 14 May 1721 and proved in Burlington] ... [205 acres] ... became the Right of William Fenimore by ... the last Will ... of his Father Richard Fenimore and ... [7.5 acres the William purchased of Charles French and Thomas Middleton on 19 May 1719 and 2 acres more which William bought of Hugh Sharp by deed dated 4 May 1719] ... And whereas John Buzby late of Willing borough dec^d in his Lifetime ... was ... seized ... in a certain Piece of Meadow Ground ... [on Northampton River of 4.5 acres] ... and being so thereof seized he the Said John made his ... Will ... [on 7 January 1754 and appointed William Buzby his

BURLINGTON COUNTY DEEDS - BOOK "C"

****

Executor and which Will was recorded in the Perogative office in Liber 8-folio 298] ... and the Said Joshua Fenimore ... [was seized of several tracts sold with his Wife, Rebecca, on 9 October 1769 of 165 acres] ... being part of the before recited Lands unto Isaac Anderson ... [in Liber AB-folio 228 and Anderson and wife Sarah sold on 21 November 1774, 146 acres to John Irick, who sold it on 25 August 1778 to Samuel Kimble the Testator ... [[adjoining land owners or names - Rancocas Creek, Richard Fenimore line, line of Solomon Ridgway, land formerly Coates] ... [156 acres including the above 7.5 acres, the 4.5 acres and the remainder out of the above 205 acres] ... And whereas the said Samuel Kimble being so ... Seized by his last Will ... executed on ... [29 December 1786] ... did order the Executors ... to wit his Sons, William, Thomas and Samuel Kimble and his Son in Law Abraham Stockton ... And ... [his sons] ... became seized of the said Plantation as Tenants in Common ... [and Abraham Stockton and Thomas Kimble renouced on 14 March 1787 and 6 August 1787] ... And ... Thomas Kimble was by the Will legally entitled to one equal and undivided ... [1/3 part of the Plantation and Tract of Land and the said] ... Thomas Kimble and Priscilla his Wife ... conveyed [the same to William Kimble and William & Samuel Kimble became seized of the whole estate with 2/3 to William and 1/3 to Samuel] ... Now this Indenture ... [William & Samuel for 1200 pounds sold to] ... Joseph Read ... all the above bounded ... Land and Plantation as aforesaid purchased by the said Samuel Kimble from John Irick ...; [Signed - William, Kimble, Ruth Kimble, Samuel Kimble, Mary Kimble; witnesses - Zach[a] Rossell, Sam[l] I. Read.]

[10 February 1792 - William & Ruth Kimble and Mary Kimble, widow of Samuel Kimble, appeared and acknowledged the above deed in Court before Judge Peter Shiras, Esq[r].]

[p 171] JOSEPH READ ESQ[R] to WILLIAM KIMBLE

25 October 1788 - Joseph Read Esqr & Martha his Wife ... Township of Northampton ... Burlington ... New Jersey ... [sold to] ... William Kimble ... Township of Evesham ... Whereas the said Joseph read by ... [an indenture dated before this date] ... under the hands of William Kimble and Samuel Kimble Executors of the last Will ... of Samuel Kimble late of the City of Burlington deceased and their respective Wives Ruth and Mary Kimble became seized ... of Fee of ... a certain ... Plantation and Tract of Land ... in ... Township of Willingborough ... [166 acres] ... [which Samuel Kimble bought of John Irick on ... [25 August 1778] ... unto which the said William Kimble and Samuel Kimble had a legal Title ... by Virtue of the Said Will devising one third then of the said Samuel Kimble the Younger one third to William Kimble and one other third Part unto Thomas Kimble of whom the Said William Kimble had purchased ... Now this Indenture ... [sells for 700 pounds] ... all that certain ... Portion of the said Farm and Plantation ... [Rancocas Creek, Richard Fenimous[?], Solomon Ridgway's line formerly Coates, Ancocas Creek, Samuel O. Kemble] ... [158 acres, 10 square perches] ...; [Signed - Jos. Read, Martha Read; witnesses - Zacha Rossel, Saml. I. Read.]

[10 February 1792 - Both Joseph Read and Martha acknowledged the above deed in court.]

BURLINGTON COUNTY DEEDS - BOOK "C"

****

[p 174]   **JOSEPH MULLEN, SHERIFF to DANIEL DOUGHTY SMITH**

21 March 1785 - Joseph Mullen Esqr high Sheriff ... Burlington ... New Jersey ... [sold to] ... Daniel Doughty Smith ... Township of Springfield ... Burlington ... Whereas Joseph Lippincott ... Township of Springfield Son and Devisee of Job Lippincott late of the Said Township Deceased by virtue of the Will of his Said Father became lawfully Seized ... in a certain Tract of Land ... in the Said Township of Springfield ... [adjoining land owners or names - Barkers Creek, Jacob Shinn, land late John Wests (now belonging to William Lovet Smith), Charles Reads land (now said Daniel Doughty Smith), Thomas Foster, Samuel Bullus] ... [125 acres] .... which tract of Land became the Right of the Said Job Lippincott by ... the last Will ... of his Father Job Lippincott ... [who bought it from William Shinn on 5 April 1749] ... And Whereas one Thomas Gaskill ... [recovered against Joseph Lippincott a debt, as did Job Renear and William Pullen; the Sheriff confiscated property of Joseph Lippincott to pay same and sold it to the highest bidder, Daniel Doughty Smith for 1650 pds] ...; Signed - Joseph Mullen; witnesses - George West, Ezra Black.

[p 180]   **HANNAH LIPPINCOTT'S RELEASE OF DOWER**

23 March 1785 - ... Hannah Lippincott Widow of Job Lippincott late of Springfield deceased ... [for 5 shillings] ... paid by Danial Doughty Smith ... [relinquishes her Dower rights in the above land] ...; [Signed - Hannah Lippincott; witnesses - George West, Ezra Black.]

[p 182]   **WILLIAM ELDRIDGE to RICHARD COX**

12 September 1788 - ... William Eldridge Son of Jabez Eldridge late of the Township of Northampton ... Burlington ... New Jersey Deceased Cordwainer ... [sold to] ... Richard Cox of the Place aforesaid Merchant ... Whereas ... Jabez Eldridge ... by his last Will ... [dated 31 May 1780] ... devised unto his Son William Eldridge ... the House and Lot where the said Jabez Eldridge then lived ... on the South side of Mill Street in Mount Holly ... [which Jabez bought from Haron Brian and Johannah his Wife on 4 September 1756] ... which Said Lot of Land and Premises Thomas Bryant Father of the Said Haron Briant became seized ... and made his last Will ... [on 4 February 1733] ... and therein did give and devise the ... Lot of Land unto his four Sons ... Haron, Samuel, Joseph and Benjamin ... And whereas the Said Benjamin and Joseph dying without Issue so the aforesaid Land descended to the Said Haron and Samuel Bryant ... [and Samuel sold his share on 1 August 1753 to Haron] ... Now this Indenture ... [sells the land to Richard Cox for 50 pounds and 10 shillings] ... one ... Lot ... on the South Side of Mill Street in Mount Holly ... [adjoining land owners or names - Jabez Eldridge's land, John West, Wall of the cellar of the late dwelling House of Said Jabez Eldridge] ... [18 sq. Perches] ...; [Signed - William Eldridge; witnesses - Patrick Gamble, Moses Kempton.]

[11 February 1792 - Moses Kempton acknowledged the above deed before the Court.]

BURLINGTON COUNTY DEEDS - BOOK "C"

[p 186] THOMAS HAINES ET AL to RICHARD COX

2 April 1792 - Thomas Haines ... Township of Northampton ... Burlington ... New Jersey Husbandman and Thomas Rogers ... Township of Burlington ... Husbandman ... [sell to] ... Richard Cox of Mount Holly ... in the Township of Northampton ... Merchant ... Whereas Joseph Kimble ... [by deed dated 3 October 1772] ... purchased from Abraham Pricket and Esther his Wife ... land in Mount Holly ... [And the Said Kimble on 16 November 1772 purchased of John Budd land] ... adjoining the first mentioned Lot of Land & Premises ... And whereas ... Kimble ... did Mortgage the aforesaid two Lots ... to Solomon Ridgway, Robert S. Jones and John Black Esquire Commissioners of the Loan Office ... And whereas ... Joseph Kimble neglected the Payment of the Interest ... [and the land was sold by Joseph Kimble and Martha his Wife on 10 October 1791 to Thomas Haines and Thomas Rogers party to these Presents in Trust ... [for his debts] ... Now this Indenture ... [Haines and Rogers sell the land for 236 pounds to Richard Cox] ... [adjoining land owners or names - road leading from Philadelphia to Moutn Holly, Ancocas Creek, Church lot] ... [1 acre, 1 rod, 1 sq. Perch] ...; [Signed - Thomas Haines, Thomas Rogers Junr; witnesses - George Budd, Moses Kempton, Thomas Haines signed before Peter Shiras and Joseph Cooper.]

[p 191] JOHN BISPHAM to RICHARD COX

8 April 1792 - John Bispham of Mount Holly ... Township of Northampton ... Burlington ... New Jersey Tanner acting Executor of the Estate of his Father John Bispham late of the Same Place deceased ... at the time of his Death was seized ... in two Lots of Land and Premises ... in Mount Holly ... [which Bispham owned by deeds dated 28 September 1776 and 26 April 1777] ... the former ... [bought from William Calvert and Martha his Wife and the latter from William Calvert] ... And ... John Bispham ... by his last Will ... [dated 9 May 1791 appointed] ... his Son the Said John Bispham party to these Presents to be acting Executor in the whole of his Estate untill his Son William Bispham Should attain the Age of ... [21 years] ... and ... [empowered John to convey the above land] ... Now this Indenture ... [sells for 45 pounds the land to Richard Cox] ... [adjoining land owners or names - Ancocas Creek below the Bridge in Mount Holly, formerly land of William Calvert and since occupied by William Stretch, road leading over the Bridge to Philadelphia, Lot formerly of Henry Paxson Esqr now Alexander Shiras] ... [1 rod, 131/360 sq. Parts of a perch] ... which two lots ... [are a part of the larger Land William Calvert bought from Henry Paxson and Martha his Wife on ... [14 December 1772 and Paxson purchased it from Patrick Reynolds on ... [10 June 1754] ... with the other part a part of larger land bought by Paxson of John Woolman who purchased it from Thomas Reynolds and John Bispham Executors of the last Will ... of Patrick Reynolds ... with other lands purchased of Daniel Wells, who purchased it from Nathaniel Cripps to whom the Same was Surveyed...; [Signed - John Bispham; witnesses - Jos. Hatkinson, Peter Shiras.]

BURLINGTON COUNTY DEEDS - BOOK "C"

[p 196]   **LOAN OFFICE to JOSEPH KEMBLE**

4 March 1788 - Commissioners of the Loan Office ... Burlington ... New Jersey ... [sold to] ... Joseph Kemble of Northampton ... [for 300 pounds] ... Lots of Land ... in the Township of Northampton ... Burlington ... [adjoining land owners or names - Ancocas Creek, land late of Caleb Shinn now of Joseph Kemble] ... The second Lot ... [adjoining land owners or names - land late of Thomas Ivins] ...; [Signed - Solomon Ridgway, R. Shettel Jones, John Black; witnesses - John Lee, John Taylor, Thos Rodman.]

[p 197]   **GEORGE BOWNE to JAMES VERREE**

18 September 1780 - George Bowne ... City of Burlington ... New Jersey and Abigail his Wife ... [sold to] ... James Verree of the same Place ... Whereas Mahlon Stacy late of the County of Burlington by Virtue of a Deed ... [from John Robertson and Thomas Lambert became seized of two whole properties and sold on 29 January 1677 1/15 part unto Thomas Foulk which he had surveyed 320 acres of land in 1684 and he sold on 10 March 1724] ... the tract of land unto his son Thomas Foulke ... And Whereas the said Thomas Fouolke the Younger ... [sold on 29 September 1737] part of the said tract ... unto Richard Skirm ... [who sold it on 15 May 1739 unto Joseph Gardiner, who by his last Will dated 5 June 1742 gave his Executors the power to sell the land and they sold it on 2 May 1743 to Ephram Lockwood, who sold it on 1 April 1746 to Jacob Lawrence, who sold it on 25 March 1764 to his brother John Lawrence, who] ... so seized Died, having first made his last Will ... [on 16 January 1767] ... and appointed his Wife Hannah and his Sons Benjamin and Jacob his Executrix and Executors giving them full power to sell ... [50 acres of the said Tract for payment of debts] ... and the residue there of he gave and devised unto his Son Jacob Lawrence ... Whereas the said Executors ... did by deed ... dated 25 March 1768 sell the 50 acres to William Potts, who on the 36 of March in the said year ... [sold it to Jacob Lawrence] ... who became seized of the whole tract ... [Excepting .25 acre lot sold to Charles McClean; and Joacob Lawrence and Elizabeth his Wife sold on 17 March 1724 the tract to Saml Buntin, who with his wife Septeme sold it on 23 September 1776] ... to Henery Haydock and George Bowne The partt heretofore as Tenants in Common ... [and Haydock sold his share to George Bowne] ... Now this Indenture ... George Bowne and Abigail his Wife ... [sell for 1500 pounds] ... his Farm, Plantation and ... Land ... in the Township of Chesterfield ... Burlington ... [adjoining land owners or names- Crosswicks Creek, road leading to the Hose of Joseph Douglass, Joel Middleton, Amos Ellisons Lot, land formerly of John Lovells, land formerly William Bunting now Middleton] ... [220 acres] ...; [Signed - George Bowne, Abigail Bowne; witnesses - Jas. Smith, Daniel Ellis.]

[James Verree released George Bown from all claims Verre has on the .25 acres sold to McClean; dated - 1 March 1783; witnesses - Joseph Smith, Daniel Ellis.]

BURLINGTON COUNTY DEEDS - BOOK "C"

****

[10 July 1792 - Joseph Smith ... "one of the People called Quakers" ... declared before James Kinsey, the Chief Justice of the Supreme Court of New Jersey, that he saw the Bowes sign the above deed.]

[p 205]   **JAMES VERRE to JEREMIAH SMITH**

26 March 1783 - James Verree ... City of Burlington ... Burlington ... New Jersey Gentleman ... [sold to] ... Jeremiah Smith ... [of the same place] ... Yeoman ... Whereas George Bowne ... and Abigail his wife ... [on 18 September 1780 sold to James Verree] ... All that certain Farm Plantation and tract of Land ... in Chesterfield ... [this is the same land as in the above deed] ...; [Signed - James Verree; witnesses - Joseph Bloomfield, John Phillips, Edward Collins.]

[p 209]   **JEREMIAH SMITH to DOCT^R FRANCIS BOWES SAYRE**

6 April 1792 - Jeremiah Smith late of the City and County of Burlington ... New Jersey yeoman but now of ... Philadelphia ... Pennsylvania Shopkeeper and Margaret his Wife ... [sold to] ... Francis Bowes Sayre of Crosswicks ... Township of Chesterfield ... Burlington ... New Jersey aforesaid Doctor of Physick ... [for 700 pounds] ... Certain Plantation ... and meadow ... in ... Chesterfield ... [adjoining land owners or names - Crosswicks Creek, Samuel Radford, the great road, Joseph Meir, Nathan Middleton] ... [60 acres] ... [which was part of 220 acres Jacob Lawrence of Chesterfield ... Farmer and Elizabeth his Wife sold on 17 March 1774] ... with an exception of ... [.25 acres] ... property of Charles Mc Clean unto ... Samuel Bunting ... [and his wife Septime, who sold it on 23 September 1776 to Henry Haycock and George Brown as Tenants in Common and Haycock sold his share to George Brown and Abigail his wife, who sold it on 18 September 1780 to James Verree, who sold it on 26 March 1783 to Jeremiah Smith] ...; [Signed - Jeremiah Smith; Margret Smith; witnesses - Benjamin Lenton, Lyhern Warren.]

[p 215]   **JOSEPH WARTON JUN^R ET AL to JOSEPH TALMAN, JUN^R**

28 June 1763 - Joseph Warton Junr ... City of Philadelphia ... Pennsylvania Merch^t and Sarah his wife (late Sarah Talman), John Lawrence ... City of Burlington ... New Jersey Esqr and Martha his Wife (late Martha Talman) which same Sarah & Martha are Coheirs & Devisees of Job Tallman late of Mansfield ... Burlington ... deceased ... [sold to] ... Joseph Talman Junr of the township of Mansfield ...Whereas John Talman of Long Island ... New York was ... seized ... of and in two Certain ... Tracts of Land and Meadow ... in Burlington ... [which was sold on 2 December 1727 to] ... Job Talman then of Long Island ... and which two parcels of Land are a part of ... [500 acres] ... know by the name of Spring hill formerly Surveyed by John Underhill ... the first piece ... of Land ... [adjoining land owners or names - Land late Joseph Shreves, James Antrim] ... [112 acres] ... The Other Parcel ... [12.5 acres] ... And Whereas Samuel Andrews late of Mansfield deceased ... seized of ... Land ... at a Place Called Spring hill in Mansfield ... [and Andrews made his Will, dated 20 September 1693 and devised to his Daughter Mary Andrews 100 acres when she should reach 21 years] ... and Soon

BURLINGTON COUNTY DEEDS - BOOK "C"

after dyed the said ... [100 acres] ... being part of the lands of the Said Samuel at Spring hill ... And ... [on 7 May 1710, the 100 acres] ... was ... Surveyed to Mary Andrews pursuant to the Will ... Out & from others of the land Whereof the Said Samuel Andrews Dyed Seized ... and by a Certificate ... it is ... described ... as ... Surveyed to Mary Andrews ... [adjoining land owners or names - Nathan Folwell, Spring hill Brook] ... And Whereas the Said Mary Andrews ... by deed ... [sold to Joseph Talman on 21 April and 22 April 1732 to Job Talman as Joint Tenants, who then divided the land on 16 March 1747, with Joseph quit claiming his share of the land to Job Talman] ... [adjoining land owners or names - land on the South side of Spring hill Brook, William Black, John Folwell] ... [52.5 acres] ... And ... [Job Talman now seized of the three tracts made his Will on 6 January 1758] ... and devised unto his two daughters ... Sarah Talman & Martha Talman ... and soon after died ... [and the two daughters became seized of the land and premises and then married] ... Now This Indenture ... [the two daughters and their husbands sell the land for 1,100 pounds to] ... Joseph Talman Junr ...; [Signed - Joseph Warton Junr, Sarah Warton; John Lawrence, Martha Lawrence; witnesses - Robt Smith, Frans Gibbon.]

[p 225]   **DIVISION OF PROPERTY**

6 August 1792 - Jacob Shinn & Samuel Atkinson ... township of Springfield ... Burlington ... New Jersey ... for the final Settling ... the lines of our adjoining lands ... [adjoining land owners or names - South Branch of Assisskunk or Barkers Creek, land Jacob Shinn purchased of Henry Lishman, John Ridgway] ...; [Signed - Jacob Shinn made his mark when signing, Saml Atkinson; witnesses - Daniel D. Smith, Moses Kempton.]

[p 227]   **JOSEPH BLOOMFIELD to CAPT. PETER HODGKINSON**

20 May 1792 - Joseph Bloomfield ... City and County of Burlington ... New Jersey Esquire Counsellor at Law & Mary his Wife ... sold to] ... Captain Peter Hodgkinson of the Same place ... [for 750 pounds] ... Land ... in the City of Burlington .. [adjoining land owners or names - Delaware River, High Street, Pearl Street, land in possession of Col. John Cox, land sold by Bloomfield to Bethanah Hodgkinson, Third Street] .. [land which Bloomfield purchased of William Skies on 17 October 1782 and Margaret Morris on 12 October 1781] ... Excepting ... [land sold to Bethanah Hodgkinson] ...; [Signed - Joseph Bloomfield, Mary Bloomfield; witnesses - Mary Ann Mc Ilvaine, Joseph Mc Ilvaine; Silvester D. Russell, Fred Kissleman.]

[p 232]   **BENJAMIN SYKES to SAMUEL STILES**

15 December 1784 - Benjamin Sykes ... Township of Chesterfield ... Burlington ... New Jersey and Hannah his Wife ... [sold to] ... Samuel Stiles ... City of Burlington ... Cordwainer ... Whereas John Sykes late ... Township of Chesterfield ... Deceased ... was seized of several lots of land by deed dated 23 January 1735 from Isaac DeCou late of Burlington deceased] ... And ... John Sykes ... so

BURLINGTON COUNTY DEEDS - BOOK "C"

seized made his Will ... 1 November 1769] and ... did give ... his House and Lot & Water Lot ... unto his son Benjamin Sykes ... Now This Indenture ... [they sell for 30 pounds, the house, land and water lot fronting the Delaware River and Pearl Street] ... [adjoining land owners or names - land formerly of Jeremiah Bass now to the Estate of John Watson, Pearl Street] ...; [Signed - Benjamin Sykes, Hannah Sykes; witnesses - Peter Talman, George Hulme.]

[p 236]   **SAMUEL STILES to JAMES MILLER**

29 August 1792 - Samuel Stiles ... City of Burlington ... Burlington ... New Jersey Cordwainer and Jane his Wife ... [sold to] ... James Miller ... City of Philadelphia ... Pennsylvania Weaver ... Whereas John Sykes late of the Township of Chesterfield ... Burlington Deceased ... [was seized of several lots in the City of Burlington and he made his Will on 1 November 1769 and devised the lots to Son Benjamin, who sold them to Samuel Stiles on 15 December 1784] ... Now This Indenture ... [for 200 pounds sold the property in the above deed] ... ; [Signed - Samuel Stiles, Jane Stiles; witnesses - Thos Rodman, Samuel Rogers.]

[p 242]   **ABRAHAM HEWLINGS JUN^R, SHERIFF to NATHAN COMBS**

26 June 1790 - Abraham Hewlings Junr Esquire late High Sheriff ... Burlington ... New Jersey ... [sold to] ... Nathan Combs of the Same Place ... [the Sheriff was directed to confiscate the property of Stillman Chapman by a Judgment won by Joseph Milnor, and the Sheriff took a brick dwelling House, blacksmith shop and land and sold it to Nathan Combs, the highest bidder for 25 pounds, 10 shillings] ... [adjoining land owners or names - Front Street, Berney Johnson, the Alley from Water Street to Second Street] ... [for 60 perches] ...; [Signed - Abraham Hewlings, Sheriff; witnesses - John How, Joel Gibbs, Jacob Wolcott.]

[p 246]   **RELEASE OF THE EXECUTORS OF JEREMIAH HAINES**

17 August 1792 - ... Jeremiah Haines late ... township of Northampton ... Burlington ... West New Jersey deceased by his last Will ... [dated 19 September 1774] ... bequeath ... unto his two daughters Rebecca Haines who since married John White late of mount Holly deceased & Frances Haines who Since married John Hilliard late of the township aforesaid deceased ... Also ... unto his three daughters ... Sarah the wife of Isaac Hilliard and the aforesaid Rebecca "now relict & widow of John White deceased" & Frances "now Relict widow of John Hilliard deceased" ... [and made] ... his Son William Haines and the above ... Isaac Hilliard Executors ... Now Know ye that we ... Isaac Hilliard, Rebecca White & Frances Hilliard ... received of & from ... William Haines one of the Executors ... [100 pounds ... and also all shares of the Personal estate of Jeremiah Haines] and Release ... [the Executors] ...; [Signed - Rebecca White in presence of Moses Kempton, Frances Hilliard in the presence of Charlotte Haines, and Isaac Hilliard in the presence of Rheuban Hilliard.]

BURLINGTON COUNTY DEEDS - BOOK "C"

[p 250] **SETTLEMENT OF LAND BOUNDARIES**

9 November 1766 - I, Micajah Reeve of Northampton ... Burlington ... West New Jersey (Yeoman) ... [for 5 shillings, sell to] ... Jeremiah Haines of the Same place (Yeoman) ... [for settling the line of Partition] ... between our lands & Plantations where we now dwell in Northampton ... I ... quit claim ... unto Jeremiah Haines ... all that tract of Land ... where he now dwelleth ... [adjoining land owners or names - land Henery Paxson purchased of Walter Reeve, South main branch of Ancokus Creek] ...; [Signed - Micajah Reeve; witnesses - Henery Paxson, John Burr Junr.]

[p 252] **ABRAHAM HEWLINGS, SHERIFF to NATHAN COMBS**

18 May 1790 - Abraham Hewlings high Sheriff ... Burlington ... New Jersey ... [sold to] ... Nathan Combs of Lamberton ... County & State aforesaid ... [the Sheriff obtained a writ from the Sheriff of Hunterdon County to seize the property of] ... Elijah Bond in possession of Isaac DeCou Executor ... which William C. Housten one of the Attornies ... recovered ... whereof ... [and against] ... Isaac DeCou Executor of Elijah Bond deceased ... [and where the Hunterdon Sheriff returned saying Isaac DeCou had none of the property and Houston testified that DeCou had the goods of Elijah Bond dec'd, but Abraham Hewlings seized one House & Lot of land in Lumberton and sold it for 500 pounds] ...; [Signed - Abraham Hewlings, Sheriff; witnesses - Geor. Mitchell, Thos D. Hewlings, Abr^m Hewlings, Junr.].

[p 258] **ELIJAH B. JERVIS to NATHAN COMBS**

28 July 1789 - Elijah B. Jervis of Chester County ... Pennsylvania & Elizabeth his Wife ... [sold to] ... Nathan Combs ... township of Nottingham ... Burlington ... New Jersey ... [for 60 pounds] ... two lots ... of Land ... in Lumberton ... township of Nottingham ... part of a Lot of five acres Late Elijah Bond ... [sold to Elijah B. Jervis on 23 August 1784] ... 1st Lott ... [adjoining land owners or names - Water Street, Nathan Combs] ... [.25 acres & 4 perches] ... 2nd lott ... [adjoining land owners or names - Water Street, Delaware River] ... [33 perches] ...; [Signed - Elijah B. Jervis, Elizabeth Jervis; witnesses - Jacob Servoss, William Dean.]

[p 261] **POWER OF ATTORNEY**

21 January 1792 - We, Thomas Cooper and Elizabeth Cooper ... Wife ... Township of Northampton ... Burlington ... West New Jersey ... appoint Jno Cooper & Jno Butterworth ... [both of the same place aforesaid] ... our true & Lawful Attorneys ... [re: the selling of their lands ...; [Signed - Both Thomas and Elizabeth Cooper made their marks when signing; witnesses - Mary Eyre, John Burr Junr.]

[Mary Eyre & John Burr Junr were identified as "of the People called Quakers".]

(91)

BURLINGTON COUNTY DEEDS - BOOK "C"

[p 264] JAMES MILLER to RICHARD GIBBS

26 October 1792 - James Miller ... City of Burlington ... New Jersey and Ann his Wife ... [sold to] ... Richard Gibbs of Bensalem ... Bucks ... Pennsylvania ... Whereas John Sykes late of Chesterfield ... Burlington Deceased ... [was seized of several lots and he made his Will on 1 November 1769 & he sold land to Samuel Stiles, who with his wife, Jane, sold to James Miller, on 29 August 1792, the lot with the building] ... Now This Indenture ... [sells for 180 pounds] ... [adjoining land owners or names - Delaware River, Pearl Street, River Street] ...; [Signed - James Miller, Anne Miller; witnesses - Thos Rodman, Daniel Ellis.]

[p 269] SETH LUCAS to OKEY HOAGLAND

10 January 1792 - Seth Lucas ... Philadelphia ... Pennsylvania ... [sold to] ... Okey Hoagland ... City of Burlington ... New Jersey ... Whereas Robert Lucas late of Willingborough ... Burlington ... [was seized at his death of plantation and land in Willingborough and he left a Will and bequeathed unto his] ... son Benjamin Lucas & to my grand Son Seth Lucas ... my farm and Plantation whereon I now Dwell ... to be Equally divided between them ... [And] ... Seth Lucas ... [so seized made his Will on 25 January 1773 & gave his plantation to his two] sons Robert & Seth to be divided between them] ... Now This Indenture Seth Lucas ... [sold for 163 pounds] ... [adjoining land owners or names - Jacob Perkins, Delaware River, land purchased of Samuel Newton] ... [27 acres and 28 perches] ... [Signed - Seth Lucas; witnesses - George Eyre, Henery P. Haines, Jacob Wolcott.]

[p 273] ROBERT LUCAS QUIT CLAIM

12 January 1792 - Robert Lucas ... Township of Willingborough ... Burlington ... New Jersey Yeoman ... [for 5 shillings quit claimed his interest in the above property] ... to Okey Hoagland.

[p 275] SAMUEL NEWTON to OKEY HOAGLAND

8 November 1791 - Samuel Newton ... Township of Willingborough ... Burlington ... West New Jersey Farmer ... [sold to] ... Okey Hoagland ... City of Burlington ... [County and State aforesaid] ... In Keeper ... [for 650 pounds] ... all this Messuage and Plantation ... in the Township of Willingborough ... [adjoining land owners or names - [Delaware River, Robert Lucas, Joseph Fenimore, Jn° Peaches] ... [100 acres] ... Secondly ... [adjoining land owners or names - Delaware River, Henery Dill, road from Burlington to Joseph Fenimores] ... [9.75 acres] ... The Third ... tract is ... [21 acres] ... of Flatts frontin the before recited lands and Plantation ... on the River Delaware Surveyed to Henery Dill ... [all the tracts contain 130 acres, 3 rods] ... [and Samuel Newton is vested in the land by deed from Joseph Fenimore and Ann his Wife on 12 April 1771] ...; [Signed - Samuel Newton; witnesses - Robt Pearson, Henery P. Haines.]

BURLINGTON COUNTY DEEDS - BOOK "C"

****

[p 279]   **MANUMISSION OF SIRO**

9 September 1789 - ... William Wood ... Township of Chesterfield ... Burlington ... did this day ... Manumit and set Free his Slave named Siro ... before Isaac Cowgill and George Anderson - Justices.

[p 279]   **MANUMISSION OF JACK**

9 September 1789 - ... William Wood ... Township of Chesterfield ... Burlington ... did this day ... Manumit and set Free his Slave named Jack ... before Isaac Cowgill and George Anderson - Justices.

[p 280]   **MANUMISSION OF GEORGE DILLON**

19 April 1790 - We the subscribers, two ... Justices of the Peace ... Burlington ... Joseph Woodward ... Township of Chesterfield ... did Manumit and set free his Negro Slave named George Dillon ...; [Signed - Isaac Cowgill, John Pope.

[p 280]   **MANUMISSION OF JACK DILLON**

19 April 1790 - We the subscribers, two ... Justices of the Peace ... Burlington ... Joseph Woodward ... Township of Chesterfield ... did Manumit and set free his Negro Slave named Jack Dillon ...; [Signed - Isaac Cowgill, John Pope.

[p 281]   **MANUMISSION OF RUTH LIPP**

4 June 1791 - We do ... Certify that ... Benjamin Shreve ... Township of Mansfield ... Burlington ... brought before two of the Overseerers of the Poor ... and two ... Justices of the Peace ... His Negro Slave named Ruth Lipp ... also not under ... [21 years or over 35 years] ...; [Signed - John Pope, Ars Gaunt; Caleb Shreive and Clayton Newbold, Overseerers of the Poor.]

14 June 1791 - I do ... Certify that I have this day Manumitted and set free my Negro Woman named Ruth Lipp She between ... [21 and 35 years]...; [Signed - Benjamin Shreive; witnesses - John Pope, Asr. Gaunt.]

[p 282]   **MANUMISSION OF DENNIS ROCKER**

30 April 1792 - We John Davison and Abigail his Wife Administrators to the Estate of Anthony Applegate deceased do set free from Bondage Dennis Rocker a Negro man belonging to said Estate for ...[5 shillings] ... by him to us in hand paid and now do hereby release all claim to his Labour to his person and Estate he may procure ...; [Signed - John Davison, Abigail Davison made her mark when signing; witnesses - Samuel Stockton, Uz Gauntt.]

BURLINGTON COUNTY DEEDS - BOOK "C"

[7 December 1792 - Uz Gauntt ... "of the People Called Quakers" acknowledged that he saw the Davisons sign the above manumission.]

[p 283] **MANUMISSION OF WILLIAM ROCKER**

13 April 1792 - We John Davison and Abigail his Wife Administrators to the Estate of Anthony Applegate deceased do set free from Bondage William Rocker a Negro man belonging to said Estate for ...[5 shillings] ... by him to us in hand paid and now do hereby release all claim to his Labour to his person and Estate he may procure ...; [Signed - John Davison, Abigail Davison made her mark when signing; witnesses - Samuel Stockton, Uz Gauntt.]

[7 December 1792 - Uz Gauntt ... "of the People Called Quakers" acknowledged that he saw the Davisons sign the above manumission.]

[p 284] **ISRAEL HARRISON to WILLIAM PHARES**

19 March 1791 - Israel Harrison, Bricklayer of ... Township of Hanover ... Burlington ... New Jersey ... [sold to] ... William Phares Black smith ... [of the same place for 600 pounds] ... a Certain piece ... of Land ... in the Township of New Hanover ... Burlington ... [adjoining land owners or names - land of Samuel Emley, Samuel Wardel, Thomas Wright, land of heirs of James Starkey, lands of heirs of Peter Harrison, Joseph Rogers] ... [210 acres] ... [which Harrison obtained by deed from his Grand Farther Richard Harrison Deces'd] ... all except about ... [60 acres] ... of s^d land purchased by Samuel Emley and about ... [12 acres] ... purchased by Jacob Andrews deceas'd which lieth and about the Village of Jacobs Town Now in possession of Jacob Warrin ... also one Small House with ... [.25 acres] ... in possession of Edith Roberts in S^d Village and a small lot where the Skool house Now Stands for use of a Skool So long as the Neighbors Shall think proper to occupie it for that use, and Likewise the Meeting house lot ... Which Said remainder ceveyed by S^d Israel Harrison ... to ... William Phares ... [137 acres] ...; [Signed - Israel Harrison; witnesses - John Antram, Jonathan Cowperthwite.]

[p 287] **BENJAMIN THOMPSON to GEORGE LESLIE**

11 September 1792 - Benjamin Thompson ... Essex ... New Jersey ... [sold to] ... George Leslie ... Morris ... Whereas George Willock late of Amboy Deceased was ... Seized ... [of land] ... and ... made his ... Will ... [on 3 January 1723] ... [and devised a share of the property to George Leslie and John Richee in equal shares; and George Leslie made a Will on 20 May 1792 and gave his shares to his sons] ... George Willocks Leslie, John Leslie, Edmond Leslie and James Leslie ... [to be equally divided but by a Codicil set forth his having a son born Since the making of his Will, named William Leslie, he ordered William also to have an equal share] ... to his Nephew Benjamin Thompson ... And Now this Indenture ... [for $14 sells to] ... George Leslie ... all his one fifth part ... [to the property

BURLINGTON COUNTY DEEDS - BOOK "C"

devised by his Uncle William's Will, Deceased] ...; [Signed - Benjamin Thomson; witnesses - John Clark, William Boote.]

[p 290]   **MANUMISSION OF JAMES HOOPER**

12 February 1787 - We do ... Certify that ... Isaiah Hains ... Township of Evesham ... Burlington ... brought before us two of the Overseers of the Poor ... and two of the Justices of the Peace ... his Slave Named James Hooper ... who ... is not ... [under 21 or over 35 years] ...; [Signed - Enoch Evans, Wm Evans, Overseerers of the Poor; Josiah Foster, Reese Edwards, Justices of the Peace.]

We the Subscribers ... Certify that ... James Hooper is Manumitted and Set Free by his Master Isaiah Haines ... Township of Evesham ... 21 March 1787 ...; [Signed - Josiah Foster, Reece Edwards.

[p 291]   **MANUMISSION OF CLEMMONT WATERMAN**

4 August 1792 - We do ... Certify that ... Isaiah Hains ... Township of Evesham ... Burlington ... brought before us two of the Overseers of the Poor ... and two of the Justices of the Peace ... his Slave Named Clemmont Waterman ... who ... is not ... [under 21 or over 35 years] ...; [Signed - Isaiah Hains; witnesses - Nehemiah Hains, Josiah Bispham - Overseerers of the Poor; Josiah Foster, Reece Edwards - Justices of the Peace.]

[p 292]   **MANUMISSION OF GEORGE DILLON**

We do hereby Certify that on ... [19 April 1790] ... Joseph Woodward ... Township of Chesterfield ... Burlington ... brought before us ... his Negro Slave named George Dillon ... [not under 21 or over 35 years] ...; [Signed - Isaac Cowgill, John Pope - Justices of the Peace; John Thorn, John Middleton - Overseerers of the Poor.]

[p 293]   **RICHARD STOCKTON to JOHN WRIGHT**

6 June 1792 - Richard Stockton ... City of Philadelphia ... [sold to] ... John Wright ... township of Hanover ... Burlington ... New Jersey (yeoman) ... Whereas William Stockton late of Springfield ... Burlington ... deceased ... [was seized of a tract of land in said township of Springfield and resurveyed by Isaac Decow on 4 April 1740 and William made his Will on 8 April 1780 and devised the same to his two sons Samuel and Richard Stockton. They divided the same and exchanged their parts by Samuel Stockton and wife Ann by deed conveying to Richard Stockton on 18 August 1784] ... Now this Indenture ... Richard Stockton ... [sells for 1,490 pounds] ... [adjoining land owners or names - John Black, Jobe Stockton, land formerly of Joseph Newbold, Samuel Sikes/Likes] ... [113 acres and 36 perches] ...; [Signed - Richard Stockton; witnesses - Samuel Stockton, Ann Stockton, Samuel Leslie.]

BURLINGTON COUNTY DEEDS - BOOK "C"

[8 December 1795 - Samuel Stockton ... "one of the People Called Quakers" acknowledged the above deed indicating that he saw Richard Stockton sign same.]

[p 296]   **JOHN DONALDSON to NATHAN COMBES**

8 December 1792 - John Donaldson ... City of Philadelphia ... Pennsylvania ... Merchant and Sarah his Wife of the first part, George Campbell Esquire of the same place and Helen his Wife of the second part, and Nathan Combes ... Township of Nottingham ... Burlington ... New Jersey of the third part ... [John Donaldson and Sarah, and George Campbell and Helen for 1,125 pounds sold to John Donaldson and George Campbell who sell to Nathan Combes] ... in his actual Possession now being, by ... a Bargain and Sale to him ... [for 30 years] ... bearing the day of the date of these presents ... All ... that tract of land and premises ... in the Township of Nottingham ... on the river Delaware ... [adjoining land owners - John Douglass, the Old Ferry tract, John Steven's Esqr, Hugh Runyon, the road from Trenton to Crosswicks, John Cox Esq] ... [for 69.8 acres] ... also that lot of woodland ... between the Crosswicks Road and Lamberton ...[adjoining land owners or names - John Cox Esq, Moore Furman, Nathan Combes, the road from Trenton to Crosswicks, the old road from Trenton to Lamberton, Barnt De Kligns land commonly called Bonds Farms, James Mathis] ... [25.25 acres] ... Also ... woodland in Nottingham township ... [adjoining land owners or names - the road from Trenton to Crosswicks, Moore Furman, Barnt Deckligen, land late in Possession of Mrs Mary Mitchell] ...; [Signed - John Donaldson, Sarah Donaldson, George Campbell, Helen Campbell; witnesses - William Campbell, Isaac Hampole.]

[p 302]   **JOHN DONALDSON to NATHAN COMBES**

[This recording appears to be a repeat recording of the above deed.]

[p 306]   **HUGH RUNYON to EPHRAIM OLDEN**

30 May 1792 - Hugh Runyon ... township of Kingwood ... Hunterdon ... New Jersey and Sarah his Wife ... [sells to] ... Ephraim Olden of ... Township of Nottingham ... Burlington ... [for 460 pounds] ... Land ... in possession of Olden in ... Nottingham ... [adjoining land owners or names - Edmond Beakes on Broad Street, Lott's line] ... [1.5 acres] ... 2nd lot ... [adjoining land owners or names - Queen Street, Thomas Jenny, John Cox's land] ... [Signed - Hugh Runyon, Sarah Runyon; witnesses - Henry Keens, John Keens.]

[p 308]   **JOHN HAINS to JACOB AUSTIN ET AL**

11 August 1787 - John Hains ... Township of Evesham ... Burlington ... New Jersey Yeoman and Martha his Wife ... [sold to] ... Jacob Austin and Caleb Austin of the same place Yeoman ... [for 270 pounds] ... Two certain pieces ... of Land ... in the Township aforesaid near Lumberton on the South

BURLINGTON COUNTY DEEDS - BOOK "C"

****

Main Branch of Rancokes Creek opposite the Vilage called Lumberton ... [adjoining land owners or names - lands late of Samuel Moore, the road from the Country to Lamberton, the corner to Widow Moores Lott] ... [30 acres] ... The second Lott Called Moores Nook is Adjoining the first ... [adjoining land owners or names - Samuel Moore] ... [13 acres] ... land was part of the Estate of Samuel Moore Deceased and sold by John Hollinshead Esq[r] High Sheriff ... to ... John Hains ...; [Signed - John Hains, Martha Hains; witnesses - Buddl Shinn, Corneley Brunir.]

[1 November 1792 - Both John Hains and Martha Hains acknowledged the above deed.]

[p 312]   **DAVID A. OGDEN, ESQ[R] to DORCAS HAINS**

23 November 1792 - David A. Ogden ... New Jersey Esquire ... [sold to] ... Dorcas Hains ... Township of Evesham ... Burlington Widow ... Whereas Jacob Wolcott High Sheriff ... Burlington ... [seized the estate of] ... Henry Pendergrass Haines ... a plantation in the Township of Evesham ... [200 acres] ... which was Devised to the said Henry by the last Will ... of his Father Nathan Haines ... [and sold it to David A. Ogden on the 16th of August last] ... [for 700 pounds] ...; [Signed - David A. Odgen; witnesses - Robert Pearson, Joseph Hollinshead.]

[p 315]   **JACOB WOLCOTT, SHERIFF to DAVID A. OGDEN**

22 November 1792 - Jacob Wolcott High Sheriff ... Burlington ... New Jersey ... [sold to] ... David A. Ogden ... Esquire ... Whereas Henry Pendergrass Hains [by the last Will of his Father Nathan Hains late of Evesham ... Deceased] ... after the Decease of his Mother Dorcus Hains ... And whereas one Apollo Woodward and Abijah Hammond ... [obtained Judgments against Henry Pendergrass Hains , the Sheriff confiscated the land and sold it at auction to David A. Ogden for 700 pounds] ..; [Signed - Jocob Wolcott Sheriff; witnesses - Robert Pearson, Joseph Hollinshead, Jun[r].]

[p 319]   **JOHN HOLLINSHEAD, SHERIFF to JOHN HAINS**

11 August 1787 - John Hollinshead Esquire high Sheriff ... Burlington ... [sold to] ... John Hains ... Township of Evesham Farmer ... [A Judgment was obtained against Jacob Austin and Caleb Austin Executors of the Will of Samuel Moore Deceased; and Rebecca White and Thomas Rodman Executors of the Will of John White deceased] ... Whereas by ... [the last Will of] ... Samuel Moore Father to Samuel Moore ... above ... became seized of ... Land ... in the Township of Evesham ... [290 acres] ... [and the Sheriff seized and sold 43 acres of the above 290 acres ... [adjoining land owners or names - Rancocas Creek, land opposite the Village of Lamberton, Moors Nook] ... [13.25 acres] ... [for 270 pounds, 6 shillings] ..., [Signed - John Hollingshead; witnesses - Buddle Shinn, John Phillips.]

BURLINGTON COUNTY DEEDS - BOOK "C"

[p 324] **JACOB PERKINS SENIOR to BENJAMIN PERKINS**

10 January 1711 - I...Jacob Perkins Senior ... Township of Willingborough ... Burlington ... New Jersey ... [sold to] ... for the Love and good will and affection I have ... to my loving Son Benjamin Perkins ... my land ... [adjoining land owners or names - Thomas Peachies's line, Delaware River, Richard Fenimore, Ancocas Creek Alias Northampton River, line between his Brother Isaac and Jacob] ... [provided] ... my son ... getting both my corn harvest and my Hay in die season so long as my natural life shall last and is to take care of me and my ... Wife ... and ... to bury us in a Christian manner ... [and] ... shall not be altered that if ... Benjamin my Son Dye without male heirs that then my Son Isaac Perkins shall have the ... [1/2 of the above] ...; [Signed - Jacob Perkins; witnesses - John Neal, Thomas Peachee, John Ward.]

[p 326] **POWER OF ATTORNEY**

18 April 1793 - I John Abraham Denormandie ... City of Burlington ... New Jersey lately Practitioner in Physic being about to remove into the City of New York ... New York ... do ... appoint my Worthy friends Joshua Madox Wallace, John Lawrence and Daniel Ellis Esqr all of the City of Burlington ... my true and Lawful Attornies ... to recover and receive of and from Anthony Rue of Middle Town Township ... Bucks ... Pennsylvania yeoman ...; [Signed - John Ab^m Denormandie; witnesses - Esckl Hartshorne, Thomas Powell.]

[p 329] **POWER OF ATTORNEY**

19 April 1793 - I Harriot Elizabeth Gillespie ... City of Burlington ... New Jersey Widow being about to remove into the City of New York ... New York ... do ... appoint my Worthy friends Joshua Madox Wallace, John Lawrence and Daniel Ellis Esqr all of the City of Burlington ... my true and Lawful Attornies ... to recover and receive of and from John and Isaac Neal ... City of Burlington ...; [Signed - Elizabeth Gillespie; witnesses - Sarah Barton, Mary Thornburgh.]

[p 331] **MANUMISSION OF PANTILLA PARADO**

20 April 1793 - ...I do voluntarily ... manumit and make free my faithful servant and humble friend Known by name of Pantilla Parado on this condition of her serving me and my Heirs in the manner she has hither done ... to ... [1 May 1796] ... during which time I will furnish her with sufficient Clothing diet and lodging ...; [Signed - Elizabeth Gillispie; witnesses - David Greenman, Sarah Barton.]

[26 April 1793 - Elizabeth Gillespie ... City of Burlington acknowledged the above before James Kinsey.]

BURLINGTON COUNTY DEEDS - BOOK "C"

[p 332] **MANUMISSION OF ROSETTA VALENECE**

20 April 1793 - ...I do voluntarily ... manumit and make free my faithful servant ... Known by name of Rosetta Valenece on this condition of her serving me and my Heirs in the manner she has hither done ... to ... [1 November 1798] ... during which time I will furnish her with sufficient Clothing diet and lodging ...; [Signed - Elizabeth Gillispie; witnesses - David Greenman, Sarah Barton.]

[26 April 1793 - Elizabeth Gillespie ... City of Burlington acknowledged the above before James Kinsey.]

[p 333] **MANUMISSION OF WILLIAM PARADO**

20 April 1793 - ...I do voluntarily ... manumit and make free my faithful servant boy ... Known by the name of William Son of Partilla Parado on this condition of his serving me and my Heirs in the manner he has hither done ... to ... [1 May 1814] ... during which time I will furnish him with sufficient Clothing diet and lodging ...; [Signed - Elizabeth Gillispie; witnesses - David Greenman, Sarah Barton.]

[26 April 1793 - Elizabeth Gillespie ... City of Burlington acknowledged the above before James Kinsey.]

[p 334] **MANUMISSION OF BENJAMIN PARADO**

20 April 1793 - ...I do voluntarily ... manumit and make free my faithful servant ... Known by name of Benjamin Parado on this condition of his serving me and my Heirs in the manner he has hither done ... to ... [1 March 1817] ... during which time I will furnish him with sufficient Clothing diet and lodging ...; [Signed - Elizabeth Gillispie; witnesses - David Greenman, Sarah Barton.]

[26 April 1793 - Elizabeth Gillespie ... City of Burlington acknowledged the above before James Kinsey.]

[p 335] **AGREEMENT O F DIVISION LINE OF LAND**

30 March 1793 - ... we Caleb and Joshua Scattergood ... township of Mansfield ... Burlington ... New Jersey do hereby Certifie that we this ... 30 March 1793] ... established the following Corners and lines of Division between our farms or plantations (nearly agreeable to the Last Will ... of our Father Caleb Scattergood ... [adjoining land owners or names - William Pott's land, Wm. Talbert's land] ...; [Signed - Caleb Scattergood, Joshua Scattergood; witnesses - Wm Wright, Amos Ellis.]

BURLINGTON COUNTY DEEDS - BOOK "C"

[p 336]   **FINAL ARBITRATION**

26 January 1793 - ...Whereas William Richards Owner of Batsto Iron Works and Henry Drinker, Joseph [Salter?] & John Drinker Owners of Atsion Iron Works .. have by ... Bonds ... [dated 23 January 1793, will abide by the final determination of] ... Elijah Clark, John Gauntt, Joseph Willcox, Lewins Darling, and John Lacey or three of them, Arbitrators ... [to determine matters between them of variance] ... [there is then listed several decisions mentioning the names of Joshua Foster, Egg Harbor Road, William Richards, the Earls, John Estell, Charles Reed] ...; [Signed - Elijah Clark, John Gauntt, Joseph Wilcox, Lewis Darnal, John Lacey.]

[p 340]   **BURLINGTON COUNTY SHERIFFS to ABLE HARKER**

26 March 1783 - Daniel Ellis Esqr formerly High Sheriff ... Burlington ... And Joseph Mullen Esqr present High Sheriff ... [of the same county] ... [sold to] ... Able Harker ... Township of Northampton ... Burlington ... New Jersey ... Whereas Samuel Cripps late of ... Township of Northampton Deceased ... [was seized of land in the above township, and who by his Will gave to] ... his Daughter Martha Cripps the now wife of Jasper Moon ... [land being part of the Plantation where he lived bound as follows] ... [adjoining the road from Burlington to Mount Holly, John Ridgway, Henry Reeves] ... [126 acres]... the Second ... piece of meadown ... [16 acres, 2 rods, 38 perches] ... that ... Samuel Cripps purchased of Joseph Gaskill by deed ... [dated 11 September 1753] ... [adjoining land owners or names - Road from Mount Holly to Slab Town in Henry Reeves line, Christopher Shuff, James Lippincott] ... The Third Piece ... [adjoining land owners or names - Daniel Shields, Benjamin Stockton, John Ridgway, Henry Reeves] ... [30 acres] ... And Whereas ... Jasper Moon and Martha his wife did ... [sell the land] ... And Whereas ... Hannah Heartshorne ... [recovered against Henry Paxson the Executor of the Will of Samuel Cripps Deceased, the Sheriff Ellis confiscated and sold the land which settled 3/4 of the debt] ... [and John Lawrence recovered against Jasper Moon, and both sheriffs confiscated the lands, and sold to] ... Able Harker for ... [885 pounds] ... the three above Tracts ... of Land and premises ...; [Signed - Daniel Ellis, John Mullen; witnesses - Andrew Craig, William Cooper.]

[There was a Note at the end which read: Part of the above land was conveyed unto John Tilley [Lilly?] by deed, dated 27 March 1783 before Execution of the above deed by the Sheriffs the whole being mortgaged to Wm Smith.]

[p 346]   **WILLIAM WILKINS to MICAJAH WILLETS**

18 June 1784 - William Wilkins ... Township of Evesham ... Burlington ... And Sarah his wife ... [sold to] ... Micajah Willets and Elizabeth his Wife ... Township of Northampton ... Burlington ... Whereas Benj. Moore, Jo^s Moore, Jno Moore Bethrell Moore Thomas Wilkins and Benjamin Wilkins of Evesham ... [Divided the tract called Haine's Mill Tract in 1780 and conveyed to Wm Wilkins ... [430

BURLINGTON COUNTY DEEDS - BOOK "C"

acres] ... Now this Indenture ... Wm Wilkins & Sarah his wife ... [sell to] ... Micajah Willets and Elizabeth his Wife ... [for them to give] ... a release of Dower ... And ... [50 pounds] ... land ... [being part of the tract] ... on the Run called Bread and Cheese run ... [adjoining land owners or names - Mekendorn Swamp, Wm Burrs] ... [300 acres] ...; [Signed - Wm Wilkins, Sarah Wilkins; witnesses - Abraham Haines, Abm Woolman.]

[p 349] **GABRIEL ALLEN to THOMAS NIXON**

2 April 1791 - Gabriel Allen ... Township of Chesterfield ... Burlington ... West New Jersey Yeo^m ... [sold to] ... Thomas Nixon of the same place Innkeeper of Bordentown ... Gabriel Allen ... Grant ... unto Thomas Nixon ... all that his Dwelling house Still house and Stills, Store houses and wharf Barn Stables, ... land ... Situate in Bordentown ... [And] ... also ... [75%] ... of the Profits Arising from said Allen's Boat and ... [25%] ... of the profits arising from Richard Waln's Boat now occupied by John Hodgkinson ... [for one year from 15th of April next] ... for the ... full Sum of ... [85 pounds] ... Except ... Allen to pay the taxes of the Still's ... [and on the property].

[This entire item was crossed out of the book and was not completed.]

[p 350] **ABLE HARKER to ISAAC HAZLEHURST**

31 July 1793 - Able Harker ... Township of Northampton ... Burlington ... New Jersey Carpenter and Sarah his Wife ... [sold to] ... Isaac Hazlehurst ... City of Philadelphia ... Pennsylvania Merchant ... [for 173 pounds, 4 shillings, 10 pence, ½ penny] ... Land ... in the Township of Northampton ... [adjoining land owners or names - John Ridgway, land of Aaron now Daniel Zilly, Isaac Hazlehurst, Benajah Butcher, Able Harker] ... [6 square perches] ... [being part of a large tract which Able Harker purchased of Daniel Ellis Esqr, Sheriff on 26 March 1783 due to judgments against Henry Paxson Executor of Saml Cripps and Jasper Moon, who Cripps claimed the land through his wife Martha Moon, who received it from her father Samuel Cripps dec'd, who inherited it through the Will of his Father Nathaniel Cripps, who inherited it from his Father John Cripps dec'd, who made a survey of the land amounting to] ... [300 acres] ...; [Signed - Able Harker, Sarah Harker, witnesses - Sarah Kemble, Jo^s read, Martha Read.]

[p 353] **MORTGAGE RELEASE**

[This release appears to be connected to both the above and the following deed - "... William Smith Esqr, the Mortgage ... Whereas the land and premises ... released ... under Mortgage unto me will appear"; signed - William Smith.]

(101)

BURLINGTON COUNTY DEEDS - BOOK "C"

[p 354]   **WILLIAM SMITH to ISAAC HAZLEHURST**

1 August 1793 - ... William Smith for ... [106 pounds] ... paid by Isaac Hazlehurst ... Quit Claim ... unto the Said ... Hazlehurst ... the land and Premises ... [in the above deed] ...; [Signed - William Smith; witnesses - Thomson Neale, Jo^s Read.]

[p 355]   **CALEB AUSTIN ET AL to JOHN WILSON**

7 March 1791 - Caleb Austin and Jacob Austin ... township of Evesham ... Burlington ... New Jersey Yeomen .. [sold to] ... John Wilson ... [of the same place] ... Whereas Reuben Haines ... City of Philadelphia ... Lawfully ... Seized ... in one ... tract of Land ... in Township of Evesham ... Did ... [sell on 2 March 1749] ... Unto Samuel Moore Senior [and Moore made his Will and gave the land to his son Samuel Moore Junior, who by his Will appointed Caleb Austin and Jacob Austin his Executors] ... Now this Indenture ... [for 36 pounds, 11 shillings, 3 pence] ... [sell to John Wilson] ... [adjoining land owners or names - Thomas Smith, Rancocas Creek, Sarah Mills, Reuben Haines, Daniel Coate, Samuel Gaskill] ... [3 acres, 1 rod] ...; [Signed - Caleb Austin, Jacob Austin; witnesses - James Austin, Susanna Bankson.]

[p 359]   **THOMAS HOLLINSHEAD to JOSIAH REEVES**

8 April 1793 - Thomas Hollinshead and Lydia his wife ... Township of Evesham, Joseph Stokes and Abigail his Wife ... Township of Chester ... Burlington ... New Jersey ... [sold to] ... Josiah Reeves of Alloway Creek ... Salem ... Whereas Josiah Foster Esqr ... Township of Evesham ... [by the last Will of his Father William Foster Esqr dec'd ... became seized of Land Plantation ... Township of Evesham .. [370 acres] ... And being So Seized ... [sold by deed of 4 February 1783 to Charles West of the City of Philadelphia ... Pennsylvania ... In which Deed there was a Proviso that if ... Foster ... Should ... pay the Consideration money for the Same that then and from thence forth the Said Deed Should be Void ... And Whereas ... [Charles West recovered against Josiah Foster Esqr, and Abraham Hewlings Esqr then High Sheriff seized the 370 acres. And on 7th of May following, Thomas Hollinshead on behalf of himself and Joseph Stokes bid 1 shilling over the debt and costs of 1,493 pounds, 10 shillings, 9 pence] ... Now this Indenture ... [they sell for 2,700 pounds] ... a Certain part of the Above cited Land ... in Evesham ... [adjoining land owners or names - the Road in Foster Town called Land late of William Foster the Younger dec'd, Isaac Haines, Nehamiah Haines, Jacob Haines, South Branch of Ancocus Creek, John Haines, Solomon Haines] ... [amounting to 300 acres] ...; [Signed - Jos^h Stokes, Abigail Stokes, Thos Hollinshead, Lydia Hollinshead; witnesses - Mary Neal, Sarah Coat, Josiah Foster.]

[p 365]   **JOSHUA SCATTERGOOD to CALEB SCATTERGOOD**

2 June 1793 - Joshua Scattergood ... Township of Mansfield ... Burlington ... New Jersey Yeoman

BURLINGTON COUNTY DEEDS - BOOK "C"

... [sold to] ... Caleb Scattergood of the Same place Yeoman ... [for 692 pounds, 5 shillings] ... Tract of 106 acres of Land ... in the Township of Mansfield ... [adjoining land owners or names - William Potts, Joseph Scott, land of Joseph Antram deceased] ... [57 acres, 2 rods, and 30 sq. Perches] ... [land which was surveyed to James Antram in Liber A, Page 67; and being so seized at death conveyed 100 acres to Benjamin Scattergood by deed dated 10 November 1722] and ... Benjamin Scattergood ... conveyed the same unto his Son Caleb Scattergood by deed ... [dated 13 August 1737] ... And ... Caleb Scattergood ... by his Last Will ... [dated 24 October 1789] ... Devise the aforesaid ... [57 acres, 2 rods, and 30 sq perches] ... It being part of the Said Joshua Scattergood the present Grantor ...; [Signed - Joshua Scattergood; witnesses - James Sloan, John Pope, John Black.]

[p 369]   **AMOS HAINES to JOHN HAINES**

1 April 1768 - Amos Hains and Mary his Wife of Waterford ... Gloucester ... New Jersey Yeoman ... and John Hains and Mary his Wife ... Township of Evesham ... Burlington ... New Jersey ... [for 50 pounds] ... Quit Claim ... to Nathan Hains of the same place ... a certain Tract of Land ... in the Township of Evesham ... [adjoining land owners or names - Daniel Hopewell, lands late of Thom. Wallis, Charles French] ... [298 acres, 3 rods] ... whereof Nathan Hains Father of the parties hereunto Died Seized and which was Devised to them by the last Will ... [dated 4 June 175?] ...; [Signed - John Haines, Mary Haines made her mark when signing, Amos Haines, Mary Haines; witnesses - Abner Rogers, Peter Tool.]

[p 372]   **GEORGE HAINES to JOHN HOLLINSHEAD ET AL**

24 January 1794 - George Haines and Ann his Wife ... Township of Northampton ... Burlington ... New Jersey ... [sold to] ... John Hollinshead, John Bishop, Hudson Burr, William Irick, Joseph Burr, William Stockton, Joseph Hilliard, Thomas Burr, John Butterworth, George Woolston, Thomas Moon, John Woolston, John Burr and Joseph Campion ... [of the same place] ... [for 7 shillings, 6 pence] ... a certain Lot of Land to build a School House ... in the Township of Northampton ... [adjoining land owners or names - Rancocas Creek, the road from Mount Holly to Vincent Town, land late of Thomas Haines deceased, the mouth of "stop the Jades"] ... [2 rods and 19 perches] ... which Said Lot of Land is part of a large Tract of Land ... which George Haines Sen' deceased divided to his Sons George Haines and Thomas Haines by will ... And ... Thomas Haines ... [by an instrument dated 6 April 1771] did quit claim ... unto ... George Haines his Share ...; [Signed - George Haines, Ann Haines; witnesses - William Burr, Joshua Foster.]

[p 376]   **WILLIAM PETER SPRAGUE to JOHN SPRAGUE**

1 November 1786 - William Peter Sprague ... City of Burlington ... Burlington ... New Jersey Esquire and Mary his Wife ... [sold to] ... John Sprague ... now ... [of the same place] ... Gent, ... Whereas William Cuzens and Jane his wife ... became ... seized of a tract of land within ... the city ... [and sold

BURLINGTON COUNTY DEEDS - BOOK "C"

it by deed dated 28 February 1746 to] ... William Plumstead ... City of Philadelphia Esquire and ... [Plumstead sold it on 21 October 1752 to Abraham Hewlings of the city and Helwings sold 20 acres of the land on 3 January 1765 to John Haskins of the city, tanner and Haskins and wife Mary sold the 20 acres on 1 August 1783 to William Cooper of the city ... merchant; and Cooper & wife, Elizabeth, sold it on 29 November 1783 to William Peter Sprague and wife Mary ... Now this Indenture ... [for 200 pounds] ... all that ... [20 acres] ... [adjoining land owners or names - the straight road to Philadelphia, land Abraham Hewlings sold to Hugh Hartshorne now John Lawrence's] ...; [Signed - William P. Sprague, Mary Sprague; witnesses - Samuel Eyre, J. Hewitt.]

[p 380]   **THOMAS RODMAN to JOHN SPRAGUE**

2 November 1791 - Thomas Rodman ... City of Burlington ... New Jersey Esqr ... [sold to] ... John Sprague of the Same Place Yeoman ... [for 249 pounds and 15 shillings] ... Land ... in the Township of Burlington ... [adjoining land owners or names - the new road from Burlington to Philadelphia, John Lawrence Esqr., Land of Abraham Hewling Esqr, Jacob Cox, Thomas Rodman] ... [41 acres, 2 rods, and 20 perches] ...; [Signed - Thomas Rodman; witnesses - Saml Evans, Daniel Ellis.]

[p 383]   **JOHN LAWRENCE to JOHN SPRAGUE**

15 February 1794 - John Lawrence ... City of Burlington ... New Jersey Attorney at Law ... [sold to] ... John Sprague of the Same Place ... [for 150 pounds] ... Land ... in the City of Burlington ... [lands late of Thomas Rodman now John Sprague, new road from Burlington to Philadelphia, land late John Hoskins now Sprague's] ... [18 acres, 3 rods] ... Also ... [lot of 3 rods] ... which said ... [18 acres and 3 rods] ... were sold ... to John Lawrence by Charles Pettit and Sarah his Wife ... [on 1 June 1774] ... and was purchased by ... Pettit of Richard Wells and Rachel his wife ... [on 1 October 1773] ... and was purchased by ... Wells of Hugh Hartshorne and Hannah his Wife ... [on 29 January 1765] ... and was purchased by ... Hartshorne of Abraham Hewlings ... [on 24 March 1760] ... and is part of a larger Tract of Land purchased ... by ... Hewlings of William Plumstead of Philadelphia ... [on 21 October 1752] ... and was purchase by ... William Plumstead of William Cowens and Jane his Wife .. [on 28 February 1746] ... And which Said Second Lot of three rods was purchased by the Said John Lawrence of Thomas Rodman ... [on 23 October 1777] ...; [Signed - Jno. Lawrence; witnesses - Abraham Gardiner, Joseph Houseman.]

[p 386]   **JOSEPH BUTTERWORTH to JOHN BUTTERWORTH**

11 May 1793 - Joseph Butterworth of Mount Holly ... Burlington tanner and Sarah his wife, Alexander Shiras of the same place Merchant and Ann Lippincott of the Township of Springfield ... Spinster which same Sarah Butterworth, Anna Lippincott and Alexander Shiras ... Executors in the last Will ... of Anna Lippincott the elder widow late of Mount Holly ... deceased John Black Surveyor and Mary his wife of Mansfield ... Elizabeth Lippincott and Patience Lippincott of Springfield ...

BURLINGTON COUNTY DEEDS - BOOK "C"

William Rodgers, Jun[r] and Ann his wife late Anna Elton and John Mullen Carpenter and Anna his wife late Anna Butterworth of Northampton Township ... Josiah Dungan and Mary his wife late Mary Butterworth ... city of Philadelphia ... Pennsylvania Sarah Butterworth and Elizabeth Butterworth of Mount Holly ... Spinster ... [sold to] ... John Butterworth ... township of Northampton ... farmer and John Ross of Mount Holly ... Practitioner in Physic and Surveyor ... Whereas ... Anna Lippincott the testatrix ... [was seized of land from Hugh Hollinshead and Mary his Wife by deed dated 23 February 1786 and became seized of other land in Mount Holly ... [adjoining land owners or names - White Street, the Mill race, land Joseph Butterworth bought of Hollinshead] ... [20 square perches] ... which ... [Hollinshead obtained from Samuel Stockton on 25 October 1782, who bought it from his brother, William, on 9 February 1782] ... and became the right of him ... [William Stockton] ... being Heir at law to his Sister Sarah Stockton who died under lawful age without issue and was devised unto ... Sarah as an estate in Remainder ... by the will of their grandfather Benjamin Brian deceased subject to a life estate of his widow therein and the said Benjamin Brian purchased ... [the property from] ...Josiah White who purchased ... [it from Samuel Gaskill who bought it from his father Edward Gaskill who in company with Josiah Southwick purchased it from Samuel Jennings ... Whereas ... Anna Lippincott the testitrix by her ... last Will ... did devise unto her daughter Sarah Butterworth, the wife of Joseph ... and who was also one of the Executors in her said will ... and after her death ... [the house and lot to be sold and the moneys divided between] ... [her, the testatrix's] ... grand daughters namely Mary the wife of John Black, Elizabeth, Anna and Patience Lippincott daughters of her son Job Lippincott dec'd, Anna Mullen the daughter of Joseph and Sarah Butterworth and wife of John Mullen son of John, Mary, Sarah, Lettis and Elizabeth Butterworth the daughters of the said Joseph Butterworth and Ann Rogers daughter of Revel Elton deceased which Anna Rogers is wife of William Rogers above named. Whereas it is discovered that by an immediate Sale of the said house and lot ... [for 85 pounds] ... it will yield more profit eventually ... [than by renting it out] ... during the life of the said Sarah Butterworth and to wait untill her death for a sale or distribution ... Now This Indenture ... [the parties of the first part sell for 85 pounds] ... to be paid unto the serverall Devisees above named that is to say the ... [Interest at 7% by half yearly payments for Sarah Butterworth during her life and the principal sum and the future Interest by equal portions to the] ... said Ten grand daughters of the said Anna Lippincott the testatrix ...; [Signed - 11 May 1793 - Joseph Butterworth, Sarah Butterworth, Anna Mullen, Sarah Butterworth Jun[r], Lettis Butterworth, William Rodgers Jun[r], Ann Rodgers, Alex[r] Shiras, John Mullen, John Black, Mary Black, Eliza Lippencott, Anna Lippencott, Patience Lippencott, Mary Dungan, Eliza Butterworth, Josiah Dungan; witness - Jos. Read, Judge.]

[p 392]   **THOMAS HOLLINSHEAD ET AL to JOSIAH REEVES**

8 April 1793 - Thomas Hollingshead and Lydia his wife ... township of Evesham, Joseph Stokes and Abigail his wife ... township of Chester all of the County of Burlington ... New Jersey ... [sold to] ... Josiah Reeves of Alloway creek ... Salem ... Whereas Josiah Foster Esquire ... township of Evesham ... by virtue of the last will ... of his father William Foster Esquire deceased ... became seized ... in a

BURLINGTON COUNTY DEEDS - BOOK "C"

tract of land and plantation ... in ... the township of Evesham ... [of 370 acres] ... And being so seized ... [sold it by deed on 4 February 1783 to] ... Charles West of ... Philadelphia ... Pennsylvania ... And whereas ... Charles West ... [won a Judgment against Josiah Foster, the sheriff confiscated his property and offered it for sale and it was sold to the high bidder Thomas Hollinshead and Joseph Stokes] ... [for 1,493 pounds, 10 shillings, 9 pence on 18 May 1791] ... Now This Indenture ... Hollingshead & Stokes sell for ... [2,700 pounds] ... to Josiah Reeve ... [adjoining land owners or names - Foster town, land of William Foster the younger deceased, Isaac Haines, Nehemiah Hines, Jacob Haines, Ancocus creek, John Haines, Solomon Haines] ... [300 acres] ...; [Signed - Joseph Stokes, Abigail Stokes, Thomas Hollinshead, Lydia Hollinshead; witnesses - Mary Neale, Sarah Coate, Josiah Foster.]

[p 399] WILLIAM BELL to MICHAEL ROBERTS

16 January 1794 - William Bell ... Philadelphia ... Pennsylvania merchant and Margaret his wife ... [sold to] ... Michael Roberts of the same place merchant ... [for 700 pounds] ... three lots ... of land ... in the town of Lamberton ... Burlington ... [adjoining land owners or names - Front Street, Abraham Woglam deceased, William Bell, Isaac Collins, James Ewing, Achsah Lambert, Elijah Bond, Lambert Cadwallader] ... [the sale was made with the agreement that Roberts would pay a yearly amount] ...; [Signed - William Bell, Margaret Bell and Michael Roberts; witnesses - N. Combes, Joseph Watson.]

[p 404] DIVISION OF LAND WITHIN THE HILLIARD FAMILY

14 September 1793 - James Kinsey Esquire Chief Justice of the Supreme Court ... New Jersey to Aaron Wells, Joseph Budd and Moses Kempton ... County of Burlington ... [re: the tracts of land of] ... John Hilliard late of ... township of Northampton ... Burlington ... one tract of land devised by the last will of Edward Hilliard father of John ... [dated 17 May 1766] ... [adjoining land owners or names - Revel Elton, Asher Woolman, Jonah Woolman] ... secondly a piece of meadow ... of twelve acres ... thirdly devised by ... Edward to ... John ... which the testator ... had bought of Daniel Wills ... fourthly ... [55 acres] ... near Mill Creek in Northampton ... which John Hilliard bought of Daniel Ellis Esquire late Sheriff ... [on 17 March 1773] ... fifthly ... land in Northampton ... [Road leading from Mount Holly to Ancocus ferry by the farm belonging to ... John Hilliard deceased] ... [2 acres, 2 rods, 23 perches] ... being part of the lands formerly belonging to ... Edward Hilliard deceased and by him devised to his son Abraham who devised the same to the said John Hilliard ... sixthly ... land in ... township of Northampton ... [2 acres, 1 rod, and 23 perches] ... part of the two lots devised by the said Edward to his said son Abraham ... to Jacob Hilliard ... which ... [were conveyed to John Hilliard deceased by Jacob Hilliard by deed dated 22 July 1779] ... Seventhly ... an island on Rancocus Creek ... [1 acre, 2 rods, 20 perches] ... Eightly ... march ... [of 1 acre, 2 rods, 20 perches on Rancocus Creek ... Ninthly ... four acres from Joseph Burr and Joseph Woolman on 6 February 1770.]

BURLINGTON COUNTY DEEDS - BOOK "C"

And being so seized died Intestate leaving issue eight children to witt Jonathan Hilliard, Sarah wife of Revell Elton, Samuel Hilliard, Mary Hilliard, Isaac Hilliard, and Rebecca Hilliard ... whereof the ... title ... descended ... [to and became vested in the above 8 children] ... in such proportion that each of the sons is entitled to ... [2/11ths] ... and each of the daughters ... of ... John Hilliard ... [1/11th ... [per application of Jonathan Hilliard dated 16 July last past] ... And ...whereas since the decease of John Hilliard ... Sarah ... [and her husband Revell Elton sold all their rights to] ... Frances Hilliard the widow of ... John Hilliard deceased ... [Chief Justice Kinsey therefore appointed those three above to divide the various tracts into eleven shares] ... and to make a field book and a map of the tracts ...; [Signed - James Kinsey.]

[The various properties were listed with their metes and bounds]

1. The Homestead place on the Northwardly side of the road ... from Ancocus meeting House to Mount Holly ... [adjoining land owners or names - Revell Elton, Asher Woolman, Jonah Woolman, Barzillia Deacon, Richard Cox] ... [204 acres, 3 rods, 16 square perches].

2. An orchard ... [adjoining land owners or names - Revell Elton, Jacob Hilliard] ... [11 acres, 2 rods, 31 square perches].

3. A bank meadow ... of ... Ancocus creek ... [14 acres, 31 square perches].

4. A mud Island ... of Ancocus creek ... [1 acre, 2 rods, 20 perches].

5. Cedar Swamp ... in bear swamp ... [4 acres] ... [Surveyed by William Ridgway Surveyor on 16 December 1793.]

[The various parts were then listed with their metes and bounds for the division of the property and a map of the divisions was drawn into this book on pages 436 and 437. The final division and the ballots were completed on 27 January 1793.]

[p 444]   **RICHARD WELLS to CHARLES PETTIT**

2 October 1773 - Richard Wills late of the city of Burlington mow of the city of Philadelphia ... Pennsylvania merchant and Rachel his wife ... [sold to] ... Charles Pettit of the city of Burlington ... New Jersey Esquire ... [for 47 pounds, 7 shillings] ... [for 18 acres, 3 rods] ... of land ... city of Burlington ... [adjoining land owners or names - Road from Burlington to Philadelphia, Samuel Rodman, John Hankins, Abraham Hewlings] ... [Wills claimed the land by deed from Hugh Hartshorne and wife Hanah dated 29 January 1765, bought by Hartshorne of Abraham Hewlings on 24 March 1760 and part of a larger tract that Hewlings bought from William Plumstead of Philadelphia on 21 October 1752, and Plumstead bought it from William Couzens and Jane his wife

BURLINGTON COUNTY DEEDS - BOOK "C"

on 8 February 1746] ...; [Signed - Richard Wells, Rachel Wells; witnesses - Jacob Howell, Milcah Martha Moore.]

[p 448] **PROPERTY LINE ESTABLISHED**

10 April 1794 - ... William Cooke Esqr and Barzillia Newbold both of the township of Chesterfield ... Burlington ... New Jersey ... [established their lines] ... [adjoining land owners or names - branch of Chapman's Mill pond, Hill's side] ... One other tract about ... [15 acres] ... [adjoining land owners or names - William Cooke's at west end of Barzillia Newbold's plantation] ...; [Signed - William Cooke, Barzillia Newbold; witnesses - Thomas Reynolds, John Ridgway, Jos^h Stokes.]

[p 451] **ASA ENGLISH to THOMAS ENGLISH**

14 March 1794 - Asa English of Mansfield ... Burlington ... New Jersey ... [sold to] ... Thomas English of the same place ... Whereas Samuel English and Elizabeth his Wife of Mansfield aforesaid (Father & Mother of the Said Asa English) was ... seized of Land ... in Mansfield ... [and they died so seized intestate] ... and they by an Act of Assembly & descent they divided ... [the land between their children] ... [Now Asa English sells for 395 pounds and 6 shillings] ... All that ... Said Asa English ... Share of his aforesaid Father and Mothers Land ... [adjoining land owners or names - English Creek, Tabitha English, Thomas English, William White] ...; [Signed - Asa English; witnesses - Sam Woolman, Isaac Hancock.]

[p 453] **HANNAH PRYOR to JONATHAN ADAMS, JUNIOR ET AL**

14 April 1790 - Hannah Pryor ... City & County of Burlington ... New Jersey Widow ... [sold to] ... Jonathan Adams Junior and John Murray both of the Said City Coopers ... Whereas William Master of the City aforesaid Biscuit Baker by his Deed ... [dated 1 January 1762] ... did grant ... unto Thomas Pryor Junr a certain Tenement & Lot of Ground ... [adjoining land owners or names - Rearl Street, River Delaware, Anthony Elton] ... [which Thomas Pryor and Hannah his Wife sold to Saml Noble and Saml Allinson as Trustees for payment of his debts by deed 6 September 1774, and Noble & Allinson sold it on 18 June 1776 to John White, with his wife Rebecca sold it to Thomas Pryor and wife Hannah] ... Now This Indenture ... [for 40 pounds, sold it to Jonathan Adams and John Murray] ... [adjoining land owners or names - Pearl Street, John Elton] ...; [Hannah Pryor; witnesses - John Elton, Thos W. Pryor.]

[p 456] **JOHN MURRAY to JONATHAN ADAMS**

14 May 1793 - John Murray ... [for 5 shillings, sold to] ... Jonathan Adams ... his Moiety or half part ... [in the above property] ...; [Signed - John Murray, witnesses - Charles Ellis, Daniel Ellis.]

BURLINGTON COUNTY DEEDS - BOOK "C"

****

[p 457]   **ABEL HARKER to JOHN ZELLY**

27 March 1783 - Abel Harker and Damaris his Wife ... [sold to] ... John Zelly both of the Township of Northampton ... Burlington ... West New Jersey ... [for 700 pounds] ... [adjoining land owners or names - road from Burlington to Mount Holly, John Ridgway, Henry Reeves] ... [85 acres] ... Also ... [land adjoining - Henry reaves, the road from Mount Holly to Slab Town, Christopher Sheaff, James Lippincott] ... [16 acres, 2 rods, 38 perches] ... the third ... a Wood Land ... [adjoining land owners or names - the road from Mount Holly to Slab town, Daniel Shields, Benjamin Stockton, John Ridgway] ... [29 acres] ... accepted for the use of Felix Hammell whereon his dwelling House now stands the whole ... three pieces containing ... [130 acres] ... [the above land was purchased by Harker from Daniel Ellis and Joseph Mullen Esqrs former and present Sheriffs of Burlington on 26 March 1783] ...; [Signed - Abel Harker, Lucy Harker; witnesses - Joseph Mullen, Daniel Ellis.]

[p 460]   **DANIEL ZELLY to ISAIAH BISHOP**

26 November 1785 - Daniel Zelly Son of John Zelly ... Twonship of Springfield ... Burlington ... New Jersey ... [sold to] Isaiah Bishop Cordwinder ... Township of Northampton ... [for 89 pounds] ... Land ... in the Township of Northampton ... [adjoining land owners or names - John Ridgway, Abel Harker, Henry Reeve, Aaron Zelly, William Duff] ... [18 acres, 3 rods, 20 pence] ... Which Said Tract of Land the Said Daniel Zelly become Seized of by virtue of a Power of Attorney from ... his Brother John Zelly which ... John Zelly purchased of Abel Harker and Damaris his Wife ... [by deed dated 26 March 1783] ...; [Signed - Daniel Zelly; witnesses - Amos Hutchin, Saml Fenimore.]

[p 463]   **DANIEL ZELLEY to AARON ZELLEY**

13 November 1786 - Daniel Zelley Yeoman ... [sold to] ... Aaron Zelley Tay [lor?] ... of Springfield ... Burlington ... New Jersey ... [for 457 pounds, 11 shillings, 6 pence] ... Land ... in the Township of Northampton ... [adjoining land owners or names - the road from Burlington to Mount Holly, Henry Reese, Isaiah Bishop] ... John Ridgway on half acre in his corner is excepted for a Daughter of Jasper Moon ... [52.5 acres] ... the Second Piece is a Piece of Meadow ... [adjoining land owners or names - Henry Reeves, the road from Mount Holly to Slab Town, land late of Christopher Shuffs, James Lippincott] ... [16 acres, 2 rods, 38 perches] ... of Meadow ... [adjoining land owners or names - Daniel Shields, Benjamin Stockton, John Ridgway] ... [29 acres] ... one Acre only excepted for the use of Philip Hammel whereon his Widow now dwells the above three Pieces ... [total 98 acres, 1 rod, 17 perches] ... which David Zelley ... of a Power of Attorney from John Zelley and Hannah his Wife ... [dated 22 October 1785] ... [and] ... became fully impowered to convey the same ... and he ... John Zelley purchased the Same ... of Abel Harker & Damaris his Wife ... [on 27 March 1783 and Harker purchased the other from Daniel Ellis and Joseph Mullen by deed dated 26 March 1783] ...; [Signed - Daniel Zelley; witnesses - Amos Hutchin, Saml Fenimore.]

BURLINGTON COUNTY DEEDS - BOOK "C"

[p 466] JACOB WOLCOTT to DANIEL ZELLEY

6 March 1793 - Jacob Wolcott Esquire high Sheriff ... Burlington ... New Jersey ... [sold to] ... Daniel Zelley ... Township of Evesham ... Whereas William Smith Esquire ... [obtained a Judgment against Aaron Zelley and Daniel Zelley recovered against Aaron Zelley, the Sheriff confiscated Aaron Zelley's lands in Northampton and sold them at public auction with Daniel Zelley bidding the highest] ... Now this Indenture ... Wolcott ... [sold to] ... Daniel Zelley ... all of the above described pieces ... [of property in this deed] ...; [Signed - Jacob Wolcott Sheriff; witnesses - James Sloan, George Sweetman, William Hutchin.]

[p 471] DANIEL ZELLY to ISAAC HAZELHURST

25 March 1794 - Daniel Zelly ... Township of Springfield ... Burlington ... New Jersey Yeoman & Penelope his Wife ... [sold to] ... Isaac Hazelhurst ... City of Philadelphia ... Pennsylvania Merchant ... [for 500 pounds] ... All that Plantation and tract of Land ... near Mount Holly ... Township of Northampton ... Burlington ... [adjoining land owners or names - Henry Reeves, the road from Mount Holly to the Friends or Quakers old Grave Yard, John Ridgway] ... [22 acres] ... excepting ... [.5 acre] ... for the Daughter of Jasper Moon and of a Lot number four conveyed to Jacob Wolcott Esquire high Sheriff ... as the Estate of Aaron Zelley ... [on 6 March 1793, which land Aaron Zelly bought of his Brother Daniel Zelly as Attorney for his Brother John Zelly from Isaiah Bishop and Rebecca his Wife on 1 June 1787, which Bishop bought of Daniel Zelley & that John Zelly had purchased of Abel Harker and wife, and Harker bought of Daniel Ellis and Joseph Mullin who sold it to Jasper Moon and Martha his Wife formerly Martha Cripps, the Daughter of Samuel Cripps dec'd] ...; [Signed - Daniel Zelley, Penelope Zelley; witnesses - Joseph Morrell, Jos. Read.]

27 March 1794 - Know all Men ... that John Zelley the former ... owner ... and Hannah his Wife ... [for 5 shillings, sold all their rights to] ... Isaac Hazelhurst ...; [Signed - John Zelley, Hannah Zelley; witnesses Jos. Read, Abraham Zelley.]

[p 476] ABRAHAM HEWLINGS to JOSEPH SMITH JUN[R]

16 April 1794 - Abraham Hewlings of ... City of Burlington ... New Jersey Esq[r] ... [sold to] ... Joseph Smith Junr of the Same Place Carter ... Whereas Richard Wright late of the Said City deceased ... [was seized of Lotts in the City & made his Will, and devised a Lot] ... unto his Daughter Sarah Wright ... And Whereas ... Sarah Wright Intermarried with Edmond Wooley who departed this Life ... [Sarah Wooley] ... made her last Will ... [dated 8 July 1786] ... And Wherein did give ... [the Lot] ... unto Anthony F. Taylor ... And whereas ... Taylor ... [as seized sold the Lot by deed dated 8 August 1787 to] ... his Father John Taylor ... [and John Taylor & Hannah his Wife sold it on 6 November 1790 unto Okey Hoagland who with his wife Dinah sold it on 16 November 1791 to Abraham Hewlings] ... Now this Indenture ... [for 35 pounds, sold it to] ... Joseph Smith ... [adjoining

BURLINGTON COUNTY DEEDS - BOOK "C"

land owners or names - the cellar Wall lately walled by Joseph Smith, Pearl Street, Post House Alley, River Delaware] ...; [Signed - Abr^m Hewlings Sen; witnesses - Saml Stockton, Daniel Ellis.]

[p 478] **APPOINTMENT FOR DIVISION OF PROPERTY**

James Kinsey Esquire Chief Justice of the Supreme Court ... to Aaron Wills, Joseph Budd and Moses Kempton, all of the County of Burlington ... Whereas John Hilliard ...; [This recording was the actual appointment document appointing the above individuals by Kinsey regarding the Surveying, Mapping, and Division of the John Hilliard property as previously recorded.]

[p 484] **ESTABLISHING PROPERTY DIVISION LINES**

3 May 1794 - ... We William Rodgers, William Troth and Job Troth all of the township of Evesham ... Burlington ... New Jersey having lands adjoining together ... in Said Township ... Now Know Ye we ... do agreeable to the fourth Section of an Act of Assembly entitled as Act for the limitation of Suits respecting ... Land ... do hereby establish the following lines ... [adjoining land owners or names - Josiah Haines, William Rodgers of one part and Job Troth and William Troth of the other part] ...; [Signed - William Rogers, William Troth, Job Troth; witnesses - Thos Hollinshead, William Sharp Junr, Jos^h Stokes.]

[p 485] **ESTABLISHING PROPERTY DIVISION LINES**

12 May 1794 - ... Joseph Engle ... Township of Evesham ... Burlington ... New Jersey and Francis Austin ... Township of Northampton ... [they established division lines per the above mentioned Act] ... [adjoining land owners or names - Rancocus Creek, from old House, Clayton Gaskill's Kitchen Chimney, the road from Mount Holly to Philadelphia] ...; [Signed - Joseph Engle; witnesses - Joseph Stokes, William Woolman, William Sharp Junr.]

[p 486] **NOAH HOWELL to NATHAN COMBES**

28 April 1794 - ...Noah Howell House Carpenter and Hannah his Wife ... Township of Nottingham ... Burlington ... New Jersey ... [sold to] ... Nathan Combes of the same place Gentleman ... [for 487 pounds, 10 shillings] ... All that Certain ... Dwelling House Lott of Land ... in Lamberton ... Township of Nottingham ... [adjoining land owners or names - Barnt DeKlyn] ...; [Signed - Noah Howell, Hannah Howell; witnesses - David Compton, Richard Brown.]

[p 489] **BENJAMIN HOLDEN to NATHAN COMBES**

14 March 1794 - ... Benjamin Holden of the City of Trenton ... Hunterdon ... New Jersey Stone Mason and Jemima his Wife ... [sold to] ... Nathan Combes ... Township of Nottingham ... Gentleman

BURLINGTON COUNTY DEEDS - BOOK "C"

****

... [for 120 pounds] ... all that Certain ... Dwelling House ... at Lamberton ... Township of Nottingham ... [adjoining land owners or names - Front street] ... [1/8 acre] ...; [Signed - Benjamin Holden, Jemima Holden; witnesses - John Chinn, Jacob Benjamin.]

[p 491]   **JAMES HAM to JACOB BOYER**

10 June 1793 - James Ham ... Falls Township ... Bucks County ... Pennsylvania ... [sold to] ... Jacob Boyer ... township of Nottingham ... Burlington ... New Jersey ... [for 20 pounds] ... all that Certain Lott ... in the Township of Nottingham ...part of a certain tract ... lately divided into Lotts and Sold by John Donaldson and Sarah his Wife and George Campbell and Helen his Wife ... [adjoining land owners or names - Water Street] ... [.8 acres] ...; [Signed - James Ham; witnesses - Rebeckah Keen, Isaac Smith.]

[Bulah Ham ... Wife of James Ham for 5 shillings forever quit claimed unto Jacob Boyer all her dower rights to the above land; [Signed - Bulah Ham; witness - Rebeckah Keen.]

[p 494]   **SAM^L HOUGH, BARZILLAI NEWBOLD ET AL, AND ISAAC POTTS**

[The following is a long and complicated three part deed regarding numerous pieces of property; much of which is not recorded here.]

1 October 1793 - Saml Hough ... Township of Springfield ... Burlington ... and Susannah his Wife of the First Part and Barzillai Newbold, Thomas Newbold and William Newbold Junior Executors of the last Will ... of Wm Newbold Esqr late of the Township of Chesterfield of the Second Part and Isaac Potts of the Township of ... [blank] ... County of Montgomery ... Pennsylvania ... of the Third Part ... Whereas Jonathan Hough Esqr late of Springfield ... deceased ... was seized ... of Land ... at Eg harbour ... Burlington ... on which Land is erected and Built a Saw Mill commonly called ... Oswego Mill ... [and he died Intestate and it descended to Daniel Hough his Eldest Son and Hough sold it by deed on 15 July 1778 to his Brother William Hough Esqr ... Excepting ... One Tract ... of Pine land ... [91.5 acres] ... Near the New Mill ... and also one Piece of Cedar swamp at Wading River ... [10 acres] ... whereon Jonathan Hough Esqr ... usually got Cedar Rails and ... William Hough afterwards died seized ... [and he made a Will naming his] ... Brother Saml Hough ... above ... executor ... And ... the Orphan's Court ... of Burlington ... [in August Term 1790 authorized him to sell the real estate of his Father to pay debts] ... and ... [for 350 pounds] ... sold it unto William Newbold Esq ... [on 10 September 1790] ... And Whereas William Budd of New Hanover ... Burlington ... [was seized of 800 acres] ... from Abraham Hewlings in part of a Warrant granted unto him to Locate ... [1,843.75 acres] and the said William Budd and his Brother Joseph Budd By ... a purchase ... [on 10 October 1784] ... of ... [154 acres] ... from John Lee ... and in part of a Warrant unto Thomas Rodman ... John Lee ... was to locate ... [7,500 acres] ... and ... William Budd and Joseph Budd ... did locate the following tracts ... in Burlington ... [there is then a long series of pieces of property with their metes and bounds

BURLINGTON COUNTY DEEDS - BOOK "C"

covering several pages] ... Now this Indenture that Saml Hough ... and Susannah his Wife and ... Barzillai Newbold, Thomas Newbold and William Newbold Junr Executor ... of ... said Father William Newbold deceased ... [for 2,250 pounds] ... [sell to] ... Isaac Potts ... All that this said Saw mill ... [adjoining land owners or names - Collards Pond, Jonathan Hough, William Budd, Saml Hough, Wading River, Pappon Run, Beaver Run, Excepting the Cedar Swamp in the Tranquility Swamp by deed dated 8 June 1792 from Joel Bodine and Mary his Wife] ... And the said Samuel Hought for himself ... and Barzillai Newbold, Thomas Newbold and William Newbold Junior for the Heir of the said William Newbold the Elder ...; [Signed - Samuel Hough, Susannah Hough, Barzillai Newbold, Thomas Newbold, William Newbold; witnesses - Thomas Earle, Joseph Hough.]

[p 506]   **CHARLES SCHUYLER to AMOS HUTCHIN**

22 March 1793 - Charles Schuyler and his wife Rhoda ... City of Burlington ... Burlington ... New Jersey ... [sold to] ... Amos Hutchin of the Sameplace InnKeeper ... [for 135 pounds] ... A Certain Lott of Land ... City of Burlington ... [adjoining land owners or names - the new road from Burlington to Burtle Town, Assincunk Creek, Peter Schuyler] ... [20 acres, 1 rod] ... [Schuyler became seized of the land by the last Will, dated 27 May 1774, of his Father Aaron Schuyler, of the City of Burlington and] ... the said Charles Schuyler and his Brother Abraham Schuyler ...; Signed - Charles Schuyler, Rhoda Schuyler; witnesses - Saml Rogers, John Folwell.]

[p 508]   **NATHAN EYRE to AMOS HUTCHIN**

15 June 1790 - Nathan Eyre ... City and County of Burlington ... New Jersey Taylor ... [sold to] ... Amos Hutchin of the same city ... [for 75 pounds, 4 shillings, 9 pence] ... a Certain Lott of meadow ... [adjoining land owners or names - the Great Road leading over the Bridge London Bridge, ground of Nathan Eyre by the lane agreed by the Will of Saml Eyre deceased to open a lane to ground of his Son George Eyre, land devised to his Brother Samuel Benjamin Eyre, great dam by the Island of Burlington] ... [2.25 acres] ... [which Nathan owned by the Will, dated 28 October 1788, of his Father Samuel Eyre late of said City deceased, and being part of Ground given him which Samuel Eyre purchased of his brother, Benjamin G. Eyre and his wife, Esther, on 20 April 1772] ... and became the right of the said Benjamin G. Eyre by ... the Will ... of his Father George Eyre ... [dated 11 January 1761] ...; [Signed - Nathan Eyre; witnesses - Danl Smith, Robt Smith.]

[p 511]   **ABRAHAM HEWLINGS to AMOS HUTCHIN**

20 March 1793 - Abraham Hewlings ... City of Burlington ... Burlington ... New Jersey ... [sold to] ... Amos Hutchin of the same place ... [for 7 pounds, 10 shillings] ... a Certain Lot of Land ... in City of Burlington ... [adjoining land owners or names - house now in possession of Rowland Ellis] ... Abraham Hewlings became seized ... [of the property by deed from Patrick Cowin on 2 August 1763

BURLINGTON COUNTY DEEDS - BOOK "C"

and part by a deed from Thomas Beekly/Bukly Polgreen on 19 March 1768] ...; [Signed - Abraham Hewlings Senr; witnesses - Saml Fenimore, Saml Hutchin.]

[p 513] **WILLIAM ENGLISH JUN to AMOS HUTCHIN**

25 March 1794 - William English Jun ... Township of Mansfield ... Burlington ... Yeoman ... [sold to] ... Amos Hutchin ... City and County of Burlington ... Innkeeper ... [for 400 pounds] ... all his Tract of Land and Plantation whereon he now lives ... [adjoining land owners or names - English Creek, Abraham English, Thomas English, land late of Joseph English] ... which tract of land includes a small island of 48 acres which William English claims by deed of Partition, by the Orphan's Court on 28 November 1785, from John English Junr on 22 April 1786] ...; [Signed - William English, Mary English; witnesses - John Hoskins Junr, Saml Fenimore.]

[p 515] **JAMES STERLING ESQ^R to AMOS HUTCHIN**

21 March 1794 - James Sterling Esqr ... City of Burlington ... Burlington ... New Jersey Merchant and Rebekah his Wife ... [sold to] ... Amos Hutchinson of the same place Innkeeper ... [for 50 pounds] ... all that ... Farm Plantation and Tract of Land ... in ... Township of Mansfield ... [adjoining land owners or names - lands late of Samuel English, John Sutton, Joseph Ellison, James Craft] ... [230 acres] ... [which Sterling claims by deed from John Ellis and wife Elizabeth on 21 October 1776] ...; [Signed - Jam^s Sterling, Rebeckah Sterling; witnesses - Wm Coxe Junr.]

[p 519] **JOHN ELTON to AMOS HUTCHIN**

20 March 1793 - John Elton and his Wife Elizabeth ... City and county of Burlington ... New Jersey ... [sold to] ... Amos Hutchin of the same place Innkeeper ... [for 63 pounds, 15 shillings] ... a Certain Lott of ground ... in City of Burlington ... [.75 acres] ... [adjoining land owners or names - York Street, Jocob Myers Lotts, Sam'l Butters, Pearl Street] ... [Elton claims by deed from Sheriff Hollinshead dated 3 January 1789] ...; [Signed - John Elton, Elizabeth Elton; witnesses - Jam^s Sterling, Saml Fenimore.]

[p 521] **MANUMISSION OF JULIUS CEASAR**

... I Richard Potts ... Township of New Hanover ... Burlington ... manumitted and set free my molatto Slave Named Julius Ceaser ... [20 January 1794] ...; [Signed - Richard Potts; witnesses - John Hall, Israel Mitton.]

... We Certify that on the ... [20 January 1794] ... Richard Potts ... Township of New Hanover ... brought before us ... his Molatto Slave named Julius Ceasar ... [not under 21 nor over 35 years] ...;

BURLINGTON COUNTY DEEDS - BOOK "C"

[Signed - Isaac Cowgill, Joel Cook - Justices of Peace; Joshua Wright, John Wright - Overseerers of the Poor.]

... We Certify that the bearer Julius Cesar is manumitted ... by his Master Richd Potts ... of Township of New Hanover ... [signed at] ... Reckless Town ... [20 January 1794] ...; [Signed - Is. Cowgill, Joel Cook.]

[p 522]   **MANUMISSION OF POMPEY STEWARD**

... I Richard Potts ... Township of New Hanover ... Burlington ... manumitted and set free my Negro Slave Named Pompey Steward ... [20 January 1794] ...; [Signed - Richard Potts; witnesses - John Hall, Israel Mitton.]

... We Certify that on the ... [20 January 1794] ... Richard Potts ... Township of New Hanover ... brought before us ... his Negro Slave named Pompey Steward ... [not under 21 nor over 35 years] ...; [Signed - Isaac Cowgill, Joel Cook - Justices of Peace; Joshua Wright, John Wright - Overseerers of the Poor.]

[p 523]   **MANUMISSION OF ROBERT**

... I Richard Potts ... Township of New Hanover ... Burlington ... manumitted and set free my molatto Slave Named Robert ... [20 January 1794] ...; [Signed - Richard Potts; witnesses - John Hall, Israel Mitton.]

... We Certify that on the ... [20 January 1794] ... Richard Potts ... Township of New Hanover ... brought before us ... his Molatto Slave named Robert ... [not under 21 nor over 35 years] ...; [Signed - Isaac Cowgill, Joel Cook - Justices of Peace; Joshua Wright, John Wright - Overseerers of the Poor.]

[p 524]   **MANUMISSION OF GEORGE ROEN**

To all ... it may Concern ... Manumitted and set free my Negro Man named George Roen aged about thirty years ... [at Burlington the place of my Dwelling on 9 July 1794] ...; [Signed - Bowes Reed; witnesses - Thos Adams.

We do ... Certify ... [on 8 July 1794] ... Bowes Reed Esqr ... Township of Burlington ... brought before us ... George Roen ... [not under 21 nor over 35 years] ...; [Dated - 18 July 1794; Signed - John Hendry, John Stockton - Overseers of the Poor; Wm Cox Junr, Thos Adams - Justice of the Peace.]

BURLINGTON COUNTY DEEDS - BOOK "C"

****

[p 525]   **MANUMISSION OF RICHARD**

This Certifies that I Talman Pennock ... Township of Mansfield ... Burlington ... Set Free my negro Slave named Richard ... [28 July 1794] ...; [Signed - Talman Pennock; witnesses - Caleb Foster, Colen Atkinson.]

This Certifies ... on ... [28 July 1794] ... Talman Pennock ... Township of Mansfield b^{rt} before us ... his Negro Man Named Richard ... [not under 21 nor over 35 years] ...; [Signed - Caleb Scattergood - Overseers of the Poor; Israel Cowgill, Jacob Wolcott - Justice of the Peace.]

[p 526]   **REVEL ELTON to FRANCES HILLIARD, WIDOW**

25 June 1794 - Revel Elton ... Township of Northampton ... Burlington ... New Jersey Farmer and Sarah his Wife ... [sold to] ... Frances Hilliard Widow and Relict of John Hiliard of the same Place deceased ... Whereas Thomas Gardner ... surveyed and laid forth Sundry Pieces ... of Land among which is ... [7 acres of meadow in the above township] ... [by Ancocus Creek] ... and ... Gardner ... [sold it to Anthony Elton on 22 November 1698, and Elton made a Will in November 1702, where he gave it to his Son Anthony Elton; and the son Anthony sold it to his Brother Revel Elton Esqr, who sold it to his son, Revel Elton Junr on 1 January 1762] ... [adjoining land owners or names - being land late of John Hilliard deceased, Ancocus Creek] ...; [Signed - Revel Elton; witnesses - Elizabeth Haines, Moses Kempton.]

[p 530]   **REVEL ELTON to FRANCES HILLIARD, WIDOW**

15 March 1792 - Revel Elton ... Township of Northampton ... Burlington ... New Jersey Husbandman and Sarah his Wife ... [sold to] ... Frances Hilliard of the Same Place Widow ... of John Hilliard ... [who died Intestate] ... leaving the following Issue Jonathan Hilliard, Sarah Hilliard now the Wife of Revel Elton, Samuel Hilliard, Mary Hilliard, Isaac Hilliard, Hannah Hilliard, Elizabeth Hilliard, and Rebekah ... [sold for 160 pounds all their rights to all the undivided parcels of Land and Premises of John Hilliard deceased] ...; [Signed - Revel Elton; witnesses - Mary Kinsey, Moses Kempton.]

[p 533]   **JONATHAN HILLIARD to FRANCES HILLIARD, WIDOW**

25 March 1794 - Jonathan Hilliard ... Township of Northampton ... Burlington ... New Jersey Mason Son of John Hilliard late of the Place aforesaid deceased ... [sold to] ... Frances Hilliard ... Widow of ... John Hilliard ... Now this Indenture ... [is for the Release of Dower given] ... all those two Lots of Orchard ... [adjoining land owners or names - the road from Mount Holly to Ancocus Meeting House in the township of Northampton, Revel Elton, Hannah Hilliard, Isaac Hilliard] ... [2 acres, 3 rods, 20 sq. Perches] ... [Signed - Jonathan Hilliard; witnesses - Elizath Kempton, Moses Kempton.]

BURLINGTON COUNTY DEEDS - BOOK "C"

[p 537] **MANUMISSION OF BENJAMIN HALE**

... I Ann Murrell [?] Widow and Executrix of the Estate of Joseph Murrell dec'd ... County of Burlington ... New Jersey do hereby ... Set Free my Negro Slave named Benjamin Hale ... [on 2 April 1792] ...; [Signed - Ann Murrell; witnesses - Josiah Foster, Reece Edwards.]

We do hereby ... [Certify] ... that on ... [2 April 1792] ... Ann Murrell ... brought before us ... her Slave named Benjamin Hale ... [not under 21 nor over 35 years] ...; [Signed - Samuel Burrough, Nehemiah Haines - Overseers of the Poor; Josiah Foster, Reece Edwards - Justices of Peace.]

[p 538] **JASPER MOON ET AL to ISAAC HAZELHURST**

9 October 1794 - Jasper Moon ... City and County of Burlington Cooper and Martha his Wife and Sarah Moon the Daughter of the said Jasper Moon and Martha his Wife ... [sold to] ... Isaac Hazelhurst ... City of Philadelphia ... Pennsylvania Merchant ... [this is a lengthy deed with numerous sales of this same property in a title chain that was explained in length in a previous deed and is not repeated here] ... [Martha Moon was Martha Cripps, the daughter of Samuel Cripps, deceased, of the township of Northampton] ... [adjoining land owners or names - the road from Mount Holly towards Burlington, John Ridgway] ... [.5 acres] ... [sell for 5 pounds] ...; [Signed - Jasper Moon, Martha Moon, Sarah Moon; witness to Sarah Moon's signature was Mary Murray, who signed with her mark, and Joseph Read; witness to Martha Moon was Sam J. Read Junr, Jos. Read; witness to Jasper Moon was Jos. Read.]

[p 542] **MANUMISSION OF BELL**

... I John Van Emburgh of the Township of Chesterfield ... Burlington ... New Jersey have ... Set free ... my Negro Slave named Bell ... [3 January 1795] ...; [Signed - J. Van Emburgh; witnesses - Benjamin Duglass, Thomas Wallin.]

We ... certify that the Bearer hereof Negro Girl Bell is ... Set free ...; [Dated - 3 January 1795; signed - Isaac Cowgill, Jacob Wolcott.]

... We do ... certify ... John Van Emburgh of Bordentown brought before us ... his Slave named Bell who ... [is not under 21 nor over 35 years] ...; [Signed - Is^c Cowgill, Jacob Wolcott - Justices of Peace; John Middleton, Isaac Field - Overseers of the Poor.]

[END OF BOOK "C"]

INDEX

MANUMITTED SLAVES, FIRST NAME ONLY

Aaron, Slave, 64; Ann(Infant) Slave, 61; Argulus, Slave, 65; Bell, Slave, 117; Brutus, Slave, 72; Charles, Slave, 61; Chloe, Slave, 46; Cloe, Slave, 64, 65; David, Slave, 52; Dinah, Slave, 24; Grace, Slave, 72; Jack, Slave, 66, 93; Kingston, Slave, 29; Mary, Slave, 61, 65; Nanny, Slave, 29; Phebe, Slave, 66; Phillis, Slave, 34; Richard, Slave, 116; Robert, Slave, 115; Ronnia, Slave, 29; Siro, Slave, 66, 93; Thomas, Slave, 23

A

Aaronson: Benjamin, 53, 58, 59; John, 11; Thomas, 53, 59
Abbot: John, 40
Acerby[?]: Hannah, Slave, 25
Adames: Jedidiah, 82
Adams: Esther, 82; James, 82; Jedidiah, 82; John, 45, 82; Jonathan, 108; Thos., 73, 115
Adams, Junior: Jonathan, 108
Aiken: Thomas, 58
Alexander: Richard, Slave, 61, 62; Sarah, Slave, 61, 62
Allen: Abraham, 59; Eastwood, 37; Enoch, 15; Gabriel, 101; Hannah, 15; Judah, 82; Matthew, 4, 5; Nathan, 82
Allen, Esqr.: John, 53
Allinson: Elizabeth, 4; Joseph, 4; Saml., 15, 108; Wm., 15
Allinson, Junr.: Samuel, 25
Anders: Peter, 61
Anderson: David, 56; Ely, 64, 65; Geo., 64, 66, 77; George, 62, 65, 76, 77, 93; Isaac, 84; Sarah, 84
Andrew: Edward, 41
Andrews: Edward, 55; Isaac, 9; Jacob, 94; Mary, 88, 89; Mordicai, 9; Samuel, 55, 88, 89
Andries: Saml., 53
Antram: Ebenezer, 19; James, 88, 103; John, 79, 94; Joseph, 103
Antrame: Sarah, 16
Antrobus: Benjamin, 48
Antrum: Adin, 65, 66
Apelgate: George, 72
Aplegate: George, 66
Applegate: Anthony, 93, 94
Archer: Joseph, 15
Areson: John, 55
Arionson: Benjamin, 55
Arney: Lippincott, 60
Ash: James, 74
Ashmore: Elenor, 76; Nelti, 76; Thomas, 76
Atkinson: Colen, 116; Elizabeth, 22; John, 4; Mahlon, 79; Saml., 89; Samuel, 48, 89; Thomas, 12, 25, 36, 45, 58, 59
Attenger: Burget, 11
Austin: Caleb, 32, 96, 97, 102; Francis, 71, 111; Jacob, 43, 96, 97, 102; James, 102

B

Bacon, Junr.: Danl., 33, 34
Bake[r]: Ezra, 24
Baker: John, 9
Ballenger: Saml., 81
Ballinger: Samuel, 80
Bankson: Susanna, 102
Bard: Ben, 45
Bard, Esq.: Peter, 4, 5
Barnin: John, 32
Barton: Job, 32; Jonathan, 79; Sarah, 98, 99
Baslie: John, 80
Bass: Jeremiah, 90
Bates: Thomas, 19
Baynton: Elizabeth, 5; John, 4, 5; Peter, 4
Bayton: Peter, 4
Beakes: Edmond, 96

INDEX

Beatty: George, 50
Belcher: Hannah, 41
Bell: Benjamin, 62, 63; John, 62; Margaret, 106; Nicholas, 48; William, 106
Bends: Thomas, 76
Benjamin: Jacob, 112
Bennett: Abigail, 32; Henry, 31, 32, 74
Bennit: Joseph, 68
Berchanes: Henry, 4
Beveridge: Dal., 74
Biddell: Joseph, 56
Biddle: Joseph, 41, 60, 63, 65, 66, 79; Lydia, 15; Thomas, 43, 73, 74; William, 15, 55
Biddle, Junr.: Joseph, 79; William, 15
Billings: Edward, 48
Bingham: James, 22
Birchams: Henry, 5
Bishop: Abigail, 60, 70; Isaiah, 41, 109, 110; John, 103; Levina, 78; Levinah, 78; Rebecca, 110; Samuel, 78; William, 78; Wm., 81
Bispham: Benjamin, 42, 45; John, 24, 25, 35, 38, 86; Jos., 83; Joshua, 27, 44, 82; Josiah, 95; Ruth, 82, 83; Samuel, 13; William, 86
Bitto: Philip, Slave, 71
Black: Edward, 24, 25, 35; Ezra, 85; Jno., 7, 58; John, 4, 23, 24, 40, 41, 87, 95, 103, 104, 105; Mary, 4, 35, 104, 105; Thomas, 25; William, 3, 4, 67, 89
Black, Esquire: John, 86
Black, Jun'r.: John, 8
Blackham: Josiah, 37
Blair: Robert, 79
Bloomfield: Abigail, 54, 59; Ann, 62; J., 48, 59; Jno., 62; John, 62; Jos., 54; Joseph, 48, 61, 62, 88; Mary, 26, 48, 59, 89; Samuel, 53, 54; Samuel, Doctor, 59
Bloomfield, Esqr.: Joseph, 26, 43, 54
Bloomfield, Esquire: Joseph, 47, 58, 59, 62, 89

Bochm, Junr.: Phillip, 40
Bodine: Joel, 113; Mary, 113
Bonadails: William, 78
Bond: Elijah, 91, 106
Bonyer: Calvert, 10
Boote: William, 95
Borden: Joseph, 26, 55, 76
Borradaill: William, 28
Borten: Thomas, 22
Borton: Benjamin, 73; Job, 32, 74; John, 73; Joshua, 44; Josiah, 46; Obadiah, 73; Phoda, 73; Samuel, 73
Bourtis: John, 64; Richard, 64; William, 64
Bowman: George, 11; Mary, 11
Bowne: Abigail, 87, 88; George, 87, 88
Boyer: Jacob, 112
Boyner: Thomas, 10
Braddock: Brazilai, 61; Brazillai, 61, 81; Daniel, 26; Robert, 81
Bradock: Robert, 81
Brain: Haron, 85
Brainard: Elizabeth, 72; John, Rev'd, 72
Braman: Benjamin, 45; Elizabeth, 45
Brandt: John, 76
Branen: John, 63
Branin: Barzillai, 26; John, 26, 27, 32, 33, 50, 57, 61, 63; Michael, 32, 57, 61, 63, 71; Sarah, 26, 27
Brannes: Barzillai, 79
Brannin: Cornelius, 26; John, 49; Michael, 26; Sarah, 26; William, 26
Brearley: Joseph, 16
Brian: Benjamin, 40, 105; Benjn., 45; Johannah, 85
Briant: Haron, 85
Briggs: George, 42; Levi, 42
Brixton: Hannah, 1; James, 1
Brock: Oddy, 49
Brook: Thomas, 32
Brooks: Samuel, 32, 74; Thomas, 31, 32, 74
Brown: Abigail, 88; Caleb, 36, 55; George,

INDEX

88; Johanna, 41; Lancelet, 82, 83; Linden, 9; Lundon, 9; Lyndon, 1, 2, 10; Preserve, 55; Richard, 111; William, 74
Brunir: Corneley, 97
Bryant: Benjamin, 48, 85; Haron, 85; Joseph, 85; Samuel, 85; Thomas, 85
Budd: Abigail, 21; George, 20, 79, 86; Isaac, 44; James, 42, 49, 69; John, 14, 32, 86; Jonathan, 44; Joseph, 19, 21, 78, 106, 111, 112; Rebekah, 42; Samuel, 44, 79; Thomas, 10, 42; William, 21, 39, 44, 112, 113
Buffin: John, 3, 6, 7, 12; Michael, 1, 7, 12
Buffin, Sen.: John, 1
Bullock: Isaac, 21; Joseph, 64
Bullus: Fra., 48; Francis, 62; Samuel, 73, 74, 85
Buntin: Saml., 87
Bunting: Aaron, 75; James, 75; John, 75; Joshua, 21, 75; Mary, 75; Samuel, 18, 88; Septime, 88; Thomas, 53, 59; William, 87
Burchan: Robert, 9
Burley: Joseph, 81; Mary, 81; William, 81
Burling: Jane, 69
Burr: Ann, 38; Elizabeth, 63; Henry, 63, 64, 68; Hudson, 78, 103; John, 10, 22, 46, 63, 103; Joseph, 38, 39, 42, 103, 106; Mary, 63; Priscilla, 63; Sophia, 63; Thomas, 64, 103; William, 38, 103; Wm., 101
Burr, Junior: Henry, 68; Joseph, 39
Burr, Junr.: John, 42, 63, 64, 91; Joseph, 38, 42
Burr, Senr.: Henry, 64
Burrough: Samuel, 117
Burroughs: Samuel, 1
Bustisee: William, 64
Butcher: Benaiah, 67; Benajah, 40, 101; John, 67; Mary, 40, 67, 69, 70; Rachel, 40; Sarah, 40, 66, 67, 69, 70; Thomas, 38, 39, 40, 66, 69

Butcher, Junr.: Thomas, 67
Butler: Israel, 15; John, 15, 25
Butters: Sam'l, 114
Butterworth: Anna, 105; Eliza, 105; Elizabeth, 105; Jno., 91; John, 103, 105; Joseph, 41, 104, 105; Lettis, 105; Mary, 105; Sarah, 41, 104, 105
Butterworth, Junr.: Sarah, 105
Buxton: Hannah, 31; James, 31
Buzby: Jabez, 50; John, 83; William, 27, 83
Byllngee: Edward, 33

C

Cadwallader: Lambert, 106
Calvert: Martha, 40, 48, 86; William, 38, 39, 40, 48, 86; Wm., 48
Campbell: Elizabeth, 8; George, 112; Helen, 96, 112; John, 8; William, 96
Campbell, Esquire: George, 96
Campion: Joseph, 103
Canca.: Maj. Cur., 60
Carey: Catherine, 10; Lott, Slave, 31
Carey, Esquire: John, 10
Carpenter: John Mullen, 105
Carr: Calsep, 9
Carslake: William, 11
Carson: Joseph, 76, 77; Mary, 76, 77
Carty: Dennis, 57
Cary: Andrew, Slave, 44
Ceaser: Julius, Slave, 114
Cesar: Julius, Slave, 115
Chambers: Henry, 66; John, 55
Chapman: Stillman, 90
Cheshire: Benjamin, 16; Jonathan, 16, 17; Sarah, 16
Chevalier: Peter, 63
Chew: Elizabeth, 5; William, 16, 35
Chew, Esquire: Benjamin, 4, 5
Chinn: John, 112
Chiras [?]: Peter, 8
Clapp: John, 56, 57; Martha, 57

INDEX

Clark: Elijah, 100; Ephraim, 8; John, 16, 25, 35, 95; Samuel, 63; William, 72
Clarke: Henry, 43
Clayton: Richard, 48
Clement: Samuel, 59
Clifford: John, 33
Coalman: James, 77
Coate: Barzillai, 17, 18; Daniel, 72, 102; Elizabeth, 17, 18; Israel, 18; John, 19; Sarah, 106; William, 18
Coates, 84: Daniel, 72
Coleman: Nathaniel, 70
Coles, Senr.: Samuel, 28
Collins: Ebenezer, 79; Edward, 61, 88; Isaac, 106; John, 25, 30, 31
Combes: N., 106; Nathan, 96, 111
Combs: Nathan, 90, 91
Comfort: John, 69
Comforts: John, 67
Comius [?]: John, 14
Compton: David, 111
Conrow: Andrew, 46; Darling, 30, 31, 44
Cook: Joel, 115; Rebecca, 64; Rebekah, 64
Cooke, Esqr.: William, 108
Cooper: Daniel, 1; Elizabeth, 91, 104; Henry, 10, 45, 46; Jno., 91; John, 40; Joseph, 86; Saml. Atkinson, 42; Thomas, 91; William, 52, 100, 104; Willm., 23
Copperwaite: Hugh, 25; Job, 25
Cordeary: William, 14
Couzens: Jane, 107; William, 107
Cowell, Jnr.: Ebenezer, 10
Cowens: Jane, 104; William, 104
Cowgill: Is., 115; Isaac, 13, 14, 21, 36, 52, 64, 65, 66, 71, 72, 93, 95, 115, 116, 117; Isc., 117
Cowin: Patrick, 113
Cowperthwaite: Mary, 75; William, 75
Cowperthwaite, Junr.: Wm., 75
Cowperthwite: Jonathan, 94
Cox: Abigail, 55, 56; Baigail, 83; Jacob, 104; John, 9, 11, 31, 55, 56, 78, 82, 83, 96; John, Col., 89; Richard, 60, 85, 86, 107; William, 14; Wm., 11
Cox, Esq.: John, 96
Cox, Esqr.: Daniel, 23; John, 11, 77
Cox, Jun'r.: Willm., 9
Cox, Junior: William, 80
Cox, Junr.: John, 23; Wm., 115
Coxe: Rachel, 62; Rebecca, 80; William, 18, 62
Coxe, Esqr.: Tench, 80
Coxe, Junior: William, 48, 62
Coxe, Junr.: Wm., 62, 73, 114
Craft: Gershom, 26, 61, 62; James, 114
Craft, Jnr.: Gershom, 62
Craft, Junr.: Gershom, 61
Craig: Andrew, 100
Crane: John, 62
Cripps: Grace, 37; Hannah, 37; John, 37, 101; Martha, 100, 110, 117; Nathaniel, 37, 38, 86, 101; Saml., 101; Samuel, 35, 37, 38, 39, 40, 48, 100, 101, 110, 117
Crips: Ann, 37; Samuel, 38
Crispan: Jonathan, 63
Crispin: Jonathan, 79; Paul, 56
Crosby: John, 49; William, 49
Croshaw: John, 19
Crossley: William, 48
Cummings: William, 49
Cunningham: Stephen, 63
Curley: Elinor, 77; John, 77
Curtes: Marmaduke, 2; Marmaduke Watson, 8; Thomas, 2
Curtis: Alice, 67; Asa, 67; Jonathan, 16; Marmaduke W., 8; Marmaduke Watson, 3, 8; Mary, 8; Thomas, 7, 54, 67; Thos., 67
Cuzens: Jane, 103; William, 103

D

Darling: Lewins, 100

INDEX

Darnal: Lewis, 100
Darnel: Edward, 32
Darnell: Edward, 32; Lewis, 63
Davenport: Frances, 6
Davis: David, 79, 81; Robert, 82
Davison: Abigail, 93, 94; John, 93, 94
De Bray: Daniel, 32, 74
De Cou: Isaac, 70, 89, 91
De Kligns: Barnt, 96
De Klyne: Barnt, 10, 11
De Normandie: Abraham, 39
Deacon: Barzillia, 107; William, 27
Dean: William, 16, 91
Debrmandie: John Abm., 5
Deckligen: Barnt, 96
Decounedius [?]: Isaac, 12
Decow: Isaac, 95
DeKlyn: Barnt, 111
Delatush: Henry, 2, 3, 6, 7; Widow, 3; Widw, 8
Delworth: William, 2
Denormandie: Abraham, 38; John Abm., 98; John Abraham, 38, 98
Dern: Cornelius, 62
Dill: Henery, 92
Dillon: George, Slave, 93, 95; Jack, Slave, 93; Phillis, Slave, 71
Dillwyn: Wm., 19
Dilworth: Joseph, 12; William, 8
Disbrow: Joseph, 64, 65, 77
Donaldson: John, 96, 112; Sarah, 96, 112
Doorn: Cornelius, 62
Dorn: Cornelius, 62
Dotey: Ebenezr., 60
Dougherty: Jno., 77
Doughty, 69
Douglass: John, 96; Joseph, 87; Thomas, 34
Downing: Martha, 77; Samuel, 77; Saml., 77
Drinker: Henry, 43, 100; Joseph, 100
Duckworth: William, 45
Dudley: Joshua, 56; Thomas, 46, 47

Duff: William, 109
Duglass: Benjamin, 117
Dungan: Josiah, 105; Mary, 105
Dunsdale: Joseph, 10; Susanna, 10; Thomas, 10

E

Earl, 100: Caleb, 24, 34, 41, 52, 53, 65, 66; John, 27; Taunton, 41; Thomas, 57
Earl, Junr.: Thomas, 58
Earle: Thomas, 113
Eayre: Hosea, 63; Thomas, 63
Edwards: Abigail, 78; Altemus, 16; Arthur, 1; John, 76, 77; Joseph, 28; Letitia, 77; Reece, 23, 24, 25, 27, 29, 30, 31, 44, 46, 47, 50, 51, 65, 78, 117; Reese, 95; Richard, 71, 78; Sarah, 78
Edwards, Esq.: Richard, 70
Edwards, Esquire: Reece, 14
Egly: Jacob, 17
Ehernzeller: Jacob, 76
Ehrenzeller: Jacob, 76
Eiver: Mary, 18; Robert, 18
Eldridge: Jabez, 60, 85; James, 59; Mary, 60; William, 85
Ellis: Amos, 99; Charle, 41; Charles, 74, 108; Daniel, 18, 26, 27, 41, 43, 44, 70, 71, 74, 87, 92, 104, 108, 109, 110, 111; Danl., 34; Elizabeth, 114; John, 114; Joseph, Coll., 53; Peter, 79; Rowland, 113
Ellis, Esq.: Daniel, 1
Ellis, Esqr.: Daniel, 9, 18, 22, 28, 40, 74, 98, 100, 101, 106
Ellis, Esquire: Daniel, 109
Ellison: Amos, 87; Hannah, 4, 5; Joseph, 4, 5, 114
Elton: Ann, 105; Anna, 105; Anthony, 108, 116; Darcus, 51; Elizabeth, 114; John, 52, 108, 114; Revel, 105, 106, 116; Revell, 60, 107; Sarah, 107, 116

INDEX

Elton, Esqr.: Revel, 116
Elton, Junr.: Revel, 116
Emans: Job, 7
Emley: John, 18; Joseph, 42; Samuel, 94
Engle: John, 59; Joseph, 111; Robert, 59
English: Abraham, 114; Ann, 15, 73; Asa, 108; Elizabeth, 108; Isaac, 43, 73; Joseph, 43, 73, 74, 114; Mary, 114; Samuel, 108, 114; Tabitha, 108; Thomas, 43, 73, 108, 114
English, Jr.: Thomas, 15
English, Jun.: William, 114
English, Junr.: John, 114
English, Minor: Joseph, 43
English, The Elder: Joseph, 43
Erdaill: James, 33
Esdaill: James, 24
Estaugh: John, 49
Estell: John, 100
Evans: Enoch, 23, 24, 29, 30, 31, 50, 51, 71, 95; John, 59; Levi, 50; Saml., 81, 104; Samuel, 80, 81; William, 23, 24, 50, 51; Wm., 29, 30, 31, 51, 95
Evens: John, 59; Martha, 59
Eves: Joseph, 30, 31
Ewan: Absalom, 42; John, 19; Julius, 19
Ewans: Absalom, 42
Ewing: James, 106; Jams., 77
Eyre: Benjamin G., 113; Esther, 113; George, 92, 113; Mary, 91; Nathan, 113; Saml., 113; Samuel, 104, 113; Samuel Benjamin, 113

F

Falwill: John, 55
Farnsworth: Daniel, 76
Farr[?]: John, 26
Farrington: Abraham, 38, 39, 48, 49, 69; Abrm., 10, 49; Samuel, 69
Fenimore: Ann, 92; Elizabeth, 3; James, 3; Joseph, 92; Joshua, 18, 83, 84; Rebecca, 84; Richard, 18, 83, 98; Saml., 109, 114; Thomas, 17, 21, 22, 33, 45, 47, 48, 52; Thos., 20, 23, 33, 48; Tomas, 14; William, 83
Fenimore, Esqr.: Thomas, 23
Ferrills: Robert, 16
Fester: Phillip, 76, 77
Field: Benjamin, 75; Isaac, 75, 117; Robert, 9
Fisher: Phillip, 76
Fister: Philip, 77; Phillip, 76, 77
Fitz: Nathl., 73
Fitz.: Nathaniel, 80
Flekey: John, 77
Fleming: Richard, 55
Folwell: George, 2, 3, 6, 7; John, 15, 58, 59, 89, 113; Nathan, 4, 89; Sarah, 58
Folwill: John, 55
Ford: Elizabeth, 82; Thomas, 82
Fordham: Benjamin, 5; Catharine, 5
Forman: Brazillai, 53, 59; Elinor, 9; John, 8, 9
Forole [?]: Percival, 6
Foster: Anna, 78; Caleb, 116; Job, 11; John, 43; Jonah, 61, 62; Joshua, 12, 100, 103; Josiah, 23, 24, 25, 29, 30, 31, 46, 50, 51, 52, 65, 79, 95, 102, 106, 117; Thomas, 85; William, 22, 26, 49, 78
Foster, Esqr.: Josiah, 49, 102; William, 102
Foster, Esquire: Josiah, 105; William, 105
Foster, Junr.: William, 78
Foster, The Younger: William, 102, 106
Foulk: Thomas, 87
Fouolke, The Younger: Thomas, 87
Fowle: Percival, 48
Freedson [?]: William, 63
Freeland: James, 9
French: Charles, 28, 55, 83, 103; Edward, 56; Thomas, 82
Furman: Moore, 96

INDEX

G

Gale: Abel, 63
Gamble: Patrick, 85
Gardiner: Abraham, 104; Joseph, 87; T.M., 50; Tho. M., 61; Thos. M., 33
Gardner: Thomas, 116
Garwood: Japhiet[?], 79; Joseph, 26
Gaskill: Clayton, 111; Daniel, 67, 69; Edward, 38, 46, 105; Joseph, 40, 42, 100; Josiah, 42; Lucretia, 42; Nathan, 41; Samuel, 42, 102, 105; Sarah, 40; Thomas, 12, 85
Gaskill, Junr.: Edward, 38; Josiah, 42
Gaunt: A., 68; Ars, 93; Asher, 52, 65; Asr., 93; Elihu, 65, 66; John, 9
Gaunt, Esqr.: Asher, 65, 66
Gauntt: John, 100; Uz, 93, 94
Gibb: Isaac, 2; Richard, 59
Gibbon: Frans, 89
Gibbs: Elizabeth, 2, 3, 4, 7; Hannah, 2, 12; Isaac, 3, 7, 12, 53; Joel, 90; John, 6, 7, 12, 17; Joseph, 1, 2, 3, 4, 6, 7, 8, 9, 10, 11; Joshua, 2; Martin, 6; Mary, 9, 10; Rich'd, 7; Richard, 3, 6, 7, 12, 53, 92
Gibbs, The Elder: Isaac, 3, 6, 7, 8
Gibbs, The Younger: Isaac, 6
Giffing: Frances, 22
Giles: James, 59
Gill: Hannah, 19; Thomas, 19
Gillispie: Elizabeth, 98, 99; Harriot Elizabeth, 98
Githens: George, 15; Joseph, 15; Mary, 15
Goldy, Junr.: John, 60
Granger: Elizabeth, 82; Joshua, 82
Greenman: David, 98, 99
Gregon: James, 47
Gregson: James, 47, 48; Mary, 47, 48
Grice: Joseph, 72
Groom: Ezekiel, 71; John, 71
Guest: Jonathan, 33

H

Hackney: Joseph, 30, 31
Haigh: Samuel, 41
Haines: Abraham, 101; Amos, 103; Ann, 103; Benjamin, 59, 71; Caleb, 79; Caspar Wistar, 73; Casper W., 72; Charlotte, 90; Elizabeth, 116; Ephraim, 28, 78, 82, 83; Frances, 90; George, 103; Hannah, 28, 78; Henry P., 92; Henry Pendergrass, 97; Isaac, 102, 106; Isaiah, 46; Jacob, 106; Jcob, 102; Jeremiah, 90, 91; Jesse, 17; Job, 72; John, 21, 22, 78, 102, 103, 106; Jonathan, 71; Josiah, 21, 111; Mary, 103; Nathan, 29, 46, 97; Nehemiah, 82, 102, 117; Rebecca, 90; Reuben, 21, 102; Rhuben, 73; Samuel, 37; Sarah, 90; Solomon, 71, 102, 106; Thomas, 22, 83, 86, 103; William, 22, 78, 90
Haines, Senr.: George, 103
Hains: Amos, 103; Carlile, 72; Dorcas, 97; Isaiah, 95; John, 72, 96, 97, 103; Jonathan, 72; Martha, 96, 97; Mary, 103; Nehemiah, 95; Reubin, 17; Rhuben, 72; Solomon, 72
Hale: Benjamin, Slave, 117
Hall: John, 114; Jon., 72; Roland, 76
Ham: Beulah, 112; James, 112
Hammel: Philip, 109
Hammell: Felix, 109; John, 36, 53, 54
Hammell, The Elder: John, 36, 55
Hammett: Joseph, 61
Hammey: Cato, Slave, 46; Mc Intosh, Slave, 47
Hammitt: Daniel, 78
Hammond: Abijah, 97
Hamploe: Isaac, 96
Hancock: Isaac, 108
Hankins: John, 107
Hankinson: Elizabeth, 32; John, 32
Harker: Abel, 40, 41, 109, 110; Able, 100,

INDEX

101; Damaris, 109; Sarah, 101
Harrison: Israel, 94; Peter, 94; Richard, 94; Wm., 8
Hartshorne: Catharine, 4, 5; Esckl., 98; Hanah, 107; Hannah, 4, 5, 104; Hugh, 5, 104, 107; Margaret, 4, 5; Robert, 4, 5
Hartung: Wm., 74
Harvey: Ann, 6; Daniel, 58, 59; John, 6; Sarah, 58
Haskins: John, 104; Mary, 104
Hastings: George, 70
Hatkinson: John, 45, 67; Jos., 86
Haycock: Henry, 88
Haydock: Henery, 87
Hayes: Henry, 40, 41; William, 40
Hayles: Peter, 48
Hazelhurst: Isaac, 39, 40, 48, 67, 69, 81, 101, 102, 110, 117
Heartshorne: Hannah, 100
Heisler: Andrew, 44
Hendrickson: Hendrick, 62
Hendy: John, 115
Henzey: Jos., 35; Joseph, 35
Herbert: Richard, 62
Heritage: Joshua, 14
Hervey: John, 79
Heulings: Isaac, 22; John, 1; Wm., 61
Heulings, Esqr.: Abm., 22
Heustis: John, 27, 82
Hewitt: J., 104
Hewling: Abraham, 43; William, 60
Hewlings: Abraham, 34, 91, 104, 107, 112, 113; Elizabeth, 63; Elizo., 34; Thos. D., 91; William, 19, 27, 70; Wm., 19, 79
Hewlings, Esqr.: Abraham, 90, 102, 110; William, 79
Hewlings, Esquire: Jacob, 19
Hewlings, Junr.: Abraham, 63; Abram, 63; Abrm., 91
Hewlings, Sen.: Abrm., 111
Hewlings, Senr.: Abraham, 114

Higby: John, 27
Hiliard: John, 116
Hill: Peter, 73
Hilliar: Joseph, 103
Hilliard: Abraham, 106; Edward, 41, 106; Elizabeth, 116; Frances, 90, 107, 116; Hannah, 116; Isaac, 90, 107, 116; Jacob, 41, 106; John, 90, 106, 107, 111, 116; Jonathan, 107, 116; Mary, 107, 116; Rebecca, 107; Rebekah, 116; Rheuban, 90; Samuel, 107, 116; Sarah, 90
Hillier: John, 63
Hinas: Nathan, 103
Hinchman: John, 32
Hinchman, Esqr.: John, 46, 47
Hind: John, 33; Mary, 33
Hind, The Elder: John, 33
Hind, The Younger: John, 33
Hines: Nehemiah, 106
Hoagland: Dinah, 110; Okey, 23, 92, 110
Hodgkinson: Bethanah, 89; John, 101; Peter, Captain, 89
Hodkinson: Bethanah, 26; Hester, 48
Hogsett: Frances, 55; Francis, 28, 82, 83
Holden: Benjamin, 111, 112; Jemima, 111, 112
Hollingshead: Hugh, 13; John, 71; Lydia, 105; Morgan, 28; Thomas, 105
Hollingshead, Esqr.: John, 32, 71
Hollinshead: Benjamin, 19; Hugh, 105; Jno., 33, 61; Joe, 73; John, 26, 57, 63, 103; Joseph, 38, 45, 73, 97; Lydia, 102, 106; Mary, 105; Sheriff, 114; Thomas, 102, 106; Thos., 102, 111; William, 19
Hollinshead, Esq.: John, 61, 70
Hollinshead, Esqr.: John, 25, 33, 76, 97
Hollinshead, Esquire: John, 62, 97
Hollinshead, Junr.: Joseph, 97
Hooper: James, Slave, 95; Robert, 48; Robert Letter[?], 76; Robert Lettiu[?], 77
Hooper, Esqr.: Robert Lettiu[?], 76

(126)

INDEX

Hooten: Hannah, 39
Hooton: William, 83
Hopewell: Daniel, 59, 60, 103; Mary, 60
Horner: Jno., 81
Horton: Thomas, 23
Hoskins: John, 104
Hoskins, Junr.: John, 114
Hough: Benj., 34; Benjamin, 24; Daniel, 19, 34, 52, 53, 112; Elizabeth, 19; Jonathan, 34, 52, 113; Joseph, 113; Saml., 112, 113; Samuel, 19, 34, 52, 53; Susannah, 112, 113
Hough, Esqr.: Jonathan, 19, 112
Hoult: Samuel, 14
Hous[?]: John, 26
Houseman: Joseph, 104
Housten: William C., 91
How: Hannah, 27; John, 27, 33, 34, 90; Saml., 15
How, Esqr.: Samuel, 27, 56
Howell: Hannah, 111; Jacob, 108; Noah, 111
Hude, Esqr.: James, 47
Huestis: John, 82
Hugg: Jacob, 6; Jos., 72; Jsh., 8
Hulme: George, 90
Humphrey: Joshua, 28
Humphreys: Asshton, 10
Humphries: Joshua, 83
Humpries: Joshua, 83
Hunt: Joshua, 25, 27; Josiah, 30, 31
Hutchin: Amos, 109, 113, 114; Saml., 114; William, 110
Hutchins: John, 1, 2, 9, 10, 12; Sarah, 2, 9
Hutchinson: George, 6, 79

I

Imlay: Catharine, 77; Elizh., 9; J., 2, 3; John, 2, 8, 26, 77; Jos., 6; Joseph, 3, 7, 8
Imlay, Esqr.: John, 43; Joseph, 71
Imlay, Junr.: John, 3
Inon: Adam, 20; Sip, Slave, 20

Inon[?]: Gabriel, Slave, 20
Irick: John, 49, 84; Mary, 49; William, 103
Ivins: Samuel, 32; Thomas, 87

J

Janney: Thoms., 77
Jennings: Samuel, 38, 105
Jenny: Thomas, 96
Jervis: Cha., 57; Elijah B., 91; Elizabeth, 91
Job: George, 76
Jobs: George, 50
Jobs, Junr.: George, 50
Jobs, Senr.: George, 50
Johnson: Berney, 90; Elizabeth, 60, 61, 70; Ezekiel, 27; John, 47
Johnson, Esqr.: Andrew, Honorable, 47
Johnston: Ezekiel, 27
Jones: Benjamin, 17; R. Shettel, 87; R. Strettell, 40; Rd. Shettell [?], 5; Robert S., 86; Robt. Shettell, 61, 62

K

Kearness: Patrick, 16
Kearney: Isabella, 5
Keeler: Jacob, 79
Keen: Rebeckah, 112
Keens: Henry, 96; John, 96
Kemble: George, 44; Joseph, 87; Priscilla, 63; Samuel, 52; Samuel O., 84; Sarah, 101; Thomas, 63
Kempton: Elizath., 116; Moses, 37, 56, 70, 80, 81, 83, 85, 86, 89, 90, 106, 111, 116
Kerlin: Mathais, 3; Matthias, 6; Thomas, 2, 3, 12
Kesselman: Frederick, 5, 22
Kimble: George, 74, 75; Joseph, 83, 86; Martha, 83, 86; Mary, 83, 84; Ruth, 83, 84; Samuel, 83, 84; Thomas, 84; William, 83, 84
Kimble, The Younger: Samuel, 84
King: Daniel, 34; Jeremiah, 70; John, 44; Obadiah, 10

INDEX

Kinsey: Chief Justice, 107; Hannah, 33; James, 98, 99, 107; James, Chief Justice, 88, 111; Mary, 116
Kinsey, Esquire: James, Chief Justice, 80, 81, 106
Kinsey, Junr.: James, 22
Kirby: Amey, 17; Robert, 17
Kirkbride: Jos., 72; Joseph, 72; Phinehas, 63
Kissleman: Fred, 89
Knight: John, 76

L

Lacey: John, 19, 20, 24, 34, 53, 57, 58, 60, 100
Lacy: John, 21
Lamb: Jude, Slave, 13
Lamb, Junr.: Joseph, 21
Lambert: Achsah, 106; Thomas, 87
Large: Ebenezer, 9, 38, 39, 69
Laurance: John, 10
Lawrence: Benjamin, 87; Clerk, 81; Elisha, 64; Elizabeth, 88; Hannah, 26, 87; Jacob, 87, 88; Jno., 104; Joacob, 87; John, 26, 87, 89, 98, 100, 104; Martha, 88, 89; Robert, 32, 47, 57, 61, 62
Lawrence, Esq.: John, 15
Lawrence, Esqr.: Elisha, 71; John, 88, 104
Lawrie: Gawen, 33
Lawry: Gawen, 48
Lee: John, 33, 37, 87, 112; Sarah, 80
Leeds: Daniel, 16; Philo, 25, 44; Vincent, 75
Leek: John, 56; John, Captain, 56
Lenton: Benjamin, 88
Leonard: John, 64
Leslie: Edmond, 94; George, 94; James, 94; John, 94; Samuel, 95; William, 94
Lewis: Ellis, 35
Linch: John, 17; Michael, 56
Linton: John, 55; Martha, 55
Lipp: Ruth, Slave, 93
Lippencott: Anna, 105; Eliza, 105; Patience, 105
Lippincott: Abel, 59; Ann, 104; Anna, 13, 35, 105; Elizabeth, 29, 30, 104, 105; James, 49, 100, 109; Job, 12, 13, 24, 34, 85, 105; John, 29, 30, 55; Joseph, 12, 13, 85; Joshua, 46, 47; Patience, 104, 105; Saml., 55; Samuel, 55
Lippincott, Junr.: Job, 45
Lippincott, The Elder: Ann, 104
Lisman: Henry, 89
Lloyd: Isaac, 37
Lockwood: Ephram, 87
Lovell: John, 87
Lovet: Aaron, 22
Lovet, Sen.: Joseph, 22
Lovett: Aaron, 22
Lucas: Benjamin, 92; Nicholas, 33, 48; Robert, 92; Seth, 92
Luker: Benjamin, 25

M

Mac Lane: Cato, Slave, 57
Maccolloah: Henry, 45
Manes: John, 82
Marr: Peter, 1
Martin: Thomas, 48
Mason & Hartly, 18
Master: William, 108
Mathis: James, 96
Matlack: Jeremiah, 31; Reubin, 31; Thos., 56; Timy., 22
Matlock: Abraham, 65
Mattheson: Isabella, 27
Matthis: Daniel, 56; Micajah, 56; Nehemiah, 56
Matthis, Junr.: Job, 56; Nehemiah, 56
Mayberry: Mary, 70; Thomas, 70, 71
Mc Clean: Charles, 88
Mc Clutche: James, 37
Mc Elroy: Herbert, 49
Mc Ilvaine: Jos., 48; Joseph, 89; Mary Ann,

INDEX

89
Mc Ilvaine, Jr.: Joseph, 47
Mc Lane: Cato, Slave, 58
McClean: Charles, 87
McCleary: Robert, 77
McIlvaine: J., 59; Joseph, 62
McNair: Solomon, 8
Means: Jane, 82; John, 82, 83
Meir: Jsoeph, 88
Mew: Richard, 48
Middleton: Abel, 18; Joel, 13, 14, 18, 21, 72, 87; John, 95, 117; Nathan, 27, 28, 83, 88; Thomas, 59, 83; Timothy, 59; William, 59
Middleton, Junr.: John, 71, 72
Middletown: Joel, 66
Mill: Ebenezer, 47
Miller: Ann, 92; Anne, 92; Charles, 16; James, 90, 92; Sarah, 21
Mills: Sarah, 72, 102
Milnor: Joseph, 90
Mintus: George, Slave, 52, 53; Hannah, 31
Mitchell: Colonel, 77; Geo., 91; George, 23; John, 10; Mary, 64, 65; Mary, Mrs., 64, 65, 96; Randle, 10
Mitton: Israel, 114
Moon: Jasper, 38, 39, 100, 101, 109, 110, 117; Martha, 39, 40, 100, 101, 110, 117; Robert, 60; Sarah, 117; Thomas, 103
Moore: Benj., 100; Benjamin, 49, 50, 60; Bethrell, 100; Bethuel, 49, 50; Elizabeth, 17, 76, 82; Hannah, 69; John, 49, 50, 69; Jos., 100; Joseph, 49, 50; Milcah Martha, 108; Samuel, 17, 21, 97; Thomas, 21, 28, 55, 76, 82; Widow, 97
Moore, Junior: Samuel, 102
Moore, Senior: Samuel, 102
Moore, Senr.: Saml., 17
Morgan: Benjamin, 70; Mary, 67; Sarah, 67
Morgan, Junior: Joseph, 66
Morr: Thomas, 14
Morre: Jno., 100

Morre, Junr.: Benjamin, 21
Morrell: Joseph, 110
Morrey: Sarah, 14
Morris: L.M., 72; Lawrence, 37; Luke, 53; Margaret, 89; William, 47
Morton: Thomas, 56; Thos., 83
Mullen: Ann, 37; Anna, 105; Anne, 38, 39; Edward, 38, 39; John, 105; Joseph, 37, 38, 39, 44, 54, 109
Mullen, Esqr.: Joseph, 32, 43, 53, 73, 74, 85, 100
Mullen, Esquire: Joseph, 12, 13, 109
Mullin: Joseph, 110
Murray: John, 108; Mary, 117
Murrel: Joseph, 117
Murrell [?]: Ann, 117
Myers: Jocob, 114

N

Neal: Isaac, 98; John, 98; Mary, 102
Neale: Mary, 106; Thomson, 39, 102
Newbold: Barzillai, 112, 113; Barzillia, 108; Clayton, 93; Joseph, 95; Joshua, 79; Rebeckah, 79; Rebekah, 79; Thomas, 75, 112, 113; William, 67
Newbold, Esqr.: William, 24, 112
Newbold, Junior: William, 112
Newbold, Junr.: William, 113
Newbold, The Elder: William, 113
Newton: Samuel, 18, 92
Nightingale: Sarah, 4; Simon, 4
Nixon: Thomas, 101
Noble: Saml., 108
Norcross: William, 49
Noulton: Isaac, 17
Nursley: John, 68; Sarah, Slave, 68
Nutt: John, 8; Phillip, 2, 6; Thomas, 7; William, 2

O

Oakford: Aaron, 37
Oaxson: Henery, 91

INDEX

Odell: Ann, 33; Jonathan, 33
Ogbourn: John, 38
Ogden: David A., 97
Olden: Ephraim, 96
Oliphant: David, 71; Jonathan, 17
Olive: Mary, 18; Thomas, 17, 18
Oliver: Jno., 16, 75
Ong: Jacob, 45

P

Page: Abner, 58, 59; Edward, 18; Harvey, 58
Pancoast: Aden, 79; John, 79; Joseph, 12; William, 12, 79
Pancoast, Junr.: Joseph, 6, 7
Parado: Benjamin, Slave, 99; Pantilla, Slave, 98; William, Slave, 99
Parker: Adam, 33, 34; Elizabeth, 33, 34
Parrish: Mary, 72; Robert, 72
Patton: Jno., 74
Paxson: Henry, 10, 24, 25, 35, 38, 42, 60, 100, 101; Samuel, 25
Paxson, Esqr.: Henry, 35, 86
Paxton: James, 76
Peachee: Thomas, 98
Peaches: Jno., 92
Peachie: Thomas, 98
Peachy: Thopmas, 37; William, 37
Peacock: John, 22
Pearson: Abel, 83; James, 83; Joseph, 66; Robert, 70, 97; Robt., 92
Pearson, Junr.: Robert, 59
Peer: Darcus, Slave, 51, 52; Michael, 51
Pemberton: James, 56, 57; Phebe, 56; Sarah, 57
Penn: William, 33, 70
Pennock: Talman, 116
Pere[Pero?]: Patience, 24
Perkins: Benjamin, 98; Isaac, 98; Jacob, 92
Perkins, Senior: Jacob, 98
Pettit: Charles, 104; Sarah, 104

Pettit, Esquire: Charles, 107
Phares: William, 94
Pharo: Amos, 56, 79; Gervas, 55
Phillips: Elizabeth, 22; Ephraim, 22; Jacob, 43, 53; Jno., 64, 65; John, 8, 14, 19, 20, 21, 23, 24, 25, 26, 29, 30, 31, 33, 34, 41, 44, 46, 47, 50, 51, 52, 53, 55, 58, 61, 62, 66, 71, 88, 97
Phillips, Esqr.: John, 67, 74
Pierson: Benjamin, 33, 34
Pine: Benjamin, 1
Platt: Thomas, 16, 17
Pleasants: Samuel, 18
Plumstead: William, 104, 107
Plumstead, Esquire: William, 104
Polgreen: Thomas Beekly, 114; Thomas Bukly, 114
Pope: John, 1, 2, 3, 4, 6, 8, 9, 11, 12, 15, 20, 54, 71, 72, 93, 95, 103; Joseph, 11, 12; Mary, 20; Nathaniel, 2, 3, 6, 7, 11, 20, 21; Sarah, 3
Pope, The Elder: Joseph, 11, 12
Pope, The Younger: Joseph, 11, 12
Potts: Arney, 25; Isaac, 112, 113; Joseph, 2; Mary, 2; Richard, 58, 114, 115; Richd., 57, 115; Thomas, 25, 26; William, 25, 87, 99, 103
Powell: Thomas, 18, 98
Pricket: Abraham, 86; Esther, 86; Jacob, 25, 35; John, 71
Prickett: Baraham, 83; Zacharia, 22
Prosses[?]: William, 27
Pryor: Elizabeth, 69; Hannah, 69, 108; Jane, 69; Joseph, 69; Samuel, 69; Thomas, 69, 108; Thos. W., 108
Pryor, Junr.: Thomas, 108
Pullen: William, 12, 85

R

Radford: Samuel, 88
Rainey: George, 19

(130)

INDEX

Randolph: Benjamin, 10
Read: Ann, 40; Charles, 26, 47, 49, 85; Jos., 13, 16, 33, 35, 39, 40, 48, 54, 57, 60, 68, 70, 75, 84, 101, 102, 105, 110, 117; Joseph, 16, 35, 46, 49, 60, 67, 84, 117; Martha, 84, 101; Saml., 35, 78; Saml. I., 84
Read, Esq.: Charles, 38; Joseph, 45
Read, Esqr.: Charles, 71; Joseph, 25, 27, 28, 73, 83, 84
Read, Esquire: Joseph, 13, 14, 48
Read, Junr.: Sam J., 117
Reade: Jos., 14
Reaves: Henry, 109
Redman: John, 10
Reed: Bowes, 115; Charles, 100; Jos., 15; Saml., 70; Thomas, 76
Reed, Esqr.: Bowes, 115
Reed[?]: Zach. R., 75
Reese: Henry, 109
Reeve: Henry, 109; Josiah, 106; Micajah, 91; Peter, 57; Walter, 91
Reeves: Henry, 42, 100, 109, 110; Josiah, 105; Rachel, 42
Renear: Job, 85
Renshaw: John, 19
Reynolds: Chichester, 60; Patrick, 86; Thomas, 21, 24, 70, 86, 108; Thos., 19, 34
Reynolds, Esqr.: Thomas, 35, 71
Richards: Thomas, 1, 6, 7, 12; William, 100
Richee: John, 94
Ridgeway: John, 9; Joseph, 69; Phoebe, 9
Ridgway: David, 59; Henry, 9, 52, 53; Jacob, 79; John, 8, 38, 39, 40, 48, 68, 89, 100, 101, 108, 109, 110, 117; Jos., 39, 67, 70; Joseph, 37, 38, 39, 40, 48, 66, 67; Mary, 39; Phoebe, 8; Solomon, 17, 40, 84, 86, 87; William, 107, Wm., 18
Riely: John, 28
Risdon: John, 83

Robert: George, 39, 40
Roberts: Edith, 94; George, 40; John, 15; Michael, 106; Thomasine, 40
Robertson: John, 87
Robeson: David, 2
Robin: George, Slave, 21
Robins: Aaron, 4; Isaiah, 62; Nathan, 55, 58, 59; Nathaniel, 35
Robinson: John, 45
Rocker: Dennis, Slave, 93; William, Slave, 94
Rockhill: John, 55
Rodgers: Ann, 105; William, 111
Rodgers, Junr.: William, 105
Rodman: Clark, 82; John, 49, 69, 82; Samuel, 107; Thomas, 1, 12, 43, 49, 59, 69, 97, 112; Thos., 87, 90, 92
Rodman, Esqr.: Thomas, 18, 104
Roen: George, Slave, 115
Rogers: Abner, 103; Ann, 105; Elizabeth, 59; Isaac, 27; John, 57, 58, 70; Joseph, 94; Saml., 113; Samuel, 33, 64, 72, 90; Thomas, 83, 86; William, 59, 80, 81, 105, 111; Wm., 81
Rogers, Junr.: Thomas, 83, 86
Ross: Jno., 75; John, 67, 74, 75, 81, 105
Rossel: Zacha., 84
Rossell: William, 13; Wm., 68; Zacha., 84; Zachariah, 13, 35, 37
Rossell, Junr.: Zachariah, 45
Rue: Anthony, 98
Runyan: Evan, 10
Runyon: Hugh, 10, 77, 96; Sarah, 77, 96
Rush: Michael, 63
Russell: Silvester D., 89
Ryle: John, 28
Rynear: Job, 12

S

Salter: Ann, 37
Salter, Esqr.: Richd., 47

INDEX

Salter[?]: Joseph, 100
Sarah: Coat, 102
Satterthwaite: David, 77; Jane, 55, 58; Joseph, 55; Meribah, 77; Richard, 31; William, 55, 58, 77
Satterwaite: Jane, 36; William, 36
Saville: George, 3
Sayre: Francis Bowes, Doctor, 88
Sbiras[?]: Peter, 83
Scattergood: Benjamin, 103; Caleb, 68, 99, 103, 116; Jos., 49; Joshua, 99, 102, 103; Saml., 45; Samuel, 49, 53; Tho., 53; Thomas, 55, 58, 59
Schuyler: Aaron, 113; Abraham, 113; Charles, 113; Peter, 113; Rhoda, 113
Scott: Joseph, 103
Selsey: Phillis, Slave, 67
Sergeant: Jonan., 74
Servoss: Jacob, 91
Sexton: Peter, 64
Sharp: Amos, 80, 81; Ann, 80; Barzillai, 81; Barzillia, 80; Deborah, 80; Dinah, 80; Elizabeth, 81; Hannah, 80; Hugh, 18, 83; Isaac, 80, 81; John, 80, 81; Mahlon, 80, 81; Mary, 80; Priscilla, 80; Samuel, 81; Tho., 81; Thos., 80; William, 81
Sharp, Junr.: Samuel, 80, 81; William, 81, 111
Shaw: John, 79
Sheaff: Christopher, 109
Shettle: Amos, 70
Shields: Daniel, 100, 109; John, 48, 55; Margaret, 48
Shin: Joseph, 60; William, 60
Shinn: Aaron, 60; Aquila, 24, 25, 35, 37; Aquilla, 72; Buddell, 72; Buddl, 97; Caleb, 87; Christopher, 35; Earl, 69; Henry, 57; Jacob, 85, 89; Jos., 42; Joseph, 42, 60; Rebecca, 69; Sam., 42; Samuel, 41; Solomon, 16, 37; Thomas, 38, 39, 45, 60, 61, 81; William, 42, 85

Shinn, Esq.: Thomas, 38
Shinn, Esqr.: Thomas, 12, 13, 34, 45, 46
Shinn, Junr.: William, 42
Shippen: Francis Wm., 50; Margaret, 80
Shippen, Esqr.: Edward, 76
Shiras: Alexander, 86, 104; Alexr., 105; John, 19; Peter, 16, 20, 46, 47, 86; Rebecca, 16
Shiras, Esqr.: Peter, 84
Shires: Alexander, 35
Shoemaker: Saml., 23
Shoemaker, Esqr.: Samuel, 23
Shourds: Daniel, 9
Shreeve: Caleb, 54; Israel, 54; Johnathan, 55
Shreive: Caleb, 93
Shreve: Aquila, 16; Benjamin, 93; Hannah, 15; Israel, 16, 17, 20, 21, 27, 32, 37, 47, 54, 55, 58; James, 45; John, 15, 58; Jonathan, 15, 53; Joseph, 20, 21, 53; Thomas, 15
Shreves: Jonathan, 53; Joseph, 88
Shuff: Christopher, 37, 100; Grace, 37
Shuffs: Christopher, 109
Sikes [Likes?]: Samuel, 95
Skies: William, 89
Skirm: Richard, 87
Skyes: John, 89
Sleeper: Hannah, 38, 39; Hannah, 48; John, 38, 39, 48; Jonathan, 38
Sloan: James, 103, 110
Small: Ann, 11; Israel, 11; John, 11; Jonas, 11; Robert, 11; Ruth, 11; William, 11
Smith: Aaron, 35; Abigail, 41; Anne, 42; Daniel, 22, 23, 57; Daniel Doughty, 85; Danl., 22, 23, 57, 70, 113; Danl. D., 89; Hugh, 77; Isaac, 112; James, 70; Jas., 87; Jeremiah, 88; Joseph, 87, 88, 110, 111; Margaret, 88; Margret, 88; Mary, 42; R.R. [?], 57; R.S., 27; Richard, 5, 47; Richard S., 27; Robert, 57; Robt., 89, 113; Samuel, 41; Sarah, 35, 57, 58, 59;

INDEX

Thomas, 17, 53, 59, 102; Timothy, 35, 55, 58, 59; William, 39, 41, 60, 69, 101, 102; William Lovet, 42, 52, 67, 85; Wm., 41, 62, 100

Smith, Esqr.: William, 40, 101; William Lovet, 42

Smith, Esquire: Samuel, 5; William, 41, 110

Smith, Jr., Esqr.: Richard, 9

Smith, Junr.: Joseph, 110; Wm., 61

Sobers: John, Slave, 65

Southwick: James, 38, 39; Josiah, 38, 49, 105

Sprague: John, 103; Mary, 103; William P., 104

Sprague, Esquire: William Peter, 103

Stacy: Mahlon, 87

Starkey: James, 94

Stephens: John, 45

Sterling: James, 15, 49; James H., 14, 15; Jams., 114; Rebecca, 49; Rebeckah, 114; Rebekah, 114

Sterling, Esqr.: James, 14, 114

Stevens: John, 77

Stevens, Esqr.: John, 96

Stevenson: Elnathan, 60; Samuel, 62

Steward: Pompey, Slave, 115

Stiles: Jane, 90, 92; Samuel, 89, 90, 92

Still: Candas, Slave, 51; Cyrus, 78; Hope, Slave, 51; Phillip, Slave, 50

Stockton: Abm., 55; Abraham, 51, 52, 84; Ann, 74, 75, 95; Benjamin, 74, 75, 100, 109; Hanna, 75; Hannah, 74; Jobe, 95; John, 115; Mary, 65, 66; Richard, 14, 15, 74, 75, 95, 96; Richd., 14; Saml., 73, 111; Samuel, 14, 15, 65, 66, 67, 68, 74, 75, 93, 94, 95, 96, 105; Sarah, 105; William, 38, 39, 45, 95, 103, 105

Stokes: Abigail, 102, 105, 106; Josa., 28; Joseph, 102, 105, 106, 111; Josh., 102, 108, 111; Thomas, 14; Thos., 78

Stokes/Storkes: Jos., 32

Stratten: Enoch, 60

Stratton: Daniel, 26; Emanuel, 26, 71; Mark, 26

Stretch: P., 21, 53, 65, 66; Peter, 21, 24, 34, 53, 58, 65, 66; W., 13; William, 86

Stretch, Esq.: Peter, 57

Sullivan: Timothy, 35; Timothy A., 35

Sutton: John, 43, 73, 74, 114

Sweetman: George, 110

Sykes: Benjamin, 89, 90; Hannah, 89, 90; John, 90, 92; William, 10

T

Talbert: Wm., 99

Tallman: Benjamin, 55; Elizabeth, 53; Hannah, 1, 31, 32; Job, 88; Joseph, 6, 53, 55; Margaret, 2, 9; Perter, 31; Peter, 2, 3, 4, 7, 9, 11, 53, 61; Thomas, 1, 2, 9, 31, 32, 74

Talman: Benja., 9; Benjamin, 53; Hannah, 1; James, 53; Job, 53, 89; John, 88; Joseph, 53, 58, 59, 89; Margaret, 1; Martha, 88, 89; Peter, 1, 53, 90; Sarah, 88, 89; Thomas, 1

Talman, Junr.: Joseph, 88, 89

Tate: James, 54

Taylor: Anthony F., 110; Hannah, 110; John, 13, 40, 87, 110; Michael, 75

Test: John, 18

Thomas: Absalom, 71; Benjamin, 71; Edward, 2, 3, 8; Edwd., 7; Nathan, 59; Nathaniel, 25, 35; Rich'd, 8

Thompson: Annis, 53, 59; Benjamin, 94; John, 71, 73; William, 63

Thomson: Benjamin, 95; Henry, 53; William, 57

Thone[Thom?]: Peter, Slave, 34

Thorn: Jemima, 16; John, 71, 72, 95; Joseph, 75; Thomas, 16, 64, 71

Thornburgh: Mary, 98

Thornton: Joseph, 50, 51

(133)

INDEX

Tilley: John, 100
Tilton: Abraham, 62; Peter, 75
Tomas: Abel, 43
Tonkin: Christian, 16; Edward, 45, 46; Hepzibah, 79; Israel, 16, 55, 61, 62
Tonkins: John, 79; Phebe, Slave, 30
Tool: Peter, 103
Toule [?]: Percival, 6
Trent: William, Major, 10
Troth: Job, 111; William, 111
Tucker, Esqr.: Ebenezer, 56

U

Underhill: John, 53, 55, 88

V

Valenece: Rosetta, Slave, 99
Van Emburgh: J., 117; John, 117
VanSciver: Barnaby, 40
Vansciver: Jacob, 2, 3, 7, 8, 12
Verree: James, 87, 88
Verves [?]: James, 10

W

Walcott: Jacob, 3, 4
Wall: Humphrey, 62; Joseph, 62; Micajah, 8
Wallace: Joshau M., 74; Joshua M., 10, 11, 12, 26, 28, 64; Joshua Maddox, 80; Joshua Wallace, 98
Wallace, Esqr.: Joshua M., 22; Joshua Maddox, 26
Wallin: Thomas, 117
Wallis: Thom., 103
Waln: Richard, 101
Walsh: Humphrey, 75
Walton: Jeremiah, 17; Penelope, 17; Punelopah, 17
Ward: Isaac, 35; John, 18, 98
Wardel: Samuel, 94
Warden: Jeremiah, 77
Warren: Fretwell, 43; Lyhern, 88
Warrin: Jacob, 94

Warrington: John, 55
Warton: Sarah, 88, 89
Warton, Junr.: Joseph, 88, 89
Water: Beulah, Slave, 23
Waterford: George, SLave, 66
Waterman: Clemmont, Slave, 95
Waters: Sam, Slave, 30
Watson: John, 22, 23, 40, 77, 79, 90; Joseph, 40, 106; Mary, 22; William, 40
Weatherby: William, 56
Webb: Wm., 77
Webber: Ann, 37; Jacob, 35, 37
Webster: Thomas, 25, 44
Wells: Aaron, 106; Daniel, 86; Rachel, 104, 108; Richard, 4, 5, 104, 108
West: Beulah, 60; Charles, 69, 102, 106; George, 85; John, 59, 60, 85
Wetherill: Anna, 70; Chriser., 61; Christopher, 60, 61, 70; Christpopher, 60; Isaac, 60, 61, 70; Isaace, 60; Joseph, 70; Samuel, 70; Sarah, 70; Thomas, 49
Wetherill, Junr.: Saml., 70; Thomas, 70
Wheatcraft: Edward, 76
White: Jesse, 36; Jno. M., 48; John, 90, 97, 108; John Moore, 61, 62; Josiah, 8, 42, 105; Mary, Slave, 30; Moore, 61, 62; Peter, 14; Rebecca, 90, 97, 108; Robert, 11; William, 47, 48, 62, 108
Whitehead: James, 15
Wilcocks, Junr.: John, 40
Wilcox: Joseph, 100
Wilkens: Uriah, 32
Wilkins: Benjamin, 50, 100; Esther, 50, 51; James, 44; John, 71; Sarah, 100, 101; Thomas, 49, 50, 51, 100; Uriah, 33, 50, 57; William, 23, 24, 49, 50, 100; Wm., 100, 101
Willas: Saly, 11
Willcox: Joseph, 100
Willets: Elizabeth, 100, 101; Micajah, 100, 101

INDEX

Williams: Abbot, 27; Abbott, 23; Catherine, 76; Hannah, Slave, 30, 31; Judah, 16; Renssalaer, 76; Rensselr., 76
Willkins: Benjamin, 49
Willock: George, 94
Wills: Aaron, 18, 20, 111; Alexander, 8; Ann, 8; Daniel, 106; Rachel, 107; Richard, 107
Wilson: Andover, 76; John, 102
Winner: Abraham, 41; John, 41; Mary, 41
Woglam: Abraham, 106
Wolcott: Jacob, 4, 6, 7, 11, 17, 26, 68, 71, 74, 90, 92, 97, 116, 117; Jocob, 97
Wolcott, Esquire: Jacob, 110
Wood: Sophia, 63; William, 16, 63, 66, 92
Woodmansee: Daniel, 64; John, 64; Joseph, 64
Woodward: Apollo, 97; Joseph, 71, 93, 95
Wooley: Edmond, 110; Sarah, 110
Woolman: Abm., 101; Abrm., 73; Asher, 106, 107; John, 38, 86; Jonah, 24, 25, 35, 37, 106, 107; Joseph, 106; Sam, 108; Saml., 43; Uriah, 63; William, 25, 111
Woolston: Esther, 8; George, 103; Jaber, 8; Jabez, 70; John, 6, 103
Worral: Peter, 22
Worrall: Peter, 23
Wright: Abednego, 20, 21; Caleb, 41; John, 95, 115; Jonathan, 16; Joseph, 19, 31; Joshua, 31, 115; Mary, 16; Nathan, 67; Richard, 110; Sarah, 110; Thomas, 94; Tretwell, 16; William, 3, 73, 74; Wm., 99

Z

Zelley: Aaron, 110; Abraham, 110; Daniel, 110; Hannah, 109, 110; John, 109; Penelope, 110
Zelly: Aaron, 109; Daniel, 109, 110; John, 109, 110
Zilly: Daniel, 101

www.ingramcontent.com/pod-product-compliance
Ingram Content Group UK Ltd.
Pitfield, Milton Keynes, MK11 3LW, UK
UKHW051853200426
11947UKWH00046B/1820